Stories of Sickness

Stories of Sickness

Howard Brody

Yale University Press
New Haven and London

Excerpts from Tell Me a Riddle, *by Tillie Olsen, copyright © 1956, 1957, 1960, 1961 by Tillie Olsen, reprinted by permission of Delacorte Press/Seymour Lawrence. Excerpts from "Diabetes" and "The Cancer Match" from* The Eye-Beaters, Blood, Victory, Madness, Buckhead and Mercy, *by James Dickey, copyright © 1968, 1969, 1970 by James Dickey. "The Cancer Match" first appeared in* Poetry, *copyright © 1969 by Modern Poetry Association. Both reprinted by permission of Doubleday & Company, Inc. Excerpt from* THE CANCER WARD *by Alexandr Solzhenitsyn. Translated by R. Frank. Translation copyright © 1968 by Bantam, Doubleday, Dell Publishing Group, Inc. Reprinted by permission of the publisher. Excerpts from* Mortal Lessons, *by Richard Selzer, copyright © 1974, 1975, 1976 by Richard Selzer, reprinted by permission of Simon & Schuster, Inc. Excerpts from Sophocles'* Electra, Antigone, Philoctetes, *translated by Kenneth McLeish, copyright © Cambridge University Press, reprinted by permission of Cambridge University Press.*

Designed by Nancy Ovedovitz and set in Times Roman type with Eras display by David E. Seham Associates, Inc. Printed in the United States of America by BookCrafters, Inc., Chelsea, Michigan.

Library of Congress Cataloging-in-Publication Data
Brody, Howard.
Stories of sickness.
Bibliography: p.
Includes index.
1. Sick—Psychology. 2. Self-respect. 3. Diseases
in literature. I. Title.
R726.5.B76 1987   610   87–10657
ISBN 0–300–03977–8 (cloth)
0–300–04692–8 (pbk.)

The paper in this book meets the guidelines for permanence and durability of the Committee on Production Guidelines for Book Longevity of the Council on Library Resources.

10   9   8   7   6   5   4   3   2

Contents

Acknowledgments

I wish to acknowledge the material assistance I have received in the preparation of this book. Many have kindly reviewed portions of the manuscript and offered helpful suggestions and criticism: Joanne Trautmann Banks, Martin Benjamin, Larry Churchill, Sally Gadow, Kathryn Hunter, Lenora Finn Paradis, Tess Tavormina, and David Thomasma. I have tried, wherever possible, to give specific credit for contributions in the footnotes. Students in two philosophy of medicine seminars at Michigan State University, taught in 1984 and 1986, read portions of the manuscript, and I have benefited from their discussions and criticism. Portions of the manuscript were discussed in colloquia before the Department of Philosophy, Michigan State University, and at an informal lunch discussion at the Hastings Center in New York. I may inadvertently have failed to credit some suggestions that were received at those times. Finally, I am indebted to Cecile Watters for thorough and thoughtful editing, and to Gladys Topkis and her colleagues at Yale University Press for sympathetic and timely handling of the manuscript.

The prepublication history of this manuscript has been a complicated one; and a brief summary may help to place some features of my discussion in perspective—in particular, my citations of other works on which I have drawn. The original version of the manuscript was written primarily between 1982 and 1984. An anonymous reviewer for another publisher recommended changes that altered greatly the order in which material was presented and that seemed to me to constitute an improvement. There was, however, a delay in publishing that revised version, which was completed in the summer of 1986. Finally Yale University Press expressed interest, and this led to my final revision of early 1987. Between 1984 and 1987, the degree of interest in story and narrative substantially increased in philosophy, medicine, and other fields of study. Hence, some ideas that seemed novel to me when I committed them to paper in 1983 or 1984 now seem much more commonplace. I have tried wherever possible to cite the newer material, as well as some older discussions that I became aware of only after the first draft had been completed.

Finally, I wish to acknowledge the support I have received at the institutional level. It has become commonplace for academics to declare that they have to go away from their normal haunts for a year or more to be able to write a book. I am either blessed or cursed with a setting that allows me to combine philosophical teaching and research with medical teaching and practice, so that I have no excuse for not writing a book of this type exactly where I am. I am grateful to Roy Gerard and my clinical colleagues in the Department of Family Practice; to Bruce Miller and the faculty of the Department of Philosophy; to Andy Hunt, Tom Tomlinson, Ken Howe, and my other compatriots in the Medical Humanities Program; and to Dean Donald Weston of the College of Human Medicine, Michigan State University, for creating the environment of cross-disciplinary creativity and intellectual fellowship in which work of this sort can flourish.

Introduction

Ivan Ilich locked the door and started examining himself in a mirror—first full face, then in profile. He took down a portrait of himself with his wife and compared it with what he saw in the mirror. There was a tremendous difference. Then he pulled his sleeves up, bared his arms to the elbow, examined his forearms, and his thoughts grew blacker than night.
(Tolstoy 1969, p. 269)

Ivan Ilich, as a result of the illness that will soon end in his death, has been turned into a different person. This is true in a physical sense. If he was given a photograph of a stranger who was to pass him on the street, and a man passed who was as different from the photograph as Ivan Ilich is from the photograph of himself with his wife, he would without hesitation decide that the man who passed on the street was not the stranger he was supposed to recognize. And this is true in a psychological sense as well, as is evidenced by this entire train of morbid analysis. The Ivan Ilich who existed before the illness was never given to this sort of introspection and questioning. Later it will occur to the sick Ivan Ilich to wonder whether he has not lived his entire life the wrong way, and whether everything he had previously sought in life was not empty and trivial; the healthy Ivan Ilich never entertained any such concerns.

And yet, in a different sense, there can be no doubt that Ivan Ilich is the same person, sick or well: "He was the former little Vania with his mummy and daddy, with his brothers Mitia and Volodia, with his toys, with their coachman, with their nanny, and later with Katia, with all the joys, sorrows, and enthusiasms of youth" (p. 273).

The sick Ivan Ilich clearly remembers things that happened to the healthy Ivan Ilich and that could be remembered only by the same person to whom they happened. And the sick Ivan Ilich clearly has the same parents, the same siblings, the same wife, and the same children as the healthy one. As the sick Ivan Ilich comes to question his former life, he experiences great regret. He recalls, from his present condition of pain and suffering, his previous unthinking pursuit of pleasure and comfort, his efforts directed always toward some promotion or increase in salary, his automatic acceptance of whatever ideas were then being talked about in the correct society, and his fear that he should ever come to have an idea on his own of which that society might disapprove. These reflections on his former life cause him unspeakable anguish; and the anguish arises precisely because this life is his own life. The fact that he now looks so different from the man in the photograph—the man who lived that life that he now finds loathsome—is of no consolation whatever to Ivan Ilich in his despair.

The story of Ivan Ilich suggests that this dual nature of sickness—the way it can make us different persons while we still remain the same person—might usefully be explored further. And it also suggests that the experience of sickness might be bound up in some intimate way with a person's self-respect. This book will attempt to show that questions like these are central to a philosophical understanding of sickness and its effect upon the person.

It will not be sufficient, however, to undertake this inquiry solely by treating "sickness" and "self-respect" as abstract concepts. Philosophy of medicine, I will argue, can indeed advance by such abstract discussions; but it can advance only so far. At some point we will require a richer context for the discussion to proceed fruitfully. This context can be provided by stories of sickness. We must look at particular sicknesses that afflict particular people to begin to appreciate the complexity of the various ways in which sickness can affect their self-respect and their life plans. Real-life case studies can provide stories of this type, and some will be related here. However, at least for a preliminary inquiry, there are considerable advantages to using the insights of trained storytellers—novelists, poets, and playwrights. Much of the material discussed below, then, will come from literature dealing with sickness.

The literary works as such, however, are not the focus; this will not be a work of literary criticism. Instead the focus will be on what can be learned from them when they are approached with a particular philosophical agenda and a particular set of questions derived from philosophical analysis of the concepts of sickness and self-respect.

This book will, in effect, provide a philosophical point of departure, and then a multitude of literary examples, to understand and elaborate upon this comment by neurologist Oliver Sacks: "If we wish to know a man, we ask 'what is his story, his real, inmost story?', for each of us *is* a biography, a story. Each of us *is* a singular narrative, which is constructed continually and unconsciously by, through, and in us—through our perceptions, our feelings, our thoughts, our actions; and, not least, through our discourse, our spoken narrations. Biologically, physiologically, we are not so different from each other; historically, as narratives, we are each of us unique" (Sacks 1985, p. 12).

Sacks is here describing a patient with severe Korsakov's syndrome, whose dementia is so profound that he cannot remember his narrative, his place in the world, from one minute to the next and must wildly confabulate to restore a superficial semblance of having a story or a narrative to his life at all. For Sacks, this patient's loss of narrative amounts to a loss of personal identity as well as of personal feeling. Obviously, few sicknesses will so fundamentally alter one's personhood and the necessary conditions for personal self-respect. But, if we are to catalog the more subtle ways in which sickness changes the person, Sacks suggests we will need more than a focus on the biology and physiology that all of us have in common. We will need an appreciation for the particular narratives of individuals and how these narrratives constitute a person's life, in sickness and in health.

Briefly, our discussion will proceed as follows. Chapter 1 will investigate the relationships between storytelling and healing—how the practice of medicine can be seen in part as a storytelling enterprise, and how the telling of stories can be seen as a social activity that can serve a healing function. This will serve as a basis for an approach that seeks to understand more about sickness and medicine by investigating the stories that are told about people's sicknesses. The chapter concludes with a description of what phenomena are covered by the notion of "story."

Then will follow two chapters that lay out the philosophical analysis of the concepts that will, in turn, suggest the questions to ask of the literary texts that will be studied later on. The first of these "philosophical" chapters looks at the notion of sickness (or illness or disease; see chap. 2, n. 3) and asks: How can sickness be defined? What aspects of sickness must be understood in order to fully understand the concept? What are the various impacts that sickness has on persons? The second of these chapters will deal with the concepts of self-respect and plans of life. Here the questions will be: What does it mean for a person to have self-respect? How is self-respect related to having a life plan? How are life plans altered by sickness? What does this then do to the person's self-respect? In what sense, and to what extent, are these individual issues dependent upon social interaction? The conclusions of these two philosophical chapters will be that previous investigations into the philosophy of medicine have been hampered by an overreliance on abstract conceptual analysis, and that the gaps that result can best be filled by looking at specific stories with detailed, particularistic content. These chapters will arm us with specific questions to ask about the stories, so that we can approach them in a structured fashion.

The next chapter will discuss further the question of precisely how to read the literary works we will be turning to, so that we can get the answers to the questions that interest us and not be misled by other, irrelevant features. This will include our being aware of the metaphorical use of illness in literature so that we can be alert to whether an author is describing a ''sickness case history'' in the sense relevant to our investigation or is using sickness in a solely metaphorical manner, in which case a literal reading of the events of the story will lead to misunderstanding. Also, we will address which sorts of stories are likely to be of most use to us.

The next four chapters will consist primarily of analyses of stories of sickness arranged by important subjects and themes that have been suggested by the prior philosophical reflections. First, we will look at the idea of sick roles and the sorts of ''practices'' that define how sick people are expected to behave by themselves and by their healthy peers. Next, we will catalog various ways in which sickness may have an impact upon the life plans of individuals. How one's sense of time and space is altered by sickness will be addressed. Two apparently contradictory aspects of sickness—sickness as leading toward solitude and sickness as influencing one's social relationships—will come under study. The social judgment of sickness and the sick individual, and the relationship to self-respect, will be discussed. And finally we will look at some ways of being sick that can appropriately be judged maladaptive and undesirable from a social perspective.

The two chapters that follow will be devoted to some implications of the above discussions that carry over into medical ethics. The concept of ''story'' suggests appreciation of a narrative mode—that certain sorts of events can be fully understood only as portions of an ongoing narrative and not as disconnected events occurring in isolation. In contrast, much of modern medical ethics is "rule"- and ''decision''-oriented, suggesting that precisely such an ahistorical, nonnarrative form of ethical analysis is optimal. We will explore two ways in which a narrative focus might alter some currently popular approaches to medical ethics: first, when the life of the patient is viewed in narrative form (with separate sections dealing with the newborn and the elderly ends of this life narrative), and second, when the relationship between physician and patient is viewed in narrative form. The final chapter will recapitulate some of the most important points with an eye toward eliciting lessons for medical education.

1

Storytelling in Medicine

*In Thasus, early in autumn, the winter suddenly set in rainy before
the usual time, with much northerly and southerly winds. These
things all continued so during the season of the Pleiades, and until
their setting. The winter was northerly, the rains frequent, in tor-
rents, and large, with snow, but with a frequent mixture of fair
weather. . . .*

*Silenus lived on the Broad-way, near the house of Evalcidas.
From fatigue, drinking, and unseasonable exercises, he was seized
with fever. He began with having pain in the loins; he had heaviness
of the head, and there was stiffness of the neck. On the first day
the alvine discharges were bilious, unmixed, frothy, high colored,
and copious; urine black, having a black sediment; he was thirsty,
tongue dry; no sleep at night. . . . On the third, all symptoms ex-
acerbated; an oblong distension, of a softish nature, from both
sides of the hypochondrium to the navel; . . . no sleep at night;
much talking, laughter, singing, he could not restrain himself. On
the seventh, loss of speech; extremities could no longer be kept
warm; no discharge of urine. . . . On the eleventh, he died. At
the commencement, and throughout, the respiration was slow and
large; there was a constant throbbing in the hypochondrium; his
age was about twenty.*

—Hippocrates, *Of the Epidemics,* Book I, II:1, III:13:II

It has been charged that Hippocrates, in the process of replacing supernatural with natural theories of disease causation, laid the groundwork for a practice of medicine in which the physician does not talk to the patient (Cassell 1976, p. 56). There is certainly a strong tradition in Western medicine that regards medical practice as first and foremost the palpation of the abdomen and the inspection of urinary sediment, so that conversation, of any sort, is seen as peripheral. But this tradition fails to take into account what becomes immediately clear on a superficial reading of Hippocrates and subsequent classics of medicine: regardless of the status of conversation with patients (which we will address below), conversation among physicians is surely central to medicine, and this conversation frequently takes the form of telling stories. From Hippocrates until fairly recent times, the case history has dominated medical thinking and has been the cornerstone of the medical literature.

It might appear that the reliance on case histories has been weakened in modern medicine by the establishment of a strong scientific base. But if the transition from anecdote to scientific theory has succeeded splendidly at one level, on another, it has been marked as a failure. Kathryn Hunter, a professor of literature invited to a major eastern medical center to teach humanities to medical students, began out of curiosity to attend the grand rounds and other scientific conferences presented at the hospital. After a while, she began to discern a recurring pattern. The discussion, whatever the specific topic, would open with ritualistic praise of the scientific method and ritualistic condemnation of the anecdotal evidence on which ignorant general practitioners had had to rely until the true physiological or biochemical basis of the disease in question was discovered. The conference would proceed to consider that physiological basis, illustrated by slides packed full of data. Finally, toward the end, the speaker would shift gears: "Now, let me illustrate the relevance of these findings by means of a case from my own clinic. There once was a man who . . ." At this point the audience, having been lulled to near-somnolence by the parade of data, would suddenly rouse themselves and sit forward in their seats. The much-despised anecdote had reappeared as an informative bridge between general scientific knowledge and the particular patient problems these physicians were likely to encounter in the wards and clinics; no one seemed to perceive the irony of the contrast between the ritualistic denunciation of anecdote and the unmistakable appeal of "There once was a man who . . ." (Hunter 1986).

I will discuss in a later chapter the assertion that medicine is fundamentally a craft in which scientific knowledge is applied to particular patients for the purpose of right and good healing actions (Pellegrino and Thomasma 1981). If this is the case, then stories are essential as a means of perceiving how scientific knowledge, in its generality, can be applied to individuals, in all their particularity. But recently the emphasis on the scientific features of medicine, to the neglect of its craftlike and moral dimensions, has taken a toll. We now rarely encounter a physician like Richard Selzer, whose writing of short stories is not only a natural outgrowth of his practice of surgery but also in an important way an essential feature of that practice (Beppu and Tavormina 1981; Tavormina 1982). And we rarely encounter a physician as insightful as a surgeon of my acquaintance who has been heard to remark that the major reward in being a physician is having the opportunity to sit in an office all day while one patient after another comes in to tell him his or her life story in full, frank, and intimate detail.

The ritual need to devalue storytelling in medicine may take several forms; and as is often the case, the patient may be blamed for the results. Overworked and harried physicians display little tolerance for any information from patients that is not already formulated as, or at least easily translatable into, the standard "medical history"—as if patients have an obligation to learn this peculiar form of discourse before having the temerity to fall ill. The patient who insists on imparting information that cannot be forced into the Procrustean bed of the standard medical history and review of systems is dealt with brusquely at morning report: "The patient was a poor historian" (Coulehan 1984). If we assume that storytelling does indeed play an important role in the day-to-day subconscious world of the physician, it is small wonder that such physicians should end their day's activities feeling vaguely frustrated and unfulfilled. They might indeed succumb to temptations to tell their stories about patients in social settings removed from their practice, where they need not fear being derided for being "anecdotal," but where instead their compulsion to tell their stories to *someone* may produce important weakenings in the traditional respect for medical confidentiality (Weiss 1982; Siegler 1982; Altman 1983).

What I have to say about stories in medicine is intended to apply to the whole of medicine. But it is no surprise that psychiatry, and especially psychoanalysis, has devoted more explicit attention to storytelling and has raised interesting questions about its epistemological features. Hillman is comfortable with a denial that psychoanalysis is empirical or scientific in any sense and with the assertion that instead it is a special form of poesis ("making by imagination into words") (1975, p. 124). To do psychoanalysis is to create special kinds of stories that have a powerful impact on the people about whom and to whom they are told; the stories appear superficially to be empirical and scientific because it is this appearance that gives them much of their power. Further, the stories are especially powerful from the patients' viewpoints because these people have, by virtue of their bizarre thoughts or behavior, frightened away all others who might have offered help in understanding, or they have remained silent out of fear of driving others away. (One historian of psychiatry has commented that American psychiatry for the past three centuries can be summarized under a single "chief complaint": "No one will listen to my story.")[1]

By contrast, E. B. Brody and J. F. Tormey (1980) are unwilling to dismiss the empirical basis of psychoanalysis so readily. They admit freely that the "reality" constructed by psychoanalysis is intersubjective and depends both on psychoanalytic theory (so that the stories themselves cannot be used as an independent empirical proof of the truth of psychoanalytic theory) and on the continued reciprocity of the analyst-patient relationship. In this regard, "the analyst's interpretations are inventions aimed at making behavior intelligible"

---

1. I am indebted to Richard Mollica for this comment regarding an unnamed historian (Psychiatry Grand Rounds, St. Lawrence Hospital, Lansing, Mich., February 6, 1986).

(p. 148), where intelligibility is a function of a deep construct (a "fable" in Hepburn's [1956] terms; a "plot" in Hillman's account of psychoanalysis) which is shared by both analyst and patient. Psychoanalytic theory ought to be interpreted not as a falsifiable hypothesis (cf. Grünbaum 1980) but rather as a "theoretical construction that serves as a principle of selection and organization" in the formulation of the patient's life story (Brody and Tormey 1980, p. 149). Further, since psychoanalysis is fundamentally therapeutic and not investigative, how the newly created life story "works" in response to the patient's suffering forms an unavoidable criterion for the success of the venture. Ultimately, Brody and Tormey argue, there are thus three criteria for "truth" in psychoanalysis—coherence, in the sense of making a mere "story" into a "fable"; correspondence, in the empirical sense of the events of the story matching publicly observable history; and pragmatic. If their argument is at least plausible, we have further reassurance that an analysis of medical activity that focuses on storytelling is subject to epistemological inquiry and clarification; one has not resorted to the storytelling motif as an excuse for begging important and interesting philosophical questions.

STORYTELLING AS HEALING

Having briefly discussed medicine as storytelling, I now turn to storytelling as medicine. The project that recently produced a book on the relationship between literature and medicine (Trautmann 1982) was referred to as "Healing Arts in Dialogue." I will argue that the inclusion of literature among the healing arts has legitimacy when one sees the various ways in which storytelling can be identified in healing activities.

I will be arguing in chapter 2 that suffering is produced, and alleviated, primarily by the meaning that one attaches to one's experience. The primary human mechanism for attaching meaning to particular experiences is to tell stories about them. Stories serve to relate individual experiences to the explanatory constructs of the society and culture and also to place the experiences within the context of a particular individual's life history. The first function of storytelling allows one to label an experience as representing, say, an act of cowardice or an act of religious devotion. The second function allows one to label an experience as, say, completely in character with the early upbringing of that individual or totally atypical and out of character. The meaning of an experience for an individual person, in the sense that I will be using the term, partakes of both these individual and sociocultural dimensions.

I have argued at length elsewhere that the ubiquitous feature of medicine that may be called the placebo effect (or, alternatively, healing by symbolic means) occurs to the optimal degree when the meaning of the illness experience is altered in a positive direction (Brody 1980; Brody and Waters 1980). That this sort of healing includes actual bodily change and is not restricted to the patient's subjective impressions has been well documented in the medical literature on placebos (Brody 1980). The notion of a "positive change in the meaning the patient attaches to the illness experience" can in turn be broken down into three distinguishable but closely related components. First, the illness experience must be given an explanation of the sort that will be viewed as acceptable, given the patient's existing belief system and worldview. Second, the patient must perceive that he or she is surrounded by and may rely upon a group of caring individuals. Third, the patient must achieve a sense of mastery or control over the illness experience, either by feeling personally powerful enough to affect the course of events for the better or by feeling that his or her individual powerlessness can be compensated for by the power of some member or members of the caring group (such as the physician).[2]

2. The sociological notion of the sick role, which I will be discussing briefly in chapter 2, clarifies the close connectedness of these three dimensions of meaning. The existence of a caring group around the patient reciprocally defines the sick role that the patient occupies. But, as a rule, this group will exhibit helpful and caring behavior only when the socially approved healing authority offers an explanation for the behavior that fits everyone's preconceptions of the nature of illness. That is, the authority must certify that the sufferer is indeed a victim of forces beyond his control and is not willfully shirking his responsibilities. And, unless both victim and associates perceive the possibility of mastery and control over the illness, they cannot sustain the sick role as a temporary deviant role from which the sufferer is expected to emerge so long as he complies with "good" (that is, role-mandated) sickness behavior (Parsons 1951, 1958, 1978).

All these factors can have negative as well as positive sides; alteration in meaning or in belief state can lead to bodily dissolution as well as to bodily healing (Hahn and Kleinman 1983). The most extreme example of this is ''voodoo death'' where the combination of an absolute belief in a magical explanatory system that predicts the individual's death, the social withdrawal of the family and close friends from the ''doomed'' individual, and a feeling of total inability to control or alter events leads speedily to the individual's death (often with no clear-cut pathophysiological changes discoverable at autopsy). In contrast, the reassuring story that is commonly told by the physician to account for the illness experience (''It looks like you've picked up that virus that is running around town—you're the sixth person I've seen today with exactly the same symptoms''), coupled with the caring and solicitous attitude of physician and office nurse, and the reassuring rituals that promise control of events (''Take two aspirin four times a day, gargle with warm salt water every hour, and stay in bed till the fever goes away''), may well effect a speedier recovery than could be accounted for either by the usual spontaneous-remission rate of the illness or by the purely pharmacological efficacy of the remedies administered.[3]

Physicians are hardly the only social figures employed in the relief of suffering. Stories are used by many others in order to reassure and comfort by giving meaning to a previously inexplicable and therefore frightening experience. Religious stories and myths, with attribution of causation to past transgressions coupled with promises

3. An example of a metaphor that increases the patient's suffering may be found in the report by Richard Mollica (see n. 1, above) of his work with post–traumatic stress syndrome among Southeast Asian refugees. Many women in that group were subjected to sexual violence as a form of torture; while their current psychiatric symptoms are referable to these experiences in important ways, it has been extremely difficult to get the women to discuss (or even to admit) these episodes for therapeutic purposes. One woman explained both the shame she felt and her conviction that it could never be erased or altered by observing, ''Man is gold; woman is cotton. If you drop gold into the mud you can pick it up, wipe it off, and it will be as good as new. If you drop cotton into the mud, it is dirty forever.'' Clearly this story of the experience perpetuates the suffering and retards healing. Clearly the aim of the psychiatrist must be to find a way to replace this story with a more positive metaphor for the relationship between men and women. But the difficulty of an American psychiatrist altering this deeply rooted cultural story is obvious.

of future redemption, are obvious examples; and the importance of folk literature and epic narratives in sustaining the pride and spirit of entire cultural groups is well accepted. But since medicine is devoted to changing things for the better within a caring social setting, all three elements of meaning as described above must be present for the medical encounter to be successful, even if in other contexts suffering may be assuaged merely by the first of the three elements (providing a satisfactory explanatory account). Thus, the stories told within the medical encounter must offer explanations for illness, but must in addition do so in such a way as to facilitate caring responses from others and controlling actions. Historically, those felt to be able to foretell the future as well as to be able to recount the past were especially valued as storytellers; and so long as prognostication is felt to be a skill possessed by the physician, the medical story takes on special importance. When one has a scientifically based cure to offer for the illness, the aura of mastery and control can be easily sustained. But even if no such cure is available (as in Hippocrates' time), the ability to prognosticate accurately, to tell the story of the future of the illness, maintains a sense of control and thus may symbolically, even if not pharmacologically, lead to enhanced healing.

The sociocultural dimension that plays a role in meaning as described above suggests that the role of the physician somehow goes beyond the telling of stories to individual patients. Berger has attempted to analyze the role that a certain English country doctor plays in the life of his community (Berger and Mohr 1967). He argues that one feature of one's psychological reaction to illness is the conviction that one's illness is unique; great comfort results when the physician is able to give a name to the complaint—if it has a name, it must have an existence apart from me; so then I can struggle against it (p. 68). The unhappy person, like the ill person, feels the uniqueness of his complaint, but feels even more that he is fundamentally unrecognizable by other persons and so destined to remain unhappy. ''The unhappy patient comes to a doctor to offer him an illness— in the hope that this part of him (the illness) may be recognizable. His proper self he believes to be unknowable'' (p. 69). The physician, to heal the unhappy patient, must somehow function as an Everyman in which the patient can see reflections of his essential self, before the patient can seriously entertain the notion that the physician can recognize his personhood. The country doctor in question sometimes succeeds in this task and sometimes fails, notes Berger, but he is fundamentally a good doctor because "there is about him the constant will of a man trying to recognize" (p. 71).

These features of illness and suffering lead to the unique role the country doctor fulfills for the village, as a privilege the villagers accord to him—he is "the requested clerk of their records" (p. 103). The villagers somehow perceive a need to know that they could, if they wished, consult the stories of their lives, their past illnesses and sufferings included, secure in the knowledge that the records they consult are objectively validated accounts and not merely reflections of their own subjective impressions.[4] They wish, ideally, a record keeper who is thorough and who can relate their stories to the outside world, perhaps drawing upon a level of articulateness that they lack. This function is not the function of the parish priest; the physician claims to represent no all-powerful or omniscient being and will offer their records to no higher judge than themselves. The function is performed at the villagers' request and only upon their own initiation—hence the humble title of clerk. The villagers indeed seldom consciously think of their doctor as a witness or record keeper; yet

4. A statement by a parent suffering from a protracted grief reaction after surrendering a child for adoption illustrates how this objective validation can play a role in the relief of suffering. The patient describes her vain efforts to find out the present whereabouts of the child: "I have had one letdown after another. I can't find out anything. *It's almost as if it [the birth] never happened.* I am very frustrated. I have become obsessed with finding her. I've lost a lot of sleep and have headaches all the time" (Deykin, Campbell, and Patti 1984, p. 276; emphasis added).

One aspect of the stories mutually constructed by physician and patient that explains their comforting quality is that they fit Kermode's (1967) definition of a "concord fiction." The sick or anguished patient experiences himself as being in a terrifying and mysterious "middle" that seems to make no sense. The physician comforts and makes the experience understandable and controllable by supplying an account of a beginning and an end that make the "middle" comprehensible in relation to them. This further reinforces the importance of providing an account of disease causation and disease prognosis in all encounters with patients (Kleinman, Eisenberg, and Good 1978).

"the most frequent opening to a conversation with him, if it is not a professional consultation, are the words 'Do you remember when . . . ?' " (p. 103). "This is what I meant by his being the requested clerk of their records. . . . It has its exact if unstated meaning" (p. 103).

This argument that storytelling heals by restoring a disrupted connectedness is echoed in the views of psychoanalysis as a form of story construction. Brody and Tormey argue that psychoanalysis originally sought to help "persons whose behavior was not intelligible in terms of the usual criteria for understanding others or was not compatible with the social rules of the context in which they lived" (1980, p. 144). "The analyst's past history influences his understanding of the patient and his selection of the words with which to communicate his understanding of the patient. Insofar as it may contain elements in common with the patient, it can be a source of collective knowledge and intuitive recognition" (p. 145). And Hillman argues that in psychoanalysis "one's past . . . is retold, and finds a new internal coherence, even inevitability, through this abnormal story. A diagnosis is indeed a *gnosis:* a mode of self-knowledge that creates a cosmos in its image" (1975, p. 137). The patient comes to analysis because his old story no longer makes his life events cohere: "It doesn't make any sense; . . . I don't know where I am, or who I am" (p. 138). Therapy is a contest between the patient's old story and the therapist's newly created story, which, if it is successful, will have a "more intelligent, more imaginative plot"; a good therapeutic outcome is a "collaboration between fictions" (p. 140).[5]

Perhaps in the final analysis stories are needed to show why stories are essential to healing. Richard Selzer (1975), in an essay entitled "The Exact Location of the Soul," illustrates a theme that runs

---

5. "A psychoneurosis must be understood as the suffering of a human being who has not discovered what life means for him. . . . The doctor who realizes this truth sees a territory opened before him which he approaches with the greatest hesitation. He is now confronted with the necessity of conveying to his patient the healing fiction, the meaning that quickens—for it is this that the patient longs for, over and above all that reason and science can give him" (Jung 1933, p. 225; quoted in Spiro 1986, p. 246).

through much of his work—the idea that the surgeon must somehow enter into a fellowship of suffering with the patient and then proceed to heal himself as the patient is healed (even though, in the process, the surgeon apparently ascends to heights of insight and spirituality that the patient cannot share). The importance of being able to tell a story about the "exact location" of any bodily process is therefore essential (even if the soul itself ultimately eludes precise localization). Only by knowing that the diseased site is precisely localizable and thus potentially removable can the surgeon justify the violation of the human body that is the act of surgery and assuage the guilt that he must feel at that violation. It also helps to assuage the guilt when the diseased part can be conceptualized as irretrievably evil.

Thus, Selzer tells us the story of his amputation of the gangrenous leg of a young blind diabetic woman. Despite his valiant delaying tactics, the foot has deteriorated to a point beyond recall: "There upon her foot was a Mississippi Delta brimming with corruption, sending its raw tributaries down between her toes. . . . There is no pain like that of the bloodless limb turned rotten and festering. There is neither unguent nor anodyne to kill such a pain yet leave intact the body" (1975, p. 16). Under the touch of illness, a portion of the body has turned evil, and he knows the place that it occupies: "At last we gave up, she and I. We could no longer run ahead of the gangrene. We had not the legs for it. There must be an amputation in order that she might live—and I as well. It was to heal us both that I must take up knife and saw, and cut the leg off. And when I could feel it drop from her body to the table, see the blessed *space* appear between her and that leg, I too would be well" (p. 17).

Another time, Selzer (appropriately enough, at night) is exploring a draining abscess on the arm of an archaeologist recently returned from Guatemala. From the portal of the abscess, to Selzer's fascinated horror, "emerges a narrow gray head whose sole distinguishing feature is a pair of black pincers. . . . Abscess? Pus? Never. Here is the lair of a beast at whose malignant purpose I could but guess" (p. 20). This horror, in effect, is the surgeon's dream—totally evil and totally separate from the integral structure of the body; no violation of the body must be accomplished in order to extirpate it.[6] "And even now the irony does not escape me, the irony of my patient as excavator excavated" (1975, p. 20).

Selzer advances, clamp in hand; the creature retreats back into the wound. He tries again:

> Got him! . . . Pinned and wriggling, he is mine. I hear the dry brittle scream of the dragon, and a hatred seizes me, but such a detestation as would make of Iago a drooling sucktit. . . . It is the hatred of fear. Within the jaws of my hemostat is the whole of the evil of the world, the dark concentrate itself, and I shall kill it. For mankind. And, in so doing, will open the way into a thousand years of perfect peace. Here is Surgeon as Savior indeed.
>
> . . . "You are going to be all right," I say to my patient. "We are *all* going to be all right from now on." (p. 21)

Next day, in the laboratory, the crowing of this latter-day St. George is stilled. The pathologists identify the culprit as the larva of a botfly; the adult insect lays its eggs beneath the skin of cattle; the mature larva burrows its way out and falls to the ground. "This one happened to bite a man. It was about to come out on its own, and, of course, it would have died" (p. 23). Selzer notes, more soberly:

> I tried to save the world, but it didn't work out.
>
> No, it is not the surgeon who is God's darling. He is the victim of vanity. It is the poet who heals with his words, stanches the flow of blood, stills the rattling breath, applies poultice to the scalded flesh.
>
> Did you ask me why a surgeon writes? I think it is because I wish to be a doctor. (p. 23)

I have attempted to suggest in a preliminary way that storytelling as an activity is central to medicine.[7] I have also suggested that sto-

---

6. The theme of the disease as localizable evil is one theme that appears in Selzer, but it would be an oversimplification to say that this is his only concept of disease. Elsewhere he speaks of tumors and diseased organs having their own beauty, and he recounts a Chinese legend of a tumor that was opened and released a canary (see Tavormina 1982).

7. A small but increasing number of physicians have recently begun to focus upon the theme of story and storytelling as a way to better characterize medical activity and interactions with patients. See, for example, Hunter 1985; Cameron and Dickie 1985; Stephens 1985; Daniel 1986, and chapters 9–11.

rytelling as an activity within society is allied to healing and can serve a healing function. I have suggested that these observations can be analyzed in a meaningful way and that they can be illustrated by appropriate case studies and literary examples. I must, however, at this point, forestall a likely objection—that the notion of "story" is so vague and all-inclusive that it excludes nothing and hence cannot be useful in coming to a finer understanding of what medicine might be about. Let us turn, then, to what we mean by "story" and "narrative."

WHAT IS A STORY?

If the scientific physician is likely to resist any analysis of medical practice that thrusts storytelling onto center stage, the analytic philosopher is equally likely to object to the storytelling theme, perhaps arguing that the concept is too vague to be useful in any philosophical inquiry. Storytelling is such a broad term, it might be argued, that there is really no place in medicine where one could *not* be said to be telling stories of one sort or another, so long as one is using language; and so the metaphor of storytelling cannot be used to distinguish one set of activities from any others within medicine. It is therefore useful to be reminded that the story, in the study of literature, is a concept denoting a particular form and function, and that reasonably precise descriptions and theories of storytelling are at hand if one chooses to take advantage of them. Moreover, recently renewed interest in story and narrative in fields as diverse as medicine, philosophy, psychology, and communications theory has increased the number of authors offering helpful definitions and descriptions.

E. M. Forster has suggested one simple definition: "a story is a narrative of events arranged in a time sequence; we read on in a story to find out 'what happens next?' " (quoted in Hillman 1975, p. 127). Although a detailed review of literary theory may not suit our present purposes, Churchill and Churchill (1982) have attempted to delineate the important dimensions of the concept of "story" as it could be applied to medicine. They suggest four key points:

1. "Human beings understand their experiences in and through the telling and hearing of stories. Narration is the forward movement

of description of actions and events which makes possible the backward action of selfunderstanding'' (p. 73).

2. ''Unlike the careful factual description of history, narrative asserts the *human* meaning of events, creating, often metaphorically, the categories for interpreting those events. So, one may review past events through narration and say, 'Oh, now I see,' as if for the first time'' (pp. 73–74).

3. ''Stories are devices which bind agents and events into some intelligible pattern. They weld actors to their actions and doers to their deeds'' (p. 74).

4. ''Both distance and intimacy characterize storytelling. . . . The dialectic of distance and intimacy is what makes storytelling distinctive as a mode of self-knowledge'' (p. 74). Distance exists because the narrator is separated from the narrated events in time and thus can assume a reflective, observant posture toward those events in a way that was impossible when the events were in progress. Intimacy exists, especially in autobiographical narrative, because the narrator *is* the individual mentioned in the narrative, is responsible for the events disclosed, and thus has a personal stake in how others react to the telling of the story. Hillman argues that the soul has a basic need to tell autobiographical stories, to historicize, whether or not there is an audience; historicizing is a way of ''maintaining an event intact but removed, in a glass vessel so that it can be puzzled over without being identified with. . . . We historicize to give the events of our lives a dignity that they cannot receive from contemporaneousness'' (1975, pp. 164–65). And one philosopher interested in the nature of ethics thinks that this tendency to historicize is of philosophical and not only of psychological interest:

> Therefore any person, man and woman alike, will be interested both in explaining and in justifying their present conduct by referring to their personal history. Historical explanation, as a mode of understanding, comes naturally to everyone, because all normal men and women are interested in their own origins and their own history and the history of their family. They are not able to think of themselves, as utilitarians and Kantians demand, as unclothed citizens of the universe, merely rational and ''sentient'' beings, deposited

in no particular place at no particular time. (Hampshire 1983, p. 166)

Two additional features of story or narrative are suggested by Fisher (1984). First, he argues that resorting to narration as a means of organizing and making sense of the world is not to reject canons of truth or rationality; it is instead to modify and extend those canons beyond the limited sense implied by logical argumentation. This means that people can offer good stories and bad stories to make sense of a particular event, and that others can give well-grounded reasons for preferring one story over the others. Fisher suggests that people's choices among competing stories will be based on two factors, *narrative probability* (an inherent awareness of what constitutes a coherent story) and *narrative fidelity* (whether they story rings true in the light of one's own past experience and of other stories that one has previously accepted). The concepts of narrative probability and narrative fidelity suggest that a coherence, rather than a correspondence, theory of truth is at work in the judging of a narrative's adequacy.

Fisher also notes that storytelling has an inherently moral dimension. A story presumes both a teller and a community of listeners, such that the act of telling the story and responding to it is a reciprocal exercise designed in part to strengthen community bonds. At the crude level of Aesop's fables or *Uncle Tom's Cabin,* telling a story is saying to the listener, "Here is the way in which you ought to behave." In more subtle instances, telling a story is saying to the listener, "This is the meaning you ought to place upon events of such-and-such a sort." Implicit in the act of storytelling is the message "If you behave or interpret events as the story suggests, then you are one of us; if you don't, then you run the risk of rejection by this community." The listeners, of course, can object to the story, and its moral message, by arguing that one ought not to behave that way or to interpret events in that manner. Narrative reasoning, for Fisher, is inherently democratic—which is another moral choice implicit in the reciprocal act of storytelling. A sense of narrative probability and narrative fidelity is widely shared by lay persons, and so the interpretation of stories cannot be claimed as the exclusive province of experts. Of course, the more subtle the narrative, the more levels of meaning it possesses, which may be the same thing as saying that it anticipates multiple communities of listeners simultaneously.

Bruner (1986) takes the reciprocal nature of storytelling one step further by arguing that the reader or listener is *necessarily* involved in the narrative. "The story," so far as the listener is concerned, is not the actual text—the words uttered by the speaker—but rather the virtual text that the listener constructs for himself according to what the utterance *means to him;* and it is the virtual text that the listener will recount when asked to repeat "the story" at a later time. "That is what is at the core of literary narrative as a speech act: an utterance or a text whose intention is to initiate and guide a search for meanings among a spectrum of possible meanings" (Bruner 1986, p. 25).[8]

Some further distinctions have been suggested, although I will not find them particularly useful in most of what follows. Hepburn (1956), who is interested primarily in stories as a mode for a deeper understanding of morality, distinguishes the *story* of one's life, a bald narrative of events, from a *fable,* which is a set of coherent themes that give form and meaning to one's life. The baldly stated narrative of one's life tells of events that simply happened, but, within

---

8. Bruner, in contrast to Fisher, is interested more in *gifted* storytellers; and this may lead him to overemphasize subtlety, levels of meaning, and so on. Both Bruner and Fisher are concerned with the question of whether the narrative mode or the scientific-rational mode of understanding is more basic to human experience. Fisher seems to adhere to the view that they deserve equal status, representing different canons of rationality rather than a rationality-irrationality split. In some places Bruner agrees, for example, that "science creates a world that has an 'existence' linked to the invariance of things and events across transformations in the life conditions of those who seek to understand—though modern physics has shown this to be true within very constrained limits. The humanities seek to understand the world as it reflects the requirements of living in it" (1986, p. 50). In other places Bruner seems to opt for a more basic role of narrative, as when he notes that it is via the narrative mode that we acquire "knowledge of other minds" (p. 69; cf. MacIntyre 1981). Kermode, the literary critic, insists that our way of understanding the world is *fundamentally* via the mode of fiction and emphasizes how we insist on imposing our fictive ideas of beginning, middle, and end upon a world that, in a purely empirical analysis, presents time to us as a seamless web (1967).

the constraints of one's psychological makeup and one's cultural environment, one can choose or create one's own fable. For reasons noted earlier in this chapter, the fable ought to have much greater healing potential than the mere story.

Still thinking primarily of morality, Hepburn further distinguishes both story and fable from *parable,* which is a type of story, since it is typically richly descriptive and highly dependent upon context; but it is treated not as a unique story but as a maxim, as if it suggests that the behavior narrated is rationally justifiable in all relevantly similar circumstances. Many medical stories partake of this dimension, as the physician is always caught in the tension between the uniqueness of the individual patient and the need to explain the patient's illness by means of generally applicable laws.

It is thus possible to distinguish the storytelling mode from other modes of description and explanation in science and medicine as well as in everyday life. (It is possible to go even further and analyze particular medical events as specific types of stories, such as tragedy or comedy, although this will not be attempted here.) For example, the invocation of general scientific laws or statistical regularities is not storytelling. It is not storytelling to say on a hospital ward, "In the Mayo Clinic study several years ago, patients who were anticoagulated for deep vein thrombosis for less than six months had a 34 percent rate of occurrence of new pulmonary emboli; so we had better make sure that Mrs. Smith takes her anticoagulant medication for at least six months after she is discharged." We might remind ourselves, however, that general laws and statistical descriptions are not all there is to science. Gorovitz and MacIntyre (1976) have argued that one can have science of particulars, and that scientific descriptions encountered in fields like ecology or meteorology (descriptions of, say, the ecosystem of a particular salt marsh or the origins of a particular hurricane) begin to share more and more characteristics with narration and storytelling.[9]

9. MacIntyre and Gorovitz suggested in this paper that since they had illustrated the possibility of a science of particulars, medicine might best be viewed as such a science. However, I will discuss in the next chapter the reasons against viewing medicine as a science of any sort.

Another common mode of medical discourse that is also distinguishable from storytelling is the maxim, or "clinical pearl." These
may be general (as the traditional "First, do no harm," or the internist's standard variant of this, "Keep the patient out of the hands
of the surgeons"), or they may be more circumscribed, as "If the
thought of doing a spinal tap on a pediatric patient crosses your
mind, that probably means the tap is medically indicated." These
are not stories because they do not take into account the particularity
of the patient; they are generalizations, even if unscientific and invalid
ones. But the storytelling mode is clearly present in such discourse
as "We had better do a set of thyroid studies on Mrs. Jones. The
last late-middle-aged lady I placed on tricyclic drugs for what I
thought was her endogenous depression turned out to be hypothy-
roid." Here two particular individuals are mentioned and an analogy
is suggested between the two cases (again, an analogy that may be
valid or invalid depending on the circumstances). This example suggests a *parable* in the sense that Hepburn (1956) employs the term.

With such distinctions in mind, the storytelling mode can be invoked whenever one wishes to criticize medical practices that do not
take individual characteristics of patients sufficiently into account
while masquerading as full explanations of the phenomena. For example, Churchill (1979) has used the concept of story to good effect
in criticizing Kubler-Ross's (1969) five-stage theory of the dying
process, arguing that health professionals who are seduced by such
theories are unlikely to listen carefully as dying patients attempt to
tell us their own stories of their unique dying experiences and concerns.

A focus on story and narrative as an approach to understanding
the meaning of sickness, however, is at odds with the way that philosophy of medicine has generally been conducted in the last decade
or so since this area of inquiry has been recognized as a distinct
subspecialty within philosophy. There is a considerable literature on
"concepts of health and disease." But that literature usually begins
(and often ends) with disease and illness as abstract concepts. Detailed
stories of sick persons are seldom provided as a means to understanding the concepts.

I will urge that this predominant approach to philosophy of medicine must be modified or at least supplemented. But a review of the conclusions of philosophers and other scholars attempting to understand the nature of disease and of medicine will nevertheless be useful as a guide to looking at the stories we will consider later on. I will provide a brief overview of the most important conclusions in the next chapter.

2

Dimensions of Sickness

Philosophical investigations into the nature of health and disease have provided many insights and, conversely, have led ultimately to frustrations. I attribute many of the frustrations to the notion that only by abstracting the idea of disease from the particular context of the sickness episode and the sick person can one arrive at the "essence" of disease, which is what counts as true philosophical knowledge.[1] This approach becomes less plausible when we consider examples like this statement: "The sick person faces marked alterations in his personhood. . . . his 'worth' and sense of self-worth as a person are all subject to drastic modification" (Rollin 1979, pp. 164–65). On its face this generalization seems defensible; and yet with further thought we are bound to ask—is this true of *any* episode of illness? If we then look at a previous passage in the same paper and note

1. My approach follows Wittgenstein (1958) in being suspicious that the meaning of complex terms like *sickness* is to be found in its so-called essence rather than in its uses in human activities, and R. Rorty (1979, 1982) in being suspicious of a view of philosophy that holds that "real" knowledge is necessarily transcendental or foundational, and that philosophy, via a correct theory of knowledge, can somehow arrive at an eternal, culture-free observation platform from which "the world as it really is" can be clearly seen. Instead, in regard to sickness and personhood, I shall try to follow a philosophical method that asks "how things in the broadest possible sense of the term hang together in the broadest possible sense of the term" (Sellars 1963, p. 1).

that this author has included *warts* as an undoubted, bona fide example of a "sickness," then the generalization about "drastic modifications in self-worth" becomes almost ludicrous. But this example could be multiplied manyfold in the literature I will briefly review below.[2]

Still, the conclusions of scholars (not all of them philosophers) who have reflected upon the nature of sickness will prove invaluable in suggesting themes and issues that we can find in literary and case studies of individual instances of sickness. The works of these scholars have centered on several questions. Can a definition of sickness be given?[3] What is the nature of sickness as immediate or primary experience? How is sickness related to the nature of medical activity? How is sickness construed as a social role or relationship? And, finally, what view of sickness best ties together these disparate dimensions? As answers to these questions, I will offer the following summary conclusions, dealing with each in turn. As the discussion

2. Two major questions in philosophy of medicine that I will not address are the concept of health and the concept of mental, as opposed to physical, illness. The former is peripheral to my concerns in this book. The latter is occasionally of great interest; but I hope to show that the problems of working with so-called physical illness are sufficient to occupy our attention. Later in this chapter I will also try to soften any residual mind-body dualism that continues to infect our concepts of sickness and medicine. On the concept of health, see Kass 1975; Boorse 1975; Engelhardt 1975, 1978; Burns 1976; Erde 1979; Kelman 1980; Whitbeck 1981. For the concept of mental health, see Parsons 1958; Kraupl-Taylor 1972, 1976; Flew 1973; Sedgwick 1973; Redlich 1976; Toulmin 1977; Eisenberg 1977b; Engelhardt 1978; Ruse 1981; Edwards 1981; Culver and Gert 1982.

3. Of the terms *disease, illness,* and *sickness* I have chosen the last for the title of this book for two reasons. One is that, when the three terms are used side by side (as, for example, in Erde 1979), *sickness* is often used as the one that implies a social dimension, and I will want to focus on the social dimensions of sickness in many places. The second is that the precise meaning of the distinction between *disease* and *illness* has been much discussed, but never resolved, within the philosophy of medicine, and choosing one of these two terms might suggest that I was adopting one particular form or another of this distinction. In fact, I have identified five ways of drawing a disease-illness distinction, although the authors in every case refer to their own way as *the* disease-illness distinction (Engel 1960; Feinstein 1967; Fabrega 1972, 1979; Spiro 1975; Boorse 1975; Redlich 1976; Cassell 1976; Margolis 1976; Engelhardt 1976, 1978; Eisenberg 1977a; Kleinman, Eisenberg, and Good 1978; Rollin 1979; Aranow 1979; Bergsma and Thomasma 1982; Hahn 1983; Williams and Hadler 1983; Chrisman and Kleinman 1983). Although I hope to be able to address this matter in detail on a future occasion, I cannot do so in this book.

of each will necessarily be brief, I will indicate the undiscussed philosophical complexities in some rather lengthy footnotes.

1. To be sick is to have something wrong with oneself in a way regarded as abnormal when compared with a suitably chosen reference class.
2. To be sick is to experience both an unpleasant sense of disruption of body and self and a threat to one's integrated personhood.
3. To be sick is to have the sort of thing that medicine, as an evolving craft, has customarily treated.
4. To be sick is to undergo an alteration of one's social roles and relationships in ways that will be influenced by cultural belief systems.
5. To be sick is to participate in a disruption of an integrated hierarchy of natural systems, including one's biological subsystems, oneself as a discrete psychological entity, and the social and cultural systems of which one is a member.

Each of these statements represents a generalization of the sort criticized at the beginning of this chapter. Hence, each should be seen as an approach to a further investigation of particular sickness episodes spanning the entire range of illness experiences, and not as a shortcut making such an investigation unnecessary.

SICKNESS, EVIL, AND ABNORMALITY

The class of sicknesses or diseases includes entities as diverse as allergic rhinitis, malignant melanoma, muscular dystrophy, plantar warts, pneumococcal pneumonia, minimal brain dysfunction or hyperactivity, infertility, and schizophrenia. In addition, some closely allied entities are usually labeled instead as "injuries," "disabilities," and "impairments" less for strong conceptual reasons than for mere convention's sake (Whitbeck 1978). Such a list might well make us despair of finding a set of essential features that all share in common (Guttentag 1949; Rollin 1979; Siegler 1981). We might be led instead to suspect that "the concept of disease indicates a family of conceptually consanguineous notions" (Engelhardt 1975;

cf. Wittgenstein 1958, 1:66–67; Engelhardt 1984). Yet philosophers have resisted this "family resemblance" hypothesis in hopes of arriving at a satisfactory formal definition that includes all states usually felt to be diseases and excludes all states recognized as not being diseases.

Many formal definitions along these lines have been offered,[4] but their multiplicity suggests that none has been quite satisfactory. Several problems have recurred. Some definitions, especially those offered in medical and pathological textbooks, tend to be circular and uninformative, perhaps defining *disease* as a "morbid state." Other definitions tend to be over- or underinclusive. A definition that focuses on the symptoms experienced by the patient, for example, will leave out asymptomatic conditions such as essential hypertension. On the other hand, a definition that focuses on the undesirability or dysfunctional nature of the state may include conditions like unemployment and poor television reception (Clouser, Culver, and Gert 1981).

Two general approaches have offered more promise. One is the effort to define sickness as essentially something abnormal. This has been spurred on by the hope that we will discover a value-free concept of disease—one that is purely an empirical description of a biological state of affairs and not a judgment of the goodness or badness of that state (Boorse 1975; Kass 1975). Boorse has suggested that the "natural design" of the species can be determined by empirical and statistical means, as can a failure to function in accord with that natural design (taking the age and sex of the individual into account). If one then defines disease as the failure to function in accord with natural species design, one supposedly has a definition of a concept that is at least as value-free as any other concept in the biological sciences.

Unfortunately this search for a value-free definition leads to difficulties. Some statistically normal conditions, like atherosclerosis in middle-aged American males or dental caries, are regarded as

4. For representative definitions of *disease*, see King 1954; Redlich 1976; Margolis 1976; Kraupl-Taylor 1976; Whitbeck 1978, 1981; Fabrega 1979; Caplan 1981.

diseases; and some statistically abnormal conditions, like extremely high intelligence, are not viewed as diseases (Nordenfelt 1984; cf. Margolis 1976; Engelhardt 1976). To deal with the former examples, Boorse is reduced to speaking of a "hostile environment" as the cause of the condition, but that looks suspiciously like allowing value judgments back in again.[5]

A different and apparently more promising approach was suggested by Clouser, Culver, and Gert (1981). They offered two initial observations. First, the fundamental notion of sickness is not *functioning abnormally*, but rather *having something wrong with oneself*. Second, the idea of "having something wrong with oneself" is shared by a variety of terms—*disease, illness, sickness, injury, disability*, and so on. They suggested that *malady* be stipulated as the genus term of which all the preceding were to be viewed as species terms. They then suggested the following definition: "A person has a malady if and only if he or she has a condition, other than a rational belief or desire, such that he or she is suffering, or at increased risk of suffering, an evil (death, pain, disability, loss of freedom or opportunity, or loss of pleasure) in the absence of a distinct sustaining cause" (p. 36).[6]

---

5. Several lines of rebuttal to Boorse (1975) have been proposed. First, one can dispute Boorse's argument that the functional explanations relevant to disease states are the same sorts of value-free functional explanations that occur in biology (Margolis 1976; Bunzl 1980; Munson 1981). Second, one can assert that the concept of disease is fundamentally and necessarily value-laden (Sedgwick 1973; Engelhardt 1975, 1976, 1984; Redlich 1976; Kellert 1976; Eisenberg 1977a; Whitbeck 1978, 1981; Goosens 1980; Caplan 1981; Caplan, Engelhardt, and McCartney 1981). Third, one can note that Boorse's idea of a value-free concept of disease involves the ability to make a radical distinction between medical science and medical practice (as Boorse agrees that the latter realm is essentially value-laden). But Pellegrino and Thomasma (1981) and Munson (1981) offer compelling reasons why medicine cannot be viewed as fundamentally or primarily a science, and Temkin (1963) notes that the emergence of "scientific" medical research as a distinct activity apart from medical practice is historically a very recent development.

6. The definition excludes rational beliefs and desires because one can be suffering an evil for such a reason (for example, feeling pain because a close friend has died) without having a disease. It specifies "increased risk" of suffering an evil so as to include asymptomatic conditions like essential hypertension and the early stages of cancer. "Evil" is defined separately as the sort of thing that one avoids unless one has a reason not to. The five evils mentioned in the definition are taken to exhaust the class. Loss of freedom

In this definition, the concept of abnormality enters only indirectly. It is necessary to specify (to some degree) what is meant by "disability," "increased risk," and "distinct sustaining cause." But it plays a peripheral role rather than the central role envisioned by Boorse. The definition also suggests where Boorse has the right idea and where he has gone astray. Whether one is suffering, or at increased risk of suffering, one of the five specified "evils" is a matter of fact, open to empirical investigation, but *that* such states are evil is irreducibly a value judgment. Thus, both the value-free and the value-laden elements of the concept of disease are clarified.

For all its good points, the "malady" definition ultimately fails for being too inclusive. The unfortunately elastic phrases are primarily "increased risk" and "loss of freedom and opportunity." Because of them, conditions like pregnancy, menstruation, menopause, and indeed being asleep could all be construed as maladies (Martin 1985). In each case one suffers loss of freedom or opportunity and is at increased risk of suffering some other evil. Note that the condition of being asleep is an especially troublesome counterexample, since one would also be at increased risk if one suffered from serious insomnia. In part, the all-inclusiveness arises from the idea of "loss of opportunity," since being in any state presumably counts as the loss of the opportunity to be in some other state at that particular time.

If we ask why menopause, pregnancy, and sleeping should not be considered maladies, the most obvious answer is: *because they are normal*. This answer suggests that the concept of normality and normal functioning is more central to the concept of sickness than Clouser, Culver, and Gert have recognized. No definition combining the concept of abnormal functioning with that of having something wrong with oneself has yet been offered, however.

---

and opportunity and loss of pleasure are included because diseases like psoriasis would be left out if one insisted that a disease must cause death, pain, or disability. Finally, one may be suffering pain because a wrestler has one in a half nelson; but if the evil goes away as soon as, or shortly after, the cause is removed, it would not be considered a malady (that is, one does not have something wrong *with oneself* if the evil goes away as soon as a distinct and external cause is removed; the cause of a malady is assumed to have an internal location).

Two related points that arise from a consideration of the value-laden features of the concept of sickness should be mentioned. First, a sickness is the sort of thing that one seeks to avoid.[7] This is different from being something that is inherently to be avoided. The latter statement would suggest that one never seeks to be sick, but this is obviously untrue. People have sought to injure themselves in various ways so as to avoid military conscription, and all of us accept a mild febrile illness with local swelling as the desired outcome of an immunization. These are the sorts of things that people seek to avoid, but in specific cases, people may not actually seek to avoid them (especially if some greater evil can be prevented by accepting the smaller evil that the sickness poses). This is like saying "A hammer is the sort of thing you use to pound nails." Pounding nails defines the general *class* of hammer, but any one particular hammer may serve as a doorstop or paperweight without ceasing to be a hammer in consequence.

Second, a sickness is ascribed to an individual, but the "normal state" that helps define when one is sick is a population norm, not an individual norm. This means two things—individuals can be sick, but populations or groups cannot (except in a metaphorical sense), and an individual cannot define himself as sick unilaterally without some validating external standard. "I feel worse than usual today" is not sufficient to establish sickness; one has to add on something like a viral rhinitis or a tension headache that would be recognized as deviating sufficiently from the relevant group norms. This logical feature of the concept of sickness lays the groundwork for seeing sickness as partly dependent upon social roles and relationships.

SICKNESS AND DISRUPTION OF SELF

Defining sickness in terms of evil and abnormality suggests an analytic approach that distances the observer and describer from the immediate experience of being sick. To philosophers of a phenom-

---

7. I prefer this locution to "diseases are things that one wishes to be able to avoid" (Whitbeck 1978, 1981), and "diseases are threats of what one wishes to avoid" (Goosens 1980).

enological bent, this is ultimately incomplete; one must, in addition, strive to capture the immediacy of the sickness experience prior to the point at which the analytical distancing occurs.[8] The accounts of sickness that result from this approach have in common the idea of a disruption of self—an unpleasantly experienced break or split in a sense of personhood that ought, instead, to be felt as whole or complete.

A basic tenet underlying this phenomenology of sickness is a rejection of Cartesian dualism and an insistence upon seeing the person as a fundamental unity. Whatever the metaphysical puzzles regarding the relationship between mind and body, at the level of immediate experience, I am I, a single entity, not an admixture of mind-me and body-me. My body is not a different substance, but simply my own presence in and interaction with the world. My body moving through the world and bumping into things is simply me moving and bumping (Gadow 1980). It follows from this that, if sickness leads us to see our bodies as being something foreign, thwarting our wills by their intransigence and unmanageability, then sickness has fundamentally altered our experience of self and has introduced a sense of split and disruption where formerly unity reigned.

Neurologist Oliver Sacks tells of his climbing a mountain, falling, and breaking his leg (1984). He discovers later that he has also suffered considerable nerve damage, resulting in loss of movement and sensation and necessitating a prolonged period of recuperation. Even before he is aware of the grave extent of his injuries, however, the disruption of self sets in: "My first thought was this: that there had been an accident, and that *someone I knew* had been seriously injured" (p. 21). Later, in the hospital, he finally realizes that his quadriceps muscle is paralyzed; but he is also aware, with dread and foreboding, that his "calling out" to the muscle, his "trying" to move the muscle, constitutes by its ineffectiveness a funny sort of

8. There is a rich literature in phenomenology, and specifically in the phenomenology of medicine, which my own analytical training renders me incapable of discussing adequately. I thus rely heavily on works by philosophers who have studied this literature but who have discussed their findings in language more congenial to analytic philosophy (Gadow 1980; Pellegrino and Thomasma 1981; Bergsma and Thomasma 1982).

inability to call out or to try. In neurological terms, he has sensed a peripheral lesion but has then come to relocate the lesion as a central one: *"not just a lesion in my muscle, but a lesion in me"* (p. 67).

Later, the sensory aspect of this denervation experience hits Sacks with full force—not only can he not move his leg when he "tries," but he cannot tell without looking whether the leg is on the bed or falling off the side. Again, this peripheral phenomenon suggests experientially a central gap of existence: "In that instant . . . *I knew not my leg*. It was utterly strange, not-mine, unfamiliar. I gazed upon it with absolute non-recognition" (p. 72).[9] It is not, Sacks realizes, as if he has simply lost his leg, as if he were an amputee; in a deeper sense, he has lost the place where the leg is supposed to go; if his leg were to be returned to him he would have nowhere to put it. In short, the disruption of his sense of self and of his sense of reality is much deeper than would be suggested by "my leg is paralyzed and I can't feel anything in it." This experience persists throughout a long course of physical therapy, during which the leg slowly improves. It leaves only when Sacks discovers himself walking automatically and unthinkingly in time to music: "In the very moment when my 'motor' music, my kinetic melody, my walking, came back—in this self-same moment *the leg came back*. Suddenly, with no warning, no transition whatever, the leg felt alive, and real, and mine" (p. 144).

Another lesson from Sacks's experience is that at no time during these events was Sacks truly afraid that he would die. Death is the ultimate dissolution of self and of personhood, and it might be assumed that the experience of sickness is threatening and unpleasant

---

9. Sacks notes that this sense of not recognizing a part of one's own body, indeed feeling that a dead body part must have been put into one's hospital bed alongside oneself, has been described neurologically (Anton's syndrome) (Sacks 1984, pp. 75–80). This is not terribly rare. I was once told by a stroke patient that he had awakened to find a strange object in his bed, had thrown it out, and only then realized that the object was his arm. What is rare, if Sacks is to be believed (and is not overdramatizing for literary purposes), is the willingness of the physician to hear the depth of despair and fear this experience triggers in the patient.

simply because it reminds one of one's mortality.[10] Our discussion so far, however, reveals the incompleteness of this theory; sickness is *of itself* an unpleasant disruption of the self, independent of the possibility of death.

In sickness, the "lived body," which is simply us existing and acting in the world, turns into the "object body," a rebellious slave that thwarts our will (Gadow 1980). Illness is thus truly an "ontological assault," affecting our very being and not simply our activities (Pellegrino 1979; Pellegrino and Thomasma 1981, pp. 207–08). When ill, I can no longer take my existence as an integrated whole entity for granted, as I am wont to do when healthy, and this in turn produces undesired feelings of egocentricity and dependency (Bergsma and Thomasma 1982, p. 182). Several levels of resolution are possible. I may simply recover completely and return to the status quo ante. I may have to make an accommodation with my rebellious body and resign myself to a different way of functioning, so that I no longer experience a constant tension between my "mind's" will and expectation and my "body's" recalcitrance. Or ultimately I may come to listen more sympathetically to my body, to see it as a source of values that legitimately should play a role in how I live my life, and not simply as having value only when it carries out the wishes of other aspects of the self. Gadow (1980) feels that the latter mode of resolution may be characteristic of aging, and hence she would argue that all sickness is a sort of foreshadowing of the aging process.

On the other hand, perhaps it is overly dramatic to see, in every commonplace sickness episode, this dread and grandiose "ontological assault." Perhaps what we are describing here is not sickness per se, but sickness that is associated with true *suffering* (Cassell 1982). For example, pain per se does not equal suffering (as today's marathon runners are always demonstrating). But pain may constitute suffering when it is overwhelming, uncontrolled, unexplained, or in

10. Gorovitz (1982, pp. 60–61) suggests four reasons illness is bad, and only one is that it reminds the sufferer of human vulnerability and mortality. The others are it causes discomfort and dysfunction; it causes an undesirable egocentricity with a shrunken world-view; and the egocentricity is boring and constraining (and gives the sufferer a sense of being boring to her close friends). We will discuss these points further in chapter 6.

some other way associated with a dire *meaning* that calls into question the continued, integrated existence of the personal self. Being a person is a multidimensional enterprise. Persons have psychological identities, past histories, future plans, social relationships, spiritual and transcendental beliefs, patterns of activities, and so forth; and any one or more of these aspects of personhood can be disrupted by sickness so as to constitute suffering. For Cassell, as I argued in chapter 1, relief of suffering comes most often by changing the meaning of the experience for the sufferer and restoring the disrupted connectedness of the sufferer with herself and those around her. Indeed, modern medical practice, by focusing so exclusively on bodily pain and ignoring the multiple aspects of personhood and personal meaning, may inadvertently increase suffering while seeking to relieve it.

SICKNESS, TREATMENT, AND MEDICAL ACTIVITY

Of all the proposed definitions of sickness, ''Sickness is something that doctors treat'' may seem most hopelessly circular and uninformative. We are used to medical and policy debates that, shorn of excess verbiage, go something like this: alcoholism is a disease because the medical establishment treats it; and the medical establishment has a responsibility to treat alcoholics because they are sick. We have, furthermore, been warned by social critics that such definitions of disease represent the medicalization of society and thus are a political power play of the medical establishment rather than a true explication of puzzling conditions (Illich 1976; Lasch 1979).

And yet some conceptual link between sickness and therapy seems unavoidable. At some point along the way, to claim that something is a disease seems to imply necessarily that one would want to be able to prevent or terminate it.[11] The challenge, then, is to articulate

---

11. For arguments that the concept of therapy is necessary to understand the concept of disease, see Whitbeck 1978; H. Brody 1980, 1981, pp. 311–12; Engelhardt 1984, p. 36). For more general arguments, to show that therapy partially defines clinical activity even if not disease, see, Guttentag 1949; Parsons 1958; Kraupl-Taylor 1971; Sedgwick 1973; Veatch 1973; Redlich 1976, pp. 275–76; Siegler 1981.

this connection between sickness and therapy in an informative and noncircular fashion. This, in turn, will require a more sophisticated understanding of the nature of medical activity; and ultimately the circularity will disappear when we recall that medicine generally, and medical therapy specifically, has a history. To say "we treat alcoholism medically because it is a disease" may be uninformative. But a history of alcoholism and medicine in twentieth-century United States, detailing earlier efforts to suppress alcoholism by regarding it as sin or as crime, and elaborating on the expanded concepts of medical science and medical capabilities that arose just as the failure of these earlier efforts was being documented, might be richly informative.

We must first note what it means for medicine to be a practice.[12] Medicine has grown and evolved over centuries as an integrated and unified activity. What medicine is and is not, at any given point in time, can usually be stated satisfactorily both by its practitioners and by nonpractitioners, even in the absence of infallible rules or algorithms for making such a determination. Practitioners begin their careers in apprenticeship fashion, being trained in the rudiments of the practice and suppressing critical, independent judgment to a large

12. "By a 'practice' I am going to mean any coherent and complex form of socially established cooperative activity through which goods internal to that form of activity are realized in the course of trying to achieve those standards of excellence which are appropriate to, and partially definitive of, that form of activity, with the result that human powers to achieve excellence, and human conceptions of the ends and goods involved, are systematically extended" (MacIntyre 1981, p. 175). Crucial to MacIntyre's concept of a practice is the existence of internal standards of excellence distinguishable from the outputs of the activity. Thus medical practice might be "excellent" in two different senses—it produces better health for the patient (external standard) and it adheres to the highest qualities as developed by the practitioners themselves (internal standard). (This use of the notions of internal and external goods differs from the usage of Munson 1981; see discussion below). See also Long (1986) on why medicine can be a practice only in a fairly limited sense.

MacIntyre lists as examples of "nonpractices" tic-tac-toe, throwing a football accurately, and planting turnips, whereas chess, playing the game of football, and farming all constitute true practices as defined above. In general, excellence at a practice involves both a certain natural aptitude and also an extended period of training or apprenticeship. These concepts will become important in chapter 5 when I will want to assert that being sick, under some circumstances, could become a practice.

degree while this training occurs. Later, however, they may make new discoveries or inaugurate new methods that systematically change the nature of some part of medical activity. Medicine thus has both its conservative and its innovative aspects.

All the above could be said of the sciences, and thus it might be suggested that medicine is fundamentally a science. The value-free concept of disease addressed above (Boorse 1975) presupposes that a science of medicine exists as distinguishable from medical practice, and that the concept of disease lives comfortably and primarily in the former realm. But this view, like the value-free concept of disease that it generates, is fundamentally mistaken.[13] Medicine can be distinguished from science with regard to its internal aims, its internal criteria for success, and its internal regulatory principles (Munson 1981). Science aims at discovery of truth, and it succeeds precisely when it discovers a truth, regardless of whether that truth aids any other practical human endeavor outside of science itself. Its internal regulatory principles also have a moral flavor (as falsifying research data, for example, constitutes one of the most basic violations of the scientific code); but that moral obligation is an impersonal commitment to truth generally.

Medicine, by contrast, seeks jointly the expansion of knowledge and the use of that knowledge to cure individual patients; but the first aim is in the service of the second, and it is only with actual cure that medicine considers itself to have accomplished its criteria for success. And, furthermore, medicine recognizes a morality as a part of its internal organizing principles, but this is specifically a personal morality, and fiduciary duties are owed to particular sick

13. Medicine "is primarily an art and, dependently, a science: it is primarily an *institutionalized service concerned with the care and cure of the ill and the control of disease*" (Margolis 1976, p. 242); "clinical medicine . . . does not claim to be a science. It admits, rather, to being a practice informed by science" (E. B. Brody and Tormey 1980, p. 146). Temkin (1963) provides a basis for perceiving the ahistoric aspects of Boorse's assertion. Medical research, as an activity distinct from medical practice, arose only in the mid-1800s. If Boorse is correct, then, medicine prior to the nineteenth century must have had a radically different concept of disease from that which we have today. But such a discontinuity in the concept of disease seems poorly supported by the historical record (cf. King 1982).

persons once they come under medical treatment. Thus, although both science and medicine are social activities, medicine is *inherently* a social activity in a way that science is not (Munson 1981).

If medicine is not a science, how may it best be characterized? I would contend that medicine is best viewed as having four features. Medicine is

1. a *practical craft* that applies
2. *scientific knowledge* to
3. *individual cases* for purposes of a
4. *right and good healing action* (Pellegrino and Thomasma 1981).

Although medicine is not a science, the popular phrase "the art of medicine" seems inappropriate as well as vague; medicine is concerned not to create new works of beauty but rather to restore. The idea of a practical craft captures this aim and its attendant complexity (with the need for an extended apprenticeship) and assures a status somewhere in between science and art. Despite the fact that medicine is not a science, scientific knowledge is indispensable for its activity. Since our definition focuses on the historical continuity and the organic and gradual evolution of medicine, we must stress that what counts as medical "science" will be relative to the historical period under scrutiny. The humoral medicine of the Middle Ages was not, by our definition, "unscientific" or "prescientific" medicine; it was a practical craft that utilized the best science available to it. Since medicine is not a science, the nature of the scientific knowledge cannot by itself define what counts as expertise in the practice of the craft. Instead, that expertise lies in the *ability to apply general scientific observations to individual cases for restorative purposes* (cf. Pellegrino and Thomasma 1981, p. 63). We should note that this particular skill might remain more constant over time than the scientific knowledge that forms a necessary precondition for its practice, so that a skilled practitioner over time can change his scientific knowledge base without much altering his skills. Finally, the account of medicine includes a moral dimension, an indispensable value commitment to healing actions that count as benefits for the particular persons subject to the medical activity. Thus, if medicine can be viewed as an activity exhibiting a good deal of historical unity, one thing that gives it its unity is the relative constancy of what human members of our culture regard as "right and good healing actions" in the face of sickness and "ontological assault."

To argue for the necessity of understanding therapy to understand sickness supposes an ongoing dialogue between the society and culture at large and the profession of medicine. This has implications for problematic examples such as alcoholism, where defining disease in terms of therapy may at first seem circular (cf. Fingarette 1985). Medicine cannot unilaterally impose a new treatment upon society; society must recognize it as conforming to the existing concepts of "rightness and goodness" in the context of sickness and suffering. And society cannot unilaterally dump a problem on medicine's doorstep and demand that physicians treat it; medicine must recognize somewhere within its scientific base and its set of applied skills the appropriate tools to address that particular problem (even if the eventual results may be disappointing, as seems to be the case with alcoholism). Therefore, to say that medicine has a therapy for some condition is to make a substantially informative statement that assumes that this bidirectional dialogue and negotiation has gone on implicitly. And, as a result, when some previously unknown or unanalyzed condition is discovered, whether or not we will choose to call it a sickness will depend at least in part on whether some treatment for it is promised within medical practice as it has evolved to date as a unified and coherent practice.

SICKNESS, SOCIAL ROLES, AND CULTURAL BELIEFS

If medicine is fundamentally a social activity, and the nature of medical treatment partially determines what we call sickness, then sickness is, in part, socially defined. This is even more the case if population norms rather than individual norms determine whether a condition is "abnormal" and hence to be counted as illness. Cross-cultural studies may further cement this view. A member of another society may have symptoms that, on an individual basis, Western physicians might unanimously and ambiguously label as constituting a serious disease. But if members of that society do not regard that individual as being diseased and continue to respond to that person precisely the same as they do to healthy members of their society, then, insofar as those people are concerned, *no sickness exists*. The individual, it is true, might drop dead tomorrow, but that does not alter the case; we say within our own society, "I was shocked to hear that Sam had died in his sleep; he looked like he was in perfect health yesterday." Furthermore, as cases of so-called voodoo death illustrate, if members of a society regard an individual as ill and treat him as befits someone with a fatal illness, that individual may in fact die soon, despite the fact that Western pathologists can discover no underlying disease process. And so medical sociologists and medical anthropologists have investigated at great length precisely how social roles and cultural beliefs define and determine sickness; and many of their conclusions have been adopted by philosophers as important for a conceptual understanding of disease. A brief survey of some of these conclusions will set the stage for later discussion.

Philosophers have attended particularly to Parsons's (1951, 1958, 1978) concept of the "sick role," despite the fact that many sociologists have come to regard Parsons as incomplete and unsupported by more recent data.[14] This may be because Parsons, in his own way, makes the mistakes I have previously attributed to philosophers of medicine—overgeneralizing and overabstracting the concept of sickness so that it is excessively divorced from the real-world experiences of sick persons.

Parsons began by viewing sickness as primarily a problem of social control. This equates sickness with other forms of *deviant* behavior—behavior that violates the normative rules, understandings, or expectations of social systems (Cohen 1968). Parsons defined a "sick role" to distinguish sickness from other forms of deviant behavior

14. For sociological critiques of Parsons, see Freidson 1970; Levine and Kozloff 1978. Lenora Finn Paradis read this section critically and suggested many additional references; unfortunately, space precludes my making full use of her suggestions.

such as sin, crime, and disloyalty. The sick role has four features:

1. The sick person has an inability to perform his socially approved roles that is not correctable by his own will or actions; he cannot be held responsible for his failure.
2. The sickness is a legitimate excuse from performing role responsibilities; excusing the sick person from her duties is not to be viewed as special favoritism or as weakening role expectations generally within society.
3. The sick person shares the basic value assumptions of the rest of society. In particular, the illness state is disvalued, and the sick person is seen as deriving no pleasure or satisfaction from being sick.
4. The sick person seeks the help of the socially identified authority and puts himself under that authority's regimen as part of the desire to get well.

Parson's work has had a powerful influence on both sociology and philosophy of medicine. Parson's theory has also been attacked as incomplete in at least three respects: it fails to look critically at medical authority; it assumes there is one rather than many sick roles; and it ignores the temporal trajectory of an episode of sickness.

Parsons tends to take for granted the authority of the physician and the objective basis of a pronouncement that an individual is sick. Freidson (1970) insists that this degree of unquestioned social authority is something of a mystery, and that sociology ought to be called upon both to explain it and to question its basis critically. Freidson does not deny that illness exists or that sick people have something the matter with their bodies; but he insists, "Illness as such may be biological disease, but the idea of illness is not, and neither is the way human beings respond to it" (p. 209). The sociologist can study the idea of illness and the social reaction to illness while leaving open the question of the validity of medical science: "it seems proper for sociology of medicine to analyze illness as a form of social deviance which is *thought* to have a biophysical cause and to require biophysical treatment" (p. 212). "When a physician diagnoses a human's condition as illness, he changes the man's behavior by diagnosis: a social state has been added to a biophysical state by assigning the meaning of illness to disease. It is in this sense that a physician creates illness just as a lawmaker creates crime" (p. 223).[15]

Freidson and others have also suggested that Parsons has identified a single sick role, when available data would support a multiplicity of sick roles. Parsons does a good job of dealing with serious acute illness; his model deals poorly with chronic illness, which is not going to get better despite one's being excused from social role responsibilities and giving oneself over to the authority of the approved healer. Nor does the model address minor illnesses where excusing from responsibility seems uncalled for. Finally, Parsons fails to address the fact that some illnesses label the patient and alter social responses in a particular and permanent way. Diseases like schizophrenia and acquired immunodeficiency syndrome cannot be understood in terms of social roles unless this stigmatizing characteristic is taken into account (Freidson 1970; Levine and Kozloff 1978).[16]

A third critique of Parsons suggests that he has, in his sick role, presented a sort of time-slice of an episode of illness, but he has not accounted for the journey from health into sickness and back to health again. Freidson begins to address these issues of the temporal trajectory of sickness by calling attention to the "lay referral system" (1970, p. 290), the process by which one finds out from discussing symptoms with one's family and friends that one should be viewed as ill and that one ought to seek help from a healer. This aspect of sickness has, however, been explored in the most depth by medical

15. Freidson here uses *disease* to label the biological state and *illness* to designate the social or cultural interpretation of that state. See n. 3, above.

16. This analysis produces a table of six possible sick roles, which for short might be labeled minor acute, minor chronic, minor stigmatizing, serious acute, serious chronic, and serious stigmatizing, where serious acute corresponds roughly to Parsons's sick role (Freidson 1970, pp. 239–45). There seems no need to stop here, however. Other variables could be added: Is the patient mobile or bedridden? Is diagnosis obvious or mysterious? Is self-cure possible or is the patient totally dependent upon professional help? Could the patient have prevented the illness, or is it strictly random? See chapter 5 for a discussion of eight sick roles as described by Siegler and Osmond (1974a).

anthropologists. Chrisman has described the process as the "health-seeking process" or the "natural history of illness" (1977). For this process to begin, there must be a set of cultural beliefs that label the experiences of the sick individual as in fact constituting presumptive evidence of illness. Special problems will arise if these cultural beliefs are considerably at odds with the explanatory model of disease employed by the relevant professional healer (Kleinman, Eisenberg, and Good 1978). Of course, the anthropologists emphasize, the Western scientific healer is only one possible end point of the "lay referral system," even in our own society. Discussion of one's distress with family and friends could just as easily lead one to a folk healer, to a health food store, or to a chiropractor.

This brief discussion of the various possible sick roles and of the way that an episode of illness will unfold over time—being shaped and defined first by cultural beliefs and, perhaps later, by the "scientific" explanations of the professional healer—further reinforces our determination to seek an understanding of how sickness affects persons in stories rather than in abstract concepts. This appears necessary both because of the wide extent of individual variations among diseases and illness experiences in various cultures, and also because of the need to keep in mind the temporal or narrative dimension of the experience of sickness.

SICKNESS AND THE HIERARCHY OF SYSTEMS

We could easily stop with having described sickness as defined in terms of evils and/or abnormalities, as experienced in the form of disruption of self, as partially shaped by medical practice and therapeutics, and as altering one's social roles in ways determined by cultural beliefs. It is a bit more satisfactory, however, to observe that a model of health and disease has been proposed within medicine that offers to tie together all these disparate aspects of sickness into a somewhat more coherent package. This model arises from reformist tendencies, largely among physicians who have been dissatisfied with the mind-body dualism, the linear cause-to-effect thinking, and the reductionism of the "old" scientific medicine (as understood by most of its practitioners) of the middle decades of the twentieth century. This newer model has been mostly popularized as the biopsychosocial model (Engel 1977, 1980).[17]

The biopsychosocial model views the human organism as constituting one level in a hierarchy of natural systems. These systems range from the basic atoms and molecules up through the organelles, cells, tissues, organs, and organ systems, include the nervous system and other psychological integrating systems, and extend further to the family, community, society, and subculture of which the individual in turn is a part. These systems are linked by flows of information, the exact nature of which depends on the hierarchical level in question (for example, exchange of molecules at a synapse between cells, or symbolic information exchange between an individual and the subculture). The information flow frequently takes the form of negative feedback loops, allowing for internal regulation to occur in a way that emphasizes homeostasis.

Health, then, may be viewed within this systems perspective as both maintenance of homeostasis and orderly growth and adaptation. Disease, in contrast, occurs when the system is disrupted either by environmental challenge or by inherent weaknesses within. Both the disease disruption itself and the measures the system might take to combat it can be expected to have ripple effects up and down the hierarchical levels as carried by the pathways of information flow. When, for example, someone suffers gastritis with mucosal hemorrhages, the effect can be noted upon the stomach, upon the cells of the gastric mucosa, upon the molecules being secreted by those cells, upon the person herself, and perhaps upon the person's family and coworkers who must respond to the sufferer's altered functional

17. This model originally derives from works on cybernetics and systems theory (Weiner 1954; von Bertallanfy 1968; Churchman 1968; Koestler and Smythies 1969; Laszlo 1972; J. Miller 1977). For specific applications to medicine, see Engel 1960; Wolf 1961, 1962; Wolff 1962; Cannon 1963; Jacobs 1964; Dubos 1965; Lipowski 1968; Bakan 1968; Sheldon 1970; Fabrega 1972; Brody 1973; Akiskal and McKinney 1973; Fabrega and VanEgeren 1976; Cassell and Lebowitz 1976; Blum 1976; Eisenberg 1977b; Brody and Sobel 1979. On the relationship between systems-theoretical approaches and "holistic health," see Brody and Sobel 1979; Kopelman and Moskop 1981.

status. The gastritis itself might have its origins partly within a medication being taken for some other malady and partly within the stress that person is experiencing because of recent interpersonal pressures.

To say that this is a systems approach suggests two things about the gastritis example. First, it is neither possible nor helpful to suggest that the effects (or causes) at any particular level of the hierarchy of systems are more "real" than phenomena at other systems levels. Thus, the reductionism that would see only the biochemical effects as truly "real" is avoided. Second, it is neither possible nor helpful to pick out from among this conglomerate a single event at a single level that constitutes *the* cause of the gastritis, or any other event as *the* effect of some antecedent cause. Causes and effects make up complex, interacting networks. Something becomes *the* cause when we *choose* to isolate or manipulate it for certain practical purposes. For the physician who elects to treat the gastritis by stopping the nonsteroidal anti-inflammatory medication that had been prescribed for menstrual cramps, a medication side effect is "the cause"; but this is ultimately arbitrary from the scientific viewpoint even if helpful and necessary from the practical viewpoint.

By this model, then, we can view the various aspects of sickness just discussed—biological, psychological, medical, and social—as manifestations of the same cause-and-effect network at different levels of an integrated hierarchy of natural systems. However, for a variety of reasons beyond our scope here (but which will be alluded to briefly in the next chapter), philosophers of medicine have demonstrated relatively modest interest either in affirming or in criticizing the biopsychosocial model. For our purposes it will suffice if it warns us against any tendency to pick out one of the aspects of sickness discussed in this chapter and to isolate it as "what sickness *really* is."

We have now, in the discussion so far, highlighted a number of philosophical points about sickness that will be useful for future discussion, once we get down to specific examples of sickness stories. We need next to look at some philosophical observations about personhood, personal identity, and self-respect, which will also prove essential to understanding those stories adequately.

3

Sickness and Self-respect

IDENTITY AND THE NARRATIVE FORM OF LIFE

If Sacks (1985), as quoted in my Introduction, is correct, then who I am—my personal identity—is constituted primarily by my story, my autobiography. This in turn provides a quick answer to the puzzle of Ivan Ilich in health and sickness. Ivan Ilich, when sick, is a *different person* in the sense that there has been a major break or change in his story; there is a sense of fairly basic discontinuity. Ivan Ilich is the *same person*, nevertheless, in that the story, despite the discontinuity, remains the story of one single life.

Within the analytic school that dominates today's philosophy, however, this is not the sort of answer one expects to get to the problem of personal identity. Rather, personal identity is viewed as a serious problem that can generate a great deal of puzzlement (Penelhum 1967; A. O. Rorty 1976). One philosopher, for example, feels that the following is the sort of puzzle we ought to be called upon to explain: if some person X is going to be in pain tomorrow if event Y occurs, then why is it the case that knowing that I am identical to X gives me a *special* reason for wanting to make sure that Y does not occur (Perry 1976)? We see immediately that this is *not* the sort of puzzle that people going about their business in our culture generally feel they must explain. If analytic philosophers feel called upon to propound and explain such puzzles, then either they have achieved an insight denied to ordinary mortals or else they have gotten seriously off the track somewhere.

A possible symptom of their having gotten off the track is the fact that, within this analytic approach, the notion of a time-slice is thought to be a meaningful way of talking about a person. The problem of personal identity then could be seen as a problem either of showing how successive time-slices can be time-slices of the same person or alternatively of showing how we would have criteria for being certain that two time-slices are time-slices of the life of the same person (Penelhum 1967). (For example, how do we know that the time-slice ''Actor who starred opposite the chimpanzee in the movie *Bedtime for Bonzo*'' and the time-slice ''Commander in chief of the U.S. armed forces at the time of the invasion of Grenada'' are time-slices of the same person?) An interest in time-slices also gives rise to a puzzle presented by the hypothetical problem of Methuselah, who lives for 900 years but whose memory (let us say) can last for a span of only 133 years. Now, one suggested criterion for personal identity is continuity of memory (Penelhum 1967). But the time-slice that is Methuselah at age 750 can remember the time-slice of Methuselah at 650 but not that of Methuselah at 550. It can therefore be asked whether Methuselah is the same person or an infinite set of overlapping 133-year person-segments (Perry 1976).

The basic problem seems to be that the philosophers have first taken the step of chopping persons' lives up into time-slices, and having done so, they have a problem of showing how to string those time-slices back together again to make up an entire life of a person. If we are reluctant to get involved in the stringing-together operation, we have another choice. We can ask what possessed the philosophers to engage in the chopping-up operation in the first place.[1] We might,

---

1. This approach is suggested by R. Rorty (1979, 1982). He disagrees with Descartes, Locke, Kant, and the general post-Enlightenment trend to regard philosophy as primarily about epistemology or theory of knowledge, in which it is the task of the philosopher to discover the indubitable foundations that are a necessary precondition for human knowledge to exist. Rorty cannot without self-contradiction attack the logical coherence of Cartesian or Kantian philosophy; to do so would suggest that there is another, truer theory of knowl-

for example, compare this time-slice chopping to the impulse of Descartes and his followers to chop up a person into two distinct realms of mind and body. Descartes and the philosophers of the Enlightenment had sound reasons for doing that, and indeed the enterprise, for hundreds of years, produced some interesting and startling philosophical reflections. But those good reasons were historical, not eternal.[2] If, in our own age, mind-body dualism seems to have outlived its usefulness and to give rise to more confusion than enlightenment, we are permitted to undertake a new historical agenda and reconsider the mind-body problem as a problem we can do away with if we simply refuse to accept some of Descartes's presuppositions (Strawson 1958). The same strategy can lead us to reject the puzzle of personal identity by refusing to agree that a time-slice is a meaningful unit for consideration. We can reply to Perry, for example, by saying that if you do not know why knowing that you are X gives you a special reason to want X not to be in pain tomorrow, then you do not know how people in our culture generally use the word *pain* (cf. Wittgenstein 1958).

The antidote to Cartesian mind-body dualism is simply to note that *persons,* not minds and bodies, are real entities that exist in the world; mind and body exist simply as abstractions from the more fundamental unity of the person (Strawson 1958). A similar move is to suggest that the fundamental observable feature of a human life is that it assumes narrative form and can be understood, by humans,

---

edge waiting to be discovered, which is precisely what Rorty wishes to deny. Instead Rorty wants to adopt a ''therapeutic'' approach to their philosophy, to ''cure'' us of the desire to ask the questions that lead to thinking that the post-Enlightenment approach is the only possible way to do philosophy (1979, pp. 5–6, 33–34).

2. Part of Rorty's therapeutic approach is to show us that Cartesianism is not *wrong,* but merely *historically optional.* He devotes a good deal of effort to showing that Plato and Aristotle, among others, did perfectly acceptable philosophy without asking Cartesian sorts of questions. He notes, for example, that various questions that could be called problems of consciousness, problems of knowledge, and problems of personhood were all lumped together in the Cartesian approach as ''problems of mind.'' Plato and Aristotle, in contrast, noted that consciousness was an attribute people shared with animals, and so saw no way in which a study of consciousness per se would lead to a further understanding of *human knowledge* (R. Rorty 1979, p. 33 ff.)

only in that fashion.[3] In this view, a time-slice is an abstraction from the more basic entity of the entire life narrative, not a fundamental building block out of which the narrative is to be constructed. It is like a freeze-frame photograph of a baseball batter's swing; the fact that we can understand and identify the photograph cannot be taken to mean that the batter, in order to swing, must first have in his possession a number of such freeze-frame fragments of motion and must then put all of them together in proper order to make the swing.

There are many complexities in suggesting that a human life is fundamentally a narrative or at least that we as humans can understand it only in narrative form. One that will be of some importance later is that how the narrative is constructed, and who constructs it, will vary with the portion of the usual human life history one is considering. At birth, our narratives begin, and we are already placed within a familial, communal, and cultural context without our choosing any of it or even being aware of it. Later in life we gradually assume increasing powers to write our own narratives as we choose, although still within the constraints imposed by our beginnings. But even then we are, at best, co-authors (Long 1986). The actions of many others will shape our narratives as much as we can shape them for ourselves. Our narratives contain a large number of supporting players and bit players, just as we ourselves will be Rosencrantz or Guildenstern to somebody else's Hamlet. In short, there is a network of social reciprocity implicit in the idea of construing human lives as narratives.

To expand further, one might argue that four concepts must be viewed as mutually interdependent:

1. The concept of the individual human life, from birth to death, as assuming a narrative form
2. The concept of accountability for one's actions

---

3. This is the suggestion of MacIntyre (1981), who agrees with Rorty in rejecting at least the ethical theories of the post-Enlightenment as being largely incoherent (while disagreeing with Rorty about the possibility of philosophy providing foundational theory). For MacIntyre, only presupposing a narrative form of human life can render a system of ethics coherent and meaningful (p. 203 ff.)

3. The concept of the intelligibility of one's actions
4. The concept of personal identity (MacIntyre 1981, p. 203)

The interdependence arises for the following reasons. In order to tell a narrative of someone's life, one presupposes that the person's actions are intelligible so that the story will make sense. But, in turn, what makes the actions intelligible is partly the fact that one can place them in narrative context, thereby showing their origins, their results, and their connections with related actions. Personal identity must be assumed if the narrative is to be that of *one* life; but at the same time, what establishes the identity relation between the person at time t_1 and the same person at time t_2 (say, between Methuselah at age 550 and Methuselah at age 750) is the fact that the narrative of the lives of both persons is the selfsame narrative. One's action is truly one's *own*, for which one is responsible, because it appears in the narrative of one's life in an intelligible manner. The narrative serves to explain the connectedness of that action with one's other actions, motives, and desires. (If an action is totally unintelligible within the life narrative, we are much more likely to deny that personal responsibility should be adjudged for it.) But at the same time, personal responsibility presupposes that the person whom we are now holding responsible is the *same* person as the one who committed the act. No matter which way we enter the matter, we are led from one concept to various other concepts within the package of four.

In this alternative view of the connection between personal identity and the narrative of an entire life, there is philosophical and not just sociological significance to the opening passage of *The Education of Henry Adams:*

> Under the shadow of Boston State House, turning its back on the house of John Hancock, the little passage called Hancock Avenue runs, or ran, from Beacon Street, skirting the State House grounds, to Mount Vernon Street, on the summit of Beacon Hill; and there, in the third house below Mount Vernon Place, February 16, 1838, a child was born, and christened later by his uncle, the minister of the First Church of the tenets of Boston Unitarianism, as Henry Brooks Adams.

Had he been born in Jerusalem under the shadow of the Temple and circumcised in the Synagogue by his uncle the high priest, under the name Israel Cohen, he could scarcely have been more distinctly branded. (Adams 1961, p. 3)

Here Henry Adams starts the narrative of his life and incidentally notes that there are certain ways of beginning a narrative such that the beginning seriously limits the options of how the narrative will turn out later on. But Adams is aware of the extent to which *who he is* is bound up with where and when he was born, to whom, and under what circumstances; and this is true in most people's cases, even if the beginnings are less portentous than were Adams's. To the question of whether he is the same Henry Adams that somebody once met, he could start by noting where and when he was born. By so doing he would immediately place himself in a social and cultural context, and this would effectively establish an identity for his narrative, just like a catalog number in a library. From MacIntyre's (1981) point of view, all these observations are legitimate and *philosophical* answers to the question of Henry Adams's personal identity. Once one has made all these sorts of observations, there is little that is peculiarly philosophical left to be said; and at any rate one cannot say it by chopping up Henry Adams into slices like a rye bread.

WHAT SICKNESS DOES TO PERSONS

We have seen that sickness may possibly have some impact on personal identity. We have not, however, discussed precisely what it means to be a *person* in the first place. We can address this briefly so as to arrive at a more important question for our inquiry: Does sickness primarily affect *personhood* itself? Does it primarily affect personal identity? Or does it have its most important impact on *some other attribute* of persons?

If one is primarily interested in philosophy of mind, one may define *person* as a being capable of conscious self-awareness and of using and manipulating symbols. If one is interested primarily in ethics and social philosophy, one might define *person* as an entity capable of being said meaningfully to be a bearer of rights and interests.[4] For our purposes, it will suffice to note that these senses of *person* are complementary, and that both presuppose a basic level of consciousness, self-consciousness, and cognitive awareness. Thus there are specific cases in which a live human being may be said not to be a person. Two such cases are an infant born with anencephaly, thus lacking the neural apparatus ever to achieve even minimal conscious awareness, and a person who enters an irreversible coma or persistent vegetative state. In such cases, it could be said that a sickness or deformity had robbed the individual of personhood. But obviously such instances are rare and extreme, and serve poorly to define the more usual human reaction to sickness. So rarely will one's personhood, in this basic sense, be fundamentally affected by sickness.

What of personal identity? I discussed briefly in the Introduction Sacks's (1985) example of a patient with such severe Korsakov's syndrome that he could not remember who or where he was from one moment to the next; his conversation was a feverish string of disconnected narrative fragments as he vainly sought to find some meaning or thread of connectedness in his shattered world. To the neurologist, this man had essentially lost his personal identity, as he had lost any sense of a coherent narrative to his life. Another case that seems even more clear-cut was that of a woman struck by light-

4. On the mental-capacity sense of personhood, see Strawson 1958; Wittgenstein 1958; Frankfurt 1971; Grene 1976; Brody 1980, pp. 77–95. On the person as bearer of rights, see Feinberg 1974, 1976; Brody 1981, pp. 82–87. On the relationship between the two concepts, see especially Dennett 1976. It is of some tangential interest that some within medical ethics have objected to a personhood approach that would label some humans (as the examples in the text) as nonpersons. I think these objections are fundamentally mistaken; but the reasons are not especially pertinent here, as the concept of personhood does so little work for us in describing the human reaction to sickness. See, for representative positions, Maguire 1974; McCormick 1974a; M. Green and Wikler 1980; Brody 1981, 1983; Veatch 1981; Sapontzis 1981; Macklin 1983. One implication of personhood, however, is worth underlining. If being a person is fundamentally being a symbol user (whose act of use gives meaning to the symbols), then being a person means, necessarily and fundamentally, being a potential participant in society and culture. Our discussion of self-respect below will rely in part upon seeing persons as fundamentally social beings.

ning on a golf course. She remained physically healthy, but the lightning seemed to have scrambled and reprogrammed her brain's electrical circuits in a way usually seen only in the hypothetical puzzle cases of the philosophers. After the accident she had the mental capacities of a six-year-old girl, although her statements and memories suggested that this was a different six-year-old girl from the one the woman herself had been at an earlier age. If this case really occurred as described, it seems that the victim of this accident is still a person, and yet she is a different person from the woman who went out on the golf course.[5] For all practical purposes, that woman's husband is now a widower (assuming that the process of mental reprogramming is irreversible, as it seemed to be).

Again, however, it appears that only unusual and extreme instances of sickness or injury will truly destroy personal identity. In a more metaphorical sense we might be tempted (as we were with Ivan Ilich) to say that the sick person is now a different person. This is a possible approach to analyzing the sculptor's request to die in the play, *Whose Life Is It Anyway?* (Clark 1978).[6] And yet the same logic would require that we deny that personal identity outlasts other major life changes, such as religious conversions. There would seem to be better and philosophically sounder ways to describe the impact of sickness on persons in all but the most extreme cases.

If neither personhood nor personal identity comprises that which is most directly altered by sickness, what other personal attributes might be looked at? I will now propose that we focus on personal self-respect.

THE CONCEPT OF SELF-RESPECT

Just as the narrative form of human life turned out to be best understood as a cluster of related notions, self-respect will form a cluster. The notions crucial for an understanding of self-respect include the

5. This case was heard at second hand and described to me by Martin Benjamin.

6. This approach is defended in a paper (to my knowledge, unpublished) by Stephen Massey.

idea of a rational plan of life,[7] the idea of excellences internal to practices that can be appreciated for their own sake as a motivating factor in human psychology, and the idea of a particular form of mini–social network that I will call the self-respect peer review network. If we note further that having a rational plan of life is very much the same thing as saying how one wants one's life narrative to transpire, in effect stating in advance the detailed obituary that one would like to have written about oneself after death, then we see immediately that the narrative-form-of-life cluster of concepts and the self-respect cluster of concepts are closely linked.

7. This entire section depends heavily on the concept of self-respect as developed by Rawls (1971) as an ingredient in his theory of social justice. The notion of rationality as it applies to life plans is fundamentally an amoral notion; it simply refers to the fact that one has looked at one's options and has chosen the most efficient means, and the means most probable, to maximize one's chosen goals over the long haul. I will address below the implications this has for sickness. See also Sachs 1981.

I will regard Rawls's notion of a rational plan of life as the forward-looking or prospective aspect of MacIntyre's notion of human life viewed in narrative form—that is, the rational plan of life is the story one *plans later to be able to tell* about how one's life has turned out. I must, therefore, address briefly the fact that MacIntyre (1981) criticizes Rawls and dismisses Rawls's theories as incoherent along with all the rest of post-Enlightenment ethics. (A full defense of Rawls against MacIntyre's criticisms is possible but would take us too far afield.) Among other things, MacIntyre's dismissal of modern ethics implies that a truly coherent system of ethics would include not just a statement of human nature as it now imperfectly exists but also an account of the human telos, or ultimate end. Further, it would include a healthy sense of goods internal to practices as closely tied to the concept of virtue. I have tried to indicate briefly that Rawls's assumptions about psychological motivation include an appreciation of goods internal to practices in the form of excellences and the satisfaction that perfecting one's talents in more complex ways can bring. Furthermore, the concept of the ideal of the just, well-ordered society functions within Rawls's system as a sort of telos, even if socially rather than individually slanted (an aspect MacIntyre should sympathize with, as he regards the invention of the individual, in the modern sense of the term, as one of the particularly deleterious outrages of the Enlightenment). Although more will have to be said on this subject at a later time, Rawls's conception of morality can be shown to meet virtually every coherence criterion inferable from MacIntyre's discussion.

An otherwise perceptive account of human lives as narratives, and the implications for medicine, by Long (1986) is marred by Long's failure to see that narrative order can be placed on lives prospectively as well as retrospectively. His failure to allow for anything like a Rawlsian plan of life leads him to suggest that human lives assume narrative form only in a fictionalized version (because of selective memory of past events).

The definition of self-respect can be rendered in schematic form as follows:

Self-respect requires having

1. a sense of one's own value and a sense that one's own conception of the good (that is, one's life plan) is worth carrying out. This in turn requires
   a. having a rational plan of life, especially one that is consistent with principles of human motivation that respect excellences internal to practices; and
   b. finding one's person and one's deeds appreciated and confirmed by one's close associates, whom one esteems in turn.
2. confidence in one's ability, so far as it is within one's power, to carry out the rational plan of life that has been chosen (Rawls 1971, p. 440).

Section 1a of the definition requires us to explain how excellences internal to practices can be part of a psychology of human motivation.[8] The idea of a rational plan of life assumes that the individual has a sense of what would constitute a set of the good things in life for her, and that she has looked at her social circumstances and her natural talents and has chosen a path that will maximize her opportunities for acquiring as many of those good things as possible. Although each person's own conception of the good life may be somewhat different, it will probably make reference to two sorts of goods. The first and most obvious goods are what we might call bottom-line goods that are the result of productive human activity. One can farm and thereby grow food to eat; one can trap animals and therefore obtain furs to wear; one can work in an office and thereby get money with which to purchase the things that one wants. But (we assume according to this model), other good things in life come out of the perceived excellence with which one carries out an activity, and not from the product of the activity: "Other things being equal, human

---

8. For the notion of practices, and goods and excellence internal to practices, see chap. 2, n. 12, and MacIntyre 1981.

beings enjoy the exercise of their realized capacities (their innate or trained abilities), and this enjoyment increases the more the capacity is realized, or the greater the complexity'' (Rawls 1971, p. 426).

Goods external to practices can be acquired whether or not one engages in the practice, and whether one does so by adhering to standards of excellence or by being slovenly and cheating. One can earn one's money honestly and buy those goods; one can find money lying in the street or win the lottery and buy precisely the same goods. But one cannot enjoy the good feeling of displaying one's excellences in the area of one's talents or training unless one actually carries out the activity. Others may vicariously enjoy the display of human excellence, but this, even though it may provide a new type of external good (in that people may pay money to buy tickets to see the excellence displayed), will be another matter.

The definition of self-respect assumes that having a rational plan of life requires making provisions for acquiring a ready and adequate supply of external goods in the form of whatever income and wealth is needed to satisfy one's wants for food, shelter, clothing, and related basic needs. But one will not really have self-respect, and one's life plan will not really be rational, unless it also makes provision for acquiring the sort of practice and experience that will allow one to develop one's natural talents and abilities. If these lead to a good job with greater income, all the better; but these activities can still play an important part in one's overall enjoyment of the good life even if they do not lead to material wealth. Other things being equal, humans are presumed to desire these sorts of goods and excellences. Others, who will be looking over an individual's life plan (in the peer review network to be discussed below), will be less likely to express affirmation of a life plan that allows few or no opportunities to develop such talents and excellences.[9]

9. In this connection it is important to relocate the notion of self-respect in Rawls's (1971, 1980) overall scheme for social justice. His scheme requires several things. First, he has claimed that a widespread system of equal basic liberties for all would be the highest-priority principle of justice in his hypothetical well-ordered society. He relies for this argument on his presumption that self-respect is the most important primary good. To

Next, we come to section 1b of the definition of self-respect: the affirmation of one's life plan by a special sort of social organization. This seems to exist informally; most contemporary descriptions of social institutions do not call attention to it. The basic idea can perhaps best be illustrated if we imagine a student in a small midwestern town about to graduate from high school. Up till now, his life plan, or his narrative, has been shaped (like Henry Adams's) largely by forces not of his choosing, but he is now approaching that time in life when he can start to play a major role in determining how his narrative will turn out. Accordingly, he faces many questions. Should he go to college, try to get a job locally, or join the armed forces? Should he try to stay close to home and family, or travel widely and maximize his novel experiences? Should he plan to settle down and marry soon, or extend his bachelor freedom as long as possible? Should he try to make precise plans and follow them out, or should he simply drift and see what opportunities turn up of their own accord?

As our student wrestles with these choices and tries to relate them both to his long-range goals and to his existing talents and abilities, he is likely to turn informally for advice, or at least for sympathy and support, to a disparate group of people. Some will be friends of his own age group. Some will be respected adults, such as a favorite teacher, school guidance counselor, or clergyman. Some

---

recognize someone's basic liberties is to say that one respects that person's conception of the good life and will allow him to have a reasonable chance of carrying it out; and this is a necessary condition for self-respect as defined above. Second, Rawls wants to claim that there is a link between a just, well-ordered society in which people have reasonable allegiance to just social institutions and a system of maximizing individual self-respect by maximizing the chances that individuals can carry out their life plans and that rational life plans will be affirmed by one's peer network. Rawls must argue that part of the life-plan-accomplishment process will consist of the sorts of cooperative efforts that will cement social bonds and induce people to see that support for just social institutions is indirect support for their own ability to achieve their ideas of the good life. This will occur to the extent that people are encouraged to develop their innate talents and abilities to the maximum and can be assured that they will be rewarded for this by some combination of material wealth, internal satisfaction, and peer approval.

will be relatives; whether his parents or older siblings are within the group will depend upon his relationship with them.

Members of this group will have several things in common. One is that our student would not have chosen them for this role had he not had respect for them and a general sense of approval of how those people are pursuing their own life plans. That is, if this student is going to be able to respect *himself* to the extent that these people are going to affirm his life plan and his chances of carrying it out, then he has to respect *them* in the same way. The activity of affirming and respecting the life plans of others is in this sense a *socially reciprocal* activity.

Another feature of this peer review network is that the student has *voluntarily* elected to associate with these people and to share his hopes and concerns with them. None of them (particularly parents) could have forced themselves into this inner circle—he could simply ignore their advice. He will have self-respect to the extent that those key people *with whom he has voluntarily chosen to associate* affirm his life plan; the failure of some other people to affirm his life plan need not minimize the self-respect.

Furthermore, a key reason he has voluntarily selected this group is his conviction that their review of his life plan, although personally sympathetic and supportive, will also be dispassionate. These peers will look at his talents critically and warn him of any unrealistic goals he might have set for himself. They will also respect his own definition of the good life for himself and will not attempt to foist off their definitions of their goods onto him. (This is why parents, especially, might be excluded if they seem unable to distance themselves from their own life plans in advising their son.)

In short, we have described a reasonable sort of social activity that seems realistic in contributing to an individual's sense of self-respect in a way that is tied in closely with the idea of having a rational life plan. Because this peer review network holds no formal meetings, keeps no minutes, and so on, it is easy to overlook its existence. But our definition and the model it implies require the existence of such an informal and implicit social organization to make full sense of the idea of self-respect. This further indicates that self-respect is fundamentally a social concept; a hermit totally isolated on a desert island cannot have self-respect.[10]

Admittedly, this description of the self-respect peer review network is somewhat idealized. In the real world of a less-than-ideal society, this process could go wrong in several ways. First, one might arrive at a life plan that is rational for oneself, given one's desires and natural talents, and that is fully consistent with the principles of a just and well-ordered society, and yet fail to gain self-respect because one's peers do not affirm the plan. Second, one might arrive at a plan that is irrational or that runs counter to just social considerations, but be encouraged to follow the plan anyway because of peer approval ("falling into bad company"). Third, others might decide whether to affirm one's life plan on the basis of a rigid formula (such as a Puritan conception of a virtuous life), so that one could not really say in the end that the life plan aims toward one's *own* conception of the good. Fourth, others might bestow approval on one's life plan on such loose criteria that the whole peer review process degenerates into a you-scratch-my-back, I'll-scratch-yours system in which the

10. Another feature of this social network that I cannot develop here is its role as moral overseer. Rawls notes that good moral character could be defined as that which it is rational for members of his ideal society to want in their associates (1971, p. 437). It seems to follow from this that members of the self-respect peer review network will not impose their own moral choices as to the good life on the individual; but they will exclude from their affirmation any life plan that displays immorality as a central feature (such as a life plan that envisions making lots of money by selling cocaine at the junior high school). I develop these implications of Rawls's theory much more extensively in a volume to be entitled *Fair Morality* (in preparation).

The peer review network also resolves some apparent puzzles related to the moral duty not to be servile (Hill 1973, 1982) and to supererogatory acts (Pritchard 1982). To condemn the person whom Hill calls the "Uncle Tom" for failing to have a sufficient sense of his self-worth, or to condemn someone for failure to perform a supererogatory act that he had said he would perform, suggests the existence of an audience to whom these people are somehow morally accountable for such failings. Yet the very nature of a self-regarding duty suggests that others cannot blame an individual for releasing himself from such a duty. If we view the audience as consisting not simply of equal moral agents but specifically of the self-respect peer review network, with whom the individual has chosen voluntarily to associate as part of the socially reciprocal activity of the mutual affirming of life plans, then we begin to see where the accountability might lie. This is of some interest in our inquiry below, as servility is one way in which an individual can respond to certain sorts of sickness. See chapter 5.

very concept of self-respect loses any meaning. These problems need not, however, occupy us much for purposes of our inquiry, so long as we can show that self-respect is an attribute of persons that figures centrally in how persons respond to sickness.

SELF-RESPECT AND SICKNESS

What justifies us in suggesting self-respect, as we have defined it, as that aspect of one's personhood that may often be most relevant in understanding the impact of sickness?

First, it should be noted that what counts as a rational plan of life for any individual depends on facts about sickness in important ways. A life plan that requires perfect health for its fulfillment and that makes no allowance whatever even for minor acute illness is not a rational life plan for anyone. And of course a life plan that requires for its completion many more years of life than is usually allotted to the normal person similarly reveals its irrationality. Persons with congenital handicaps or impairments, or who develop chronic diseases later in life, will have narrower ranges of life plans to choose from and will rationally have to reexamine and revise their life plans in light of the limitations imposed. This can occur with otherwise minor conditions if those conditions are especially pertinent to particular life goals or activities (for example, tremor in a concert pianist, or a knee injury in a football player).

Naturally, the peer review network we have described must take sickness into account in affirming life plans. This arises perhaps most dramatically when a person in good health is struck by a major illness that seems to necessitate a major change in life goals and life-style. The peer review network will then be confronted with the question of what counts as someone's failing to fulfill a still-rational life plan, as opposed to someone's becoming unable to fulfill a life plan because, given a new illness, it is no longer rational. If the former is the case, the failure to carry forth a rational life plan affirmed by one's peers must reflect a flaw in one's character and determination, and one then ought rationally to feel diminished self-respect and shame (Rawls 1971, pp. 442–46). But if the latter is the case, it is acknowledged that the successful accomplishment of a life plan depends a good deal on luck; and if one is prevented from accomplishing a life plan owing to illness or some other major factor outside of one's control, then no diminution of self-respect is warranted.

Rawls paints an idealized picture of the lack of regret someone rationally ought to feel when the person can say that he chose the best life plan he could, given the data then available, even if later circumstances conspire to render the plan futile (1971, p. 422). If we take Rawls to be doing descriptive psychology, we are bound to find his account seriously flawed—a rational refusal to experience regret is a far cry from the typical human reaction to an unexpected illness that demolishes someone's fondest goals. So it is again important to see that Rawls is exploring the logical connection between such concepts as life plans and self-respect and is not doing psychology per se. The point to be taken is that even radical revisions in one's life plan occasioned by illness need not in the end lead to loss of self-respect, however difficult emotionally the transition phase may be. But the lack of regret depends upon the affirmation by the relevant peer group that the previous life plan was the most rational and that the sickness and its sequelae are truly beyond one's control. This extension of Rawls's account to include how the peer network might respond to illness squares with the idea of the sick role we reviewed in the previous chapter.

Another way of looking at the impact of sickness is to ask what sickness does to the unfolding narrative of one's life. So long as one continues to function as a person, one's life story is not over just because the life plan in its original form is no longer achievable. One may yet revise a life plan to take into account the newly limited capabilities and set out in pursuit of newly defined goals. And, if someone does so, the person will still have a single life story and, in retrospect, a single life plan, even though the narrative is marked in the middle by a radical change of direction and events in the narrative have a marked before-or-after quality to them. There will not (except in extreme cases hard to imagine, such as those in which personal identity might not be maintained) be two disconnected pieces to the life story as if it were being told of two successive individuals. Unless this individual is quite different from most human beings, the radically revised life plan will still demonstrate some fair degree of continuity with the life goals, values, and attitudes of the individual before illness struck. As MacIntyre (1981) observed, the concepts of a narrative form of life and of personal moral responsibility are closely linked; and what above all else provides continuity to the life story, bridging the occurrence of the major illness, is that the person has chosen the revision of the life plan; the person reaffirms himself as a free moral agent, as a chooser of life plans, even as he disvalues and repudiates the fact of the illness itself.[11]

Previously, we cited the principal character in the play *Whose Life Is It Anyway?* (Clark 1978) as someone whose life story takes on this radical before-and-after quality (or will, if he chooses not to allow himself to die at the end of the drama). The real-life case that could almost have served as a jumping-off point for the fictional drama, and itself much discussed in American medical-ethics circles, is that of Donald ("Dax") Cowart, the severely burned Texan whose initial desire to die because of his injuries was captured in a teaching videotape entitled *Please Let Me Die* (White and Engelhardt 1975). Clearly, personal identity, in the sense discussed in the previous chapter, was unaltered by the burn accident; and yet the radical split in the narrative is reinforced by Cowart's choice of a new first name by which to be known after his rehabilitation. But, on the other hand, a radical break in one's life narrative can arise from factors other than illness. Consider Gandhi's decision to return to devout Hinduism, to forsake his European manners and dress, and to devote his life to the cause of Indian independence.

To summarize the discussion of the last two chapters, we have surveyed some of the different implications or senses of being sick,

---

11. Kafka's story "The Metamorphosis" provides one extreme example of a life story in which personal identity is (just barely) maintained but in which a sickness or malady otherwise produces a near-total break in a person's life. For an extended discussion, see chapter 7.

and we have looked at those aspects and attributes of persons that would appear most likely to be affected significantly by sickness. This discussion now provides us with a philosophical basis from which to begin a study of some stories in which particular persons are involved with particular episodes of illness. In the next chapter I will survey briefly where such stories may be found and evaluate some strategies for reading them carefully.

4

Reading Stories about Sickness

A philosopher who elects to search literature for insights on sickness and healing is on foreign soil.[1] My goal is not literary criticism, a method for which I have no formal training, but rather the elucidation of philosophical questions by means of compelling examples, and insightful juxtaposition of differing concepts, which literature frequently provides. Before launching into the detailed investigation of sickness, some preliminary remarks will help make clear why the particular works were chosen and with what approach they were read.

A good deal of the body of work that has been identified as "literature about medicine" is not well suited for this particular inquiry, however valuable it might be for other purposes and for general study about the nature of medicine and health. Many literary works about

---

1. The literature on literature and medicine is rapidly expanding. On the definition of this cross-discipline, see Trautmann 1982. For an excellent annotated bibliography upon which I have relied heavily, see Trautmann and Pollard 1975; 1982. The journal *Literature and Medicine* is now published annually by the Johns Hopkins University Press. Convenient anthologies are Ceccio 1978; Cousins 1982. I am indebted to Kathryn M. Hunter, Joanne Trautmann Banks, Tess Tavormina, and Glenn Wright for suggesting useful readings.

medicine are primarily about physicians (for example, Cousins 1982). Naturally, a description of the life and activities of a physician is bound to reveal important things about the sick people whom she treats; and yet the viewpoint will be skewed, and we will see events not through the eyes of the sick individual but through the eyes of someone else. For our purposes we would rather see physicians as part of the general landscape of illness—a foreign species of animal, perhaps, that sick people encounter along their journeys—than as the main characters of the narrative.

Other literary works, like "The Death of Ivan Ilich," are primarily about death and how people face or prepare for death. I assume that the fact that sickness may have a fatal outcome constitutes an important feature of how we experience it and react to it, but that the fact that some sickness leads to death does not in any way exhaust the experience of sickness per se. We saw in chapter 2 that the experience of being sick is a disvalued state in and of itself, and not necessarily because it portends death or reminds us of our mortality. For our purposes, literary descriptions of illnesses that lead to death and that are expected to do so by their nature fall far short of exhausting the possibilities for a study of stories of sickness.

Still other sorts of literary works focus on health and prevention. In these works, the discussion of sickness focuses almost exclusively on etiology, with an eye toward warning the reader of what to avoid so as to lessen his chances of falling ill. This form of work seems to have been popular in Renaissance and Enlightenment times; Franklin's famous literary debate with his gout is an example.

After these various possibilities have been eliminated, we are left with stories of sickness, or "pathographies" (Hawkins 1984), in which the sickness and the sick person occupy center stage. These works of literature deal with sickness, but the sickness may constitute different sorts of themes within the work. For our purposes, we want primarily descriptive treatments, particularly those that detail the variety of ways in which sickness may affect the lives of different people. We will therefore wish to avoid, or at least to label clearly, works in which sickness plays a primarily metaphorical role, and in which individual episodes of sickness are to be read as symbols for something else rather than as literal descriptions of sick people.[2]

Thus, a work of literary criticism that helps the nonexpert navigate among the different levels of meaning to be found in such literary works will be welcome. A very useful as well as fascinating work of commentary is Sontag's *Illness as Metaphor* (1978). Since the two diseases that Sontag analyzes in detail, tuberculosis and cancer, will be the major focus of the next chapter, her warnings are especially pertinent.

Sontag points out that both in the popular mind and in literature, tuberculosis and cancer have been viewed in symbolic and metaphorical terms at least since the romantic era. Tuberculosis became rapidly demythologized in the 1950s when adequate antibiotic treatment was developed, but cancer retains its metaphorical dimension. The two diseases have had important similarities and important differences. Both have been seen as mysterious, sneaking up on their victims. Both have been sufficiently feared that doctors have felt compelled to lie about the true diagnosis to the patient. Both have been viewed as highly individualistic sorts of diseases, in contrast to, say, syphilis and plague, other diseases with heavily charged metaphorical meanings. One becomes infected with the plague because one happens to live in a time and place that is visited by an epidemic; one suffers along with a significant number of others. One becomes infected with syphilis because one engages in a certain sort of act with a certain sort of person; one usually could have chosen not to do so and avoided almost all risk of contagion. For neither plague nor syphilis does it seem to make sense to ask the question that can readily and meaningfully be asked by the tuberculosis or

2. For this reason, a recent study by Meyers, *Disease and the Novel* (1985) is less useful for our purposes than one might hope. Meyers reviews at length two of the works we will consider below. But his treatments focus on the metaphorical level, touching primarily upon the grand literary themes of love and death, and upon the individual as metaphor for the society or the state. He spends very little time viewing these literary works as more or less psychologically realistic descriptions of how humans respond to illness.

cancer victim: "Why me?" (Sontag 1978, pp. 37–39). Thus it might appear that tuberculosis and cancer carefully select their victims, and that in turn the fact that one suffers from one of these diseases might seem to promise some special insight into the psychological character of the sufferer. From this in turn have arisen various psychological views of disease causation, such as attributing cancer to depression or to repressed passions.

Sontag also details important differences between the two diseases as perceived metaphorically by both lay people and poets. Tuberculosis is a disease of the lungs, of the ethereal parts of the body; the death that eventually results is in effect the body falling away, so that only pure spirit remains. Cancer is often perceived to be a disease of the lower, heavier regions of the body that are usually not mentioned in polite conversation; in its progression toward death the body becomes solidified and opaque. Tuberculosis was popularly thought to be associated with euphoria and increased appetite and libido, even if these states were false and ultimately debilitating; cancer was stultifying and desexualizing. Death from tuberculosis was though to be painless and easy—Sontag notes the absence from popular accounts of some of the true deathbed details, such as the putrid, rotting-flesh breath of the end-stage consumptive. Death from cancer was felt to be inevitably painful and wretched.

Whereas no one has thought it fashionable to appear to suffer from cancer, one has the striking phenomenon of the "consumptive look" that was briefly popular in the nineteenth century, such that ladies sought to appear thin, pallid, and slightly flushed. This could be explained by the mythology that the tubercular patient's illness might have been originally caused by frustrated passion, and that the disease itself rendered its sufferer more passionate and exquisitely refined and sensitive. There was the further romantic notion that the consumptive, even with this newfound passion and refinement, still lacked some vital force or will, and if this will could be recovered or rediscovered, the patient might yet be cured. Tuberculosis was thus "a way of describing sensuality and promoting the claims of passion. . . . Above all, it was a way of affirming the value of being more conscious, more complex psychologically. Health becomes banal'' (Sontag 1978, p. 26).

Once one has cancer and the (supposedly) inevitable, slow progression toward death has begun, change of location or climate is thought to have no positive effect upon the disease. But the mythology of tuberculosis was made even more attractive by the accepted medical notion of climatological cure. The tubercular patient was not only hyperrefined, exquisitely sensitive, and interesting; he was also a traveler: "The TB sufferer was a dropout, a wanderer in endless search of a healthy place. Starting in the early nineteenth century, TB became a new reason for exile, for a life that was mainly traveling. . . . The Romantics invented invalidism as a pretext for leisure" (p. 33). Parsons's model included as an important social function of the sick role the isolation of the sick individual so that the healthy would not be "contaminated" by seeing and envying how the sick person was excused from burdensome responsibilities, lest the healthy lose their desire to stay healthy. The romantic myth of tuberculosis suggests strongly the need for such social controls: the traveling of the consumptive in search of cure "was a way of retiring from the world without having to take responsibility for the decision" (p. 34).[3]

With all these potential layers of meaning, many of which conveniently ignore the realities of the disease process (to say nothing of ignoring the plight of nineteenth-century consumptives whose social class and income did not permit a life of genteel exile), it is small wonder that tuberculosis, cancer, and other diseases have been used as metaphors in literary works. The contemporary penchant for using "cancer" as a metaphor for some despised social practice or social group, and of using militaristic symbolism when speaking of its medical treatment ("war" on cancer; "invasive" cells overcome the body's "defenses"; both cancer cells and "innocent bystander"

---

3. On Parsons's model of the sick role, see Parsons 1951, 1958, 1978; Levine and Kozloff 1978, and the discussion in chapter 2, "Sickness, Social Roles, and Cultural Beliefs."

cells are "bombarded" by cobalt radiation) seem to Sontag to drive home her point.

Her conclusion is to take a dim view of illness as metaphor: "My point is that illness is *not* a metaphor, and that the most truthful way of regarding illness—and the healthiest way of being ill—is one most purified of, most resistant to, metaphoric thinking" (p. 3). Sontag's distaste for metaphor primarily arises from the frequency with which metaphoric approaches to disease assume a blame-the-victim quality. Cancer, for instance, may be viewed as a disease that preferentially strikes depressed people (the "cancer-prone personality"); the implication is that if the victim had only cheered up or gone out and had a good time on occasion, she would not have gotten cancer, so it's her own fault that she did. Similarly, with the current popularity of certain psychological techniques for cancer treatment (such as visual imaging of the cancer cells), the implication might be that some people seem to be able to cure their own cancers by sheer will power, so there must be something wrong with the person who cannot. Metaphors that blame the victim serve only as a primitive, social denial mechanism; they allow us the tenuous luxury of convincing ourselves that we are "different" from the sick person and hence need not worry about falling ill or dying ourselves.

When Sontag generalizes from such destructive uses of metaphor to all attribution of meaning to illness, however, she overreaches her argument. At one point she states: "Nothing is more punitive than to give disease a meaning—that meaning being invariably a moralistic one" (p. 57). But if what we discussed in chapter 1 is on target, it is precisely by giving meaning to illness that one succeeds in alleviating suffering (Cassell 1982). Of course, Sontag is correct in part; if we attribute to illness a meaning that diminishes the person who is sick, we increase suffering instead. But the major point is that "to give disease a meaning" is not something we can choose to do or not to do. We are inevitably involved in the business of attributing meaning to illness whenever we tell stories about sick people or even if we engage merely in medical diagnosis. Her point could better be stated: When we give meaning to the experience of sick persons, let us take their suffering and their needs into account.

Let us avoid giving meaning to illness that merely makes us feel better or safer, and at the cost of increasing the suffering of the ill person.[4]

Having established a general approach for selecting literary works that can be most fruitful for telling us about sickness, and keeping in mind warnings such as Sontag's to beware metaphoric treatments of sickness that deviate substantially from accurate descriptions of the plight of the sick person, we can turn, at long last, to some stories. I will begin with two novels that provide particularly rich descriptions of how sickness affects life plans, the various roles sick persons may assume, and the complex practices of being ill.

4. For more on negative judgments applied to sick persons, see chapters 7 and 8. The insights provided by Sontag (1978) are important enough to make it mandatory that its weaknesses also be noted. Sontag seems to accept a simplistic faith in the traditional biomedical paradigm (cf. Engel 1977), so that inevitably cancer will go the way of tuberculosis as soon as research uncovers the ''germ'' that causes it and the ''magic bullet'' that will cure it. She also attacks various psychological theories of cancer causation and cure as if these were important theories influencing medical care. She fails to note that these are more in the realm of pop psychology and that legitimate psychosomatic medical research rejected the simplistic notion of the ''cancer-prone personality'' years ago.

5

Sick Roles: Practices and Life Plans

Virginia Woolf, in an essay entitled "On Being Ill," laments:

> Considering how common illness is, how tremendous the spiritual change that it brings, how astonishing, when the lights of health go down, the undiscovered countries that are then disclosed, what wastes and deserts of the soul a slight attack of influenza brings to view, . . . how we go down into the pit of death and feel the waters of annihilation close above our heads and wake thinking to find ourselves in the presence of the angels and the harpers when we have a tooth out. . . . When we think of this, as we are so frequently forced to think of it, it becomes strange indeed that illness has not taken its place with love and battle and jealousy among the prime themes of literature. (Woolf 1948, p. 9)

Two notable exceptions to Woolf's generalization are Thomas Mann's *The Magic Mountain* and Aleksandr Solzhenitsyn's *The Cancer Ward*. These two monumental twentieth-century novels have several things in common that suit them especially for our purposes in this chapter. Both show a central character or characters who are sick and who spend most of the novel in a place of sickness among those who share the same disease. To set the stage and to introduce the cast of characters, the author must show us numbers of sick persons, each suffering under or coping with his disease in a unique way. (The diseases selected, tuberculosis and cancer, are chronic conditions that behave differently at different stages of their processes and that strike different parts of the body, thus allowing maximal variability in terms of how the individuals are affected by them.) The dramatic tension of both novels depends on the variety of ways of reacting to sickness; the protagonist is presented with a smorgasbord of behaviors, as it were, from which he may choose and combine to develop his own personal reaction to the sickness (and, especially in *The Magic Mountain,* try on a variety of reactions in sequence as the novel progresses). Both authors have something important to say about the societies from which the characters have come to live in the place of sickness. Both authors see the societies as sick in an allegorical way, and both see the possibility of cure in the future—Mann's Germany through the fires of the First World War, and Solzhenitsyn's Russia through de-Stalinization. But both authors are mainly interested in people, not allegories, and hence avoid Sontag's pitfalls of dealing with illness only as metaphor. This is not to say that all descriptions of the disease are strictly realistic in the clinical sense; it is to say that both authors, while making their social comments, do so with no injustice to the realistic portrayal of what sickness does to people.

Although there will be a great deal of overlap, I will use Mann primarily to illustrate the ways and practices of being sick, and Solzhenitsyn to illustrate how sickness affects the life plans of various individuals. Given the discussion in chapter 3, we might think it better to go directly to issues around life plans. An important aspect of both novels, however, is that they take us into a foreign world, the world of the sick, where many of our healthy ways and ideas will be challenged and turned topsy-turvy. It would be helpful, then, to get our bearings in this new world first, before turning to issues of how people move between the world of the sick and the world of the healthy.[1]

1. I find these descriptions of the "world of the sick" to be of considerable philosophical interest in illuminating the notion of illness. Some, however, might question the relevance of these views to the practice of medicine in the United States in the 1980s, where we have, for the most part, eliminated such "worlds of the sick" as the tuberculosis sanatorium

VARIATIONS ON THE SICK ROLE

A useful way of approaching *The Magic Mountain* will be to touch upon the work of two medical social scientists, Siegler and Osmond, who have used the novel as a jumping-off point for an interesting critique of the sick role (1974a). Their work is a mix of social science theory and literary commentary, growing out of their concern to analyze various models used in contemporary psychiatry (1974b). They distinguish six models that inform the therapeutic relationship in psychiatry, which they call the medical, moral, impaired, psychoanalytic, social, and psychedelic models (1974b).[2] They then deduce from them six corresponding roles that may be occupied by the ill. The medical model gives rise to Parsons's "ideal" sick role (see chapter 2). The moral model leads to the "bad" role (or occasionally the "good" role, if the patient is led to feel that good behavior will be "rewarded" with a cure); the impaired model to the role of "sufferer" or "impaired person"; the psychoanalytic model to the role of "analysand"; the social model to the role of "social victim"; and the psychedelic model to that of "enlightened victim" (1974a).

Siegler and Osmond's basic message is that the sick role is a good thing for society to have and that the medical model is the best model for psychiatry to adopt.[3] They argue that one of the most socially

---

and chronic disease hospitals generally, in favor of brief in-patient treatment and maximum return of the sick person to the "world of the healthy." The extent to which this social practice has changed the *inner* world of the sick person and the experience of sickness thus becomes a very interesting question, which I cannot pursue here. Hawkins (1984) may be pertinent in comparing the experience of sickness across several centuries; see also chapter 6.

2. Siegler and Osmond also describe two other models, which will not be of importance to our discussion—the Conspiratorial and Family Interaction models (1974b).

3. Overall Siegler and Osmond's critique is disappointing. They defend their Medical model and denounce the alternative models by citing only the strong points of the former and only the weak points of the latter; they totally ignore the valid if sometimes overly strident criticisms of the Medical model from authors like Illich (1976). Their critique of the Family Interaction model is especially wide of the mark. They accept Parsons wholeheartedly despite the weaknesses of the Parsonian model detailed in chapter 2, and despite their own findings that Parsons's sick role adequately describes only one of the six roles they elicit. Their only quarrel with Parsons is that he refers to the sick role as a deviant role; they apparently fail to see that Parsons uses *deviant* in a descriptive rather than a pejorative sense (Siegler and Osmond 1974b, pp. 116–17; cf. Cohen 1968).

destructive reactions to illness is the tendency to blame either oneself or others for the misfortune; if this tendency is unchecked in a society where sickness is common, increased levels of hostility and various forms of witch-hunts could eventually lead to social breakdown (1974b, pp. 89–90). This tendency toward interpersonal hostility is countered by the sick role and the medical model, which emphasize that no blame is properly to be attached in cases of illness. The special authority of the physician, which they call Aesculapian authority, is necessary to confer the sick role; and indeed the benefits of having such a thing as the sick role seem to be the main reason for the existence of such a thing as Aesculapian authority. The suggestion is that the tendency to allot blame for sickness is so strong that only a very powerful and special social authority can counteract it.[4]

Despite its great social utility, the sick role, with its stringent and precise requirements as set out by Parsons, is a hard role to maintain. Owing to its complexity, there are many ways of "falling out of" the sick role, and the other five roles depict some of the most common alternative roles that one may occupy when one shoots for the ideal sick role but doesn't quite pull it off. Siegler and Osmond note that of their proposed roles, only the impaired role has received empirical verification in the form of sociological studies. Whereas Freidson arrived at the sick and impaired roles as two of six possible roles, based on his logical analysis of seriousness and legitimacy as major features of illness (Freidson 1970), Siegler and Osmond base their models not on any logical construct of possible dimensions of illness but rather on their observations and criticisms of various schools of psychotherapy.

Siegler and Osmond go on to illustrate their six variations on the sick role by following the career of the protagonist of *The Magic*

4. More recently, the societal panic over acquired immunodeficiency syndrome reveals both the ongoing need for such authoritative reassurance in the face of a social temptation to attack or stigmatize a minority group as being responsible for the contagion and also the fact that this Aesculapian authority is granted by social consent and can be withdrawn by social consent. For example, in local battles over allowing children known to carry the HIV virus to return to school, physicians' insistence as to the very low risk of contagion has been overtly rejected by community groups, who claim that the authorities cannot be trusted to reveal the true facts to the public.

Mountain, Hans Castorp (1974a, pp. 54–55). We meet Hans, a young German who has just finished his apprenticeship and is about to embark upon a career as a marine engineer, arriving at the Swiss tuberculosis sanatorium, the Berghof, for a three-week visit with his cousin Joachim. Hans is coaxed into adopting the ways of the Berghof—the bountiful and frequent meals, the outdoor cures, even temperature taking—as one might out of curiosity and diplomacy adopt the ways of natives in a strange land. But before the visit is done, Hans is diagnosed as actually having tuberculosis and the three-week stay turns into an extended sojourn. Siegler and Osmond suggest that at the point of his arrival, Hans occupies the social victim role. Mann has depicted Hans as really having very little desire to become an engineer and as generally hemmed in by the restrictive and archaic social structure in the German maritime city on the flatland. Hans thus exhibits the sickness of his society instead of being personally and individually symptomatic.[5]

With the diagnosis of tuberculosis conferred with the Aesculapian authority of the Berghof's presiding physician, Dr. Behrens, Hans can for a while assume the uncomplicated sick role, following the therapeutic regimen laid out for him and trying thereby to get well. Soon, however, he falls under the influence of the Russian woman, Clavdia Chauchat, with whom he becomes infatuated, and experiments with the bad role. "The patients at the Berghof are fascinated by her, because she does what many would like to do but dare not: she openly uses her illness as an excuse for badness" (Siegler and Osmond 1974a, p. 45). The Italian patient, the literary Settembrini, who often serves as Hans's Virgil through this mountaintop world, opines that Chauchat is probably incurable because the illness is "in good part, if not entirely, a moral one . . . neither the ground nor the consequence of her 'slackness,' but precisely one and the same

---

5. Contrary to the order in which Siegler and Osmond present the various roles, the social victim theme develops slowly in the novel and is difficult to discern at the outset. It is, however, unquestionably present. At one point the narrator suggests that Hans would not have been so ready to stay at the Berghof had he only been provided by his culture and education with "any reasonably satisfying explanation of the meaning and purpose of man's life" (Mann 1944, p. 230).

thing'' (Mann 1944, p. 228). Although the "slacknesses'' of which Chauchat is guilty include such minor offenses as slamming doors and exhibiting easygoing table manners as well as indulging in sexual dalliances with men to whom she is not married, she is nonetheless dangerous. The sick role grants excuse from one's normal role responsibilities only provisionally so that one may devote one's energies to the therapeutic regimen and the restoration of health. When the excuse from responsibility becomes an end in itself rather than a means toward health and the shared values of the well community, one has entered the bad role instead—a role that, in the isolated environment of the Berghof far above the moralizing flatlands, has many attractions and few penalties.

Siegler and Osmond have already noted that Hans's cousin Joachim typifies at times the flip side of the moral model, the good role. Joachim is a soldier, eager for promotion and glory, who chafes under his forced leisure and longs to return to the colors. At times he obsessively complies with the treatment in the unconscious hope that his goodness and sacrifice will cause the powers that be to grant him his health as a reciprocal reward. This, too, is a dangerous deviation from the ideal sick role. If one can, through one's good behavior, win a reprieve, one suggests that some outside power has caused one's illness in the first place, which in turn suggests that one has somebody to blame for the illness. It is partly this moralistic bargaining posture that Dr. Behrens has in mind when he tells Hans that Joachim is "no good at being ill" (Mann 1944, p. 46). True to the doctor's prediction, Joachim leaves against medical advice to rejoin his regiment, only to return to the Berghof with worsened consumption and die there.

Hans reacts against the bad role and the general frivolity and aimlessness he sees among the others by starting to visit the bedridden and dying patients, whom everyone else studiously ignores. He later formally enters the analysand role under the tutelage of Behrens's assistant, Dr. Krokowski, who gives rather bizarre lectures in which he develops his theory that all disease is caused by perverted manifestations of the power of human love, that disease is merely love transformed (a parody, as it were, of all of Sontag's worst fears!).

Then comes a major decision—Joachim has elected to leave despite Behrens's warnings, but Behrens tells Hans that he has improved enough so that he can return to the flatland, too. Hans finds reasons to discount this advice and remain at the Berghof. To Siegler and Osmond, this indicates that he has entered the enlightened role; he has reinterpreted his illness as an opportunity for taking stock and developing new sensitivities to the meaning of life; he cannot leave until this mission is fulfilled. Finally Hans, lost in a snowstorm on the mountain, achieves his peak experience and glimpses the meaning of love and death in life, but the grand message proves to be notably fleeting (Mann 1944, pp. 496–98). Hans now slips imperceptibly into the impaired role, regarding himself as a permanent resident of the Berghof and permanently cut off from life in the flatland; a new vaccine treatment proposed by Behrens is greeted with cynicism rather than hope. Hans finally and abruptly leaves the mountaintop to reenter life at the start of the war, taking up in effect the colors that Joachim longed to follow but could not. Our last glimpse of Hans is as a soldier dodging bullets at the front, in no way incommoded by any vestiges of the supposedly serious illness that kept him for seven years at the Berghof. The final message indeed seems to be that Hans's more serious illness was not pulmonary but rather derived from the prospect of a life that offered no self-respect since it would be lived according to a plan that was not really his own. The only cure would come from a restructuring of society so that a role with real meaning was available to him.

Although Siegler and Osmond's characterization of Hans's "illness career" as a succession of roles seems a bit cut-and-dried,[6] we have at least been introduced to an outline of the novel, and have been reminded of the importance of the time course of sickness, so that one's reaction to it at one point is not necessarily a good predictor of how one will behave at a later time. Apparently intending to defend and elaborate on Parsons's sick role, Siegler and Osmond inadvertently provide further ammunition for the critics of Parsons, who

6. Indeed their summary, for all its fascinating insights, is a further argument for the "primacy of stories over stages" (Churchill 1979).

hold that no single role description can capture the intricacies of human response to illness.

THE PRACTICE OF BEING SICK

A one-sidedness of any analysis of sickness in terms of roles is revealed in the case of Hans's cousin Joachim. Looked at one way, Joachim is not a good patient because his compliance with treatment arises from a bargaining posture, as if good behavior will be rewarded automatically by a cure. But that is not all there is to Joachim's attitude toward the treatment. He pursues the cure so that he may return to the service, but also "for the sake of the cure itself, which, after all, was a service, like another; and was not duty duty, wherever performed?" (Mann 1944, p. 147). And elsewhere Joachim is depicted as devoting himself to the treatment in lieu of his military service, "even . . . making of it an interim profession" (p. 207). This description of Joachim's attitude raises the question of whether somehow a life with sickness, properly lived, can have its own internal set of rewards—or, in MacIntyre's (1981) phraseology, whether there can be a practice of being sick. We might also ask what sort of life plan might emerge out of such practices and whether it is the sort of life plan that will promote its possessor's self-respect.

Asking about the practice of being sick expands upon an apparent paradox in the notion of the sick role as a form of socially deviant behavior. On the one hand, part of occupying the sick role is being excused from the expectations and responsibilities that form part of one's usual role in life (as businessman, homemaker, or whatever). On the other hand, if the sick role is to be a true social role (in the sense that it reciprocally guides and modifies the behavior of others toward oneself, and oneself toward others, over time), then there must be a new set of expectations and responsibilities that belong to the sick role in its own right. Even though being sick is a deviant and thus socially disvalued state, people can admire the "good patient" who adheres to treatment and tries hard to get well, since the goal is abandonment of the deviance and return to the socially valued state. We do not, in the same fashion, admire the "good criminal" or the "good sinner" or the "good adulterer" who occupy deviant roles from which a return to nondeviance is indirect or impossible (although we may admire the truly repentant sinner). This explains the resentment and envy with which Hans Castorp regards Chauchat and the other patients who use their sickness as an excuse for a life of empty frivolity and sexual license. The social bargain implicit in their living at the Berghof is that, in exchange for not being blamed for not carrying out their usual social duties, they are supposed to try to get well and follow orders. (They are, that is, supposed to be cheerful but not to enjoy themselves.) When they fail to turn all their energies toward cure but instead devote themselves to petty gratification, they become doubly deviant. They suffer little from this stigmatization, however, because they are isolated from the flatland world and the social values of the healthy and can surround themselves with others similarly inclined who give at least superficial assent to a life plan based on using sickness as an excuse for irresponsible pleasure seeking.

Except for his on-again, off-again infatuation with Chauchat, this is not the way Hans Castorp intends to go about the business of being sick. Although he may be stuck in a culture that gives him no room to create a life plan that can rationally reflect his individual talents and proclivities, Hans compensates by devoting himself to living the right way, to coming up to the standards that he can set for himself. The pettiness of his activities viewed more broadly only goes to show how the culture has failed to teach Hans any meaning or purpose to life; the pettiness does not detract from the fact that the activities form a practice Hans has learned over time to excel at, and at which he tries to excel for rewards that are internal to the practice. He chooses exactly the correct items of wardrobe and smokes only a particular sort of imported cigar not to impress others or to make his way ahead in the world of commerce but to live up to the standards that he sets. Hans's stay at the Berghof is marked by the gradual giving up of each of these activities (first to go are the cigars, which don't taste right in the mountain atmosphere) and the eventual substitution of a new practice of living that celebrates his commitment to life in the sanatorium. Hans now takes pride in the expert way he can wrap himself snugly in his rugs when he goes onto the outside balcony for the rest cure in his chaise longue: "Only a few old hands . . . could wield both blankets at once, flinging them into position with three self-assured motions. This was a rare and enviable facility, to which belonged not only long years of practice, but a certain knack as well" (p. 102). He is proud when he perfects the old-timers' ability to lie quietly for the hours of the rest cure, doing absolutely nothing, an unread book in his lap. Eventually he finds a new brand of cigar, available in the local village shop, that suits his taste perfectly.

Aware of the work involved in living up to these new standards, which would be totally unappreciated by anyone of the flatlands, Hans can begin to sympathize with the Berghof patient in an anecdote related by Settembrini. This patient was discharged, completely cured, and returned to his family below, only to find the flatland life totally intolerable after his years on the mountain—everything he had come to regard as important they viewed as trivial and vice versa. Eventually, despite continued absence of symptoms, he had no choice but to return to the Berghof. His family below, said Settembrini, "lacked the fundamental conception" (p. 199). Hans's calm self-assurance in the practices of the Berghof serves him well when his family makes its only serious effort to retrieve him from the mountaintop and recall him to his career and responsibilities. His uncle, the ambassador from the flatland, immediately senses that he is in a foreign environment in which he knows nothing but in which Hans is expert. Soon the uncle bolts for home, almost desperate lest he too become captive to the Berghof and extend his planned stay of days into years.[7]

---

7. A nice vignette of how Hans's concept of the practice of sickness differs from that of his undisciplined fellow patients is provided by a phonograph procured for the Berghof toward the end of the novel. The other patients pounce upon it as a new toy, play records helter-skelter, amuse themselves by such childish tricks as changing the speed of the turntable to hear the voices squeal, and then seek other amusement, leaving the records strewn about the room. Hans approaches the phonograph as a serious business, uses great care in handling the records and needles, and works his way methodically through the collection of songs.

One can get self-satisfaction from practices like these well carried out, but one cannot ultimately gain self-respect unless these practices can be elaborated into a rational life plan that is affirmed by those with whom one chooses to associate. (Hans chooses most of the time to associate with those whom, like Settembrini, he views as more intelligent than himself, showing that he seeks a deeper and more enduring self-respect than do most of his fellow patients. Thus, as a character, Hans eventually earns the reader's respect as well despite his seemingly interminable adolescent soul-searching.) Eventually, with the coming of the war, he finds the prospect of an activity that can give meaning to his life, and he is then able to abandon the practices of seven years without a qualm or a backward glance.

SELF-RESPECT IN AND THROUGH SICKNESS

The Cancer Ward, in a hospital in Soviet Central Asia in the mid-1950s, is seen mainly through the eyes of Pavel Rusanov, a loyal middle-level bureaucrat of the Stalinist system, and Oleg Kostoglotov, a Russian whom that system sent to forced labor camps for years for some imagined political infraction and who then emerged as an exile in a Central Asian village. On the ward the role of good patient is well played by Akhmadzhan, a young Uzbek who translates for the other tribesmen who do not speak Russian. Akhmadzhan's only and constant desire is to go home, and he occasionally whines or wheedles, not so much to be difficult as to express the depth of this desire. But most of the time he is cheerful and has devoted himself to learning the ward routine and to accepting the words and deeds of the doctors without question. He practices with increasing skill what closely approaches Parsons's ideal sick-role model. (Fortunately he has an early cancer that is responding well to treatment, thus allowing him the self-delusion that his cancer is a serious and acute but curable condition, for which the Parsonian sick role is most suited.)

Kostoglotov cannot perform as a good patient, not because he has no concept of adhering to standards internal to practices, but because a rational plan of life occupies his entire attention to the exclusion of almost all other considerations. The doctors are enraged with him over his failure to go along with the ward routine, especially his questioning of their treatment and his threatened refusal of consent for additional treatment. They think it totally irrational that Kostoglotov, dragged into the hospital two weeks previously more dead than alive and having recovered remarkably in so short a time, should now turn on their medical regimens with such base ingratitude. From Kostoglotov's viewpoint it is eminently rational—so long as he was almost dead he had no need to make plans. Now that he seems to be recovering, making plans is uppermost in his mind, and he is frustrated by the physicians who will not candidly answer his questions and grant him a role in deciding his treatment. From years in the forced labor camps where he dared plan no more than survival, he has emerged into a life of exile where at least he can enjoy some of the simple pleasures of village life. He is, rationally, willing to trade off some increased life expectancy in order to return reasonably intact to that village life without undue delay. He chafes at the hospital policies that will not permit him openly to consult medical books to learn about his prognosis, and he is indignant when, without informing him of the consequences, the physicians begin a course of hormone treatment that will render him impotent (thus further limiting his future life-plan options). Kostoglotov's brief flirtations with an attractive nurse and doctor are less hospital skirt-chasing episodes than "try-ons" for his life-planning process—how seriously should he consider life plans that involve marriage or sexual commitment? Eventually, for Kostoglotov, accepting his sickness involves accepting his impotence, just as he has previously accepted his status as ex-prisoner and exile—as limitations within which he must form a life plan that makes the most of what he has available.

Whereas Kostoglotov's stay in the cancer ward is marked by serious planning and chafing at the restrictions that interfere with planning, Rusanov's stay is marked at the beginning by unrelieved fear and suffering. Rusanov is a man whose self-respect has always been tenuous, whose life plan is one that he would not be willing to submit to review by his peers, and whose self-esteem depends entirely on his excellence at various practices, the ends of which he refuses to question. Basically insecure and weak, he has found a niche for himself within a totalitarian bureaucracy, following the party line without question and identifying with those in authority in order eventually to wrest some authority for himself which he can then use in selfish ways. He is very good at his work, which involves searching for damaging information among the intimate details of other people's personnel files; and in addition to the satisfaction of the work itself he enjoys the power that he has to terrorize any of his subordinates with a carefully dropped word or facial expression.

Rusanov is very jealous of this authority (since he lacks any deeper self-respect), and, for him, one of the sufferings of sickness is to be stripped of the trappings of authority and to be forced onto a par with his fellow patients. While in his office Rusanov habitually has climbed a flight of stairs to use a bathroom on another floor, feeling it would be demeaning if any of his subordinates or peers encountered him in the common facility; in the hospital he is forced to use the common latrine that has no stalls and no privacy. "In a few hours [after his admission to the ward] Rusanov had lost his whole status in life, his honors, and his plans for the future, and had become 168 pounds of warm white flesh that did not know what would happen to it tomorrow" (Solzhenitsyn 1968, p. 12). In the hospital he is deprived of the advice and companionship of his wife, the only person to whom he can speak candidly of aspects of his life he can admit to no one else. Between them, for example, they have rationalized his denunciation of a neighbor to the secret police, years ago, so that they could take over the half of the apartment formerly occupied by that neighbor and his family. His wife, therefore, is less a peer to whom he turns for approval of his life plan, and more an accomplice in a life plan that neither dare to submit for approval. Typically, on learning that this neighbor has been rehabilitated after Stalin's death, Rusanov's reaction is not a twinge of conscience or remorse but simply the purely physical fear that the former neighbor will beat him if he should find him.

Rusanov projects this same sense of a shell empty of self-respect, unsupported by a life plan that can be exposed to scrutiny, onto the nation that he professes to serve with devotion. He can understand why Beria should have to be shot after Stalin's death if Beria was really guilty of all the crimes he is said to have committed as leader of the secret police. What Rusanov cannot comprehend is that this should have been talked of openly—what should have been done, in his view, is to have shot Beria, let it be known that he had died of a heart attack, and then given him a hero's funeral.

When a tumor appears on his neck, shutting off Rusanov "like a wall" from his family, his office, and his easy and comfortable life (pp. 18–19), Rusanov has few resources to deal with his sickness. In his terror he begins by denying that his disease is cancer—to which an unsympathetic but logical fellow patient responds, "Now there's a fool! If he didn't have cancer, why would they put him in here?" (p. 10). In attempts to shore up his self-esteem by regaining a sense of authority and influence, he begs his wife to cajole additional privileges on his behalf from the hospital authorities. It turns out that his influence with the higher-ups is less than he had imagined, and the only result, at first, is that he is allowed to wear his own pyjamas that he has brought from home; the longed-for transfer to a Moscow hospital never materializes. Primarily he is reduced to blustering at the other patients, instructing them on correct socialist attitudes.

Rusanov suffers terribly with his illness (until the tumor starts to regress under therapy) because his experience lacks meaning in all the three senses alluded to in chapter 1. As he is afraid even to admit the name of the illness, he can hardly construct a satisfactory explanatory framework within which to place it. (His only available explanatory systems seem to be political; hence his desire for a cure gets expressed as a desire to be transferred to a hospital in Moscow where the specialists are presumably better.) Kept apart from his wife, he is stripped of the caring companion he is used to leaning on in times of trouble; and his obnoxious bluster helps ensure that he will find no replacement in the cancer ward among his fellow patients. And he has lost all sense of control because those practices at which he excels, and which have assured his control in his life up to this point, no longer seem applicable.

Solzhenitsyn adeptly uses the transformation of the large society to mirror Rusanov's feeling of loss of control over his personal life and future. One of the special privileges Rusanov tries to bully for himself is to be the first to read the newspaper.

> "Why should you be first?"
> "What do you mean, 'why?' Why?'' Pavel Nikolayevich was in anguish, suffering from the undeniability, the self-evidence of his right to be first, indefensible though this right might be in words. He felt something akin to jealousy if someone else unfolded a fresh newspaper with uninitiated fingers. Nobody here could understand what was in the newspaper better than he, Pavel Nikolayevich. He regarded newspapers as openly disseminating what were, in fact, coded instructions, in which it was impossible to call things by their proper names, but from which a knowledgeable and capable person could form the correct concept of the newest trend by various little hints, the page position and display of the articles, and what had been omitted or left unsaid. That was precisely why Rusanov had to be the first to read the newspaper. (pp. 243–44)

Reading a Soviet newspaper properly is thus described as a practice at which Rusanov excels, and he feels that his excellence at this practice, which others ought properly to esteem, is part of what makes him a worthwhile person. His mastery of the practice makes him feel in control of his life and his future; in the hospital, where his feeling of control has been largely stripped away, he clings even more desperately to this appearance of power. But Fate has dealt him a further blow—when he finally gets the paper he finds news of sweeping changes on an unprecedented scale. The Supreme Court has been completely replaced. Malenkov has asked that he be relieved of his post as chairman of the Council of Ministers.

> [Rusanov] grew weaker and his grip on the paper relaxed. He could not go on reading. He did not understand this news. He had ceased to understand "coded information" openly disseminated. . . . It was as though, somewhere at great, great depths, geological strata had rumbled and quivered ever so slightly in their rock bed, and the whole city, the hospital, and Pavel Nikolayevich's bed had swayed with the shock. (p. 304)

Hoping to gain some return of his inner strength by exercising a practice at which he excels, Rusanov is cruelly deceived and is left feeling even more depressed. But later, as his tumor shrinks, the old Rusanov reasserts himself. At first his inability to deal with the larger social realities had made him feel even less powerful in dealing with his sickness; conversely, once his sickness starts to remit, he regains all his old optimism about being able, with his bureaucratic wiles, to survive in the larger world. He leaves the hospital essentially the same person, the same shallow hypocrite, as when he was admitted; the future is not clear, but we are left with the impression that, when he suffers the almost inevitable relapse or metastatic growth, he will be every bit as unprepared to face that new challenge as he was with this one. By contrast, Kostoglotov leaves the hospital with a changed sense of himself and his future as a result of his self-conscious reflection upon the meaning of the sickness for his future life plans.

SICKNESS AND LIFE PLANS

Having gotten our bearings among the roles and practices that constitute the world of sickness, and having seen, in the cases of two characters from *The Cancer Ward,* how sickness might affect life plans, we might next request a more comprehensive catalog of the variety of ways in which one's life plan, or one's self-respect, may be altered by illness. *The Cancer Ward* provides an especially rich set of examples for this discussion, although *The Magic Mountain* and other literary works are also pertinent. With these examples, we can, as it were, compile a list of "possible stories of sickness."

First, sickness may be viewed as a lacuna in the narrative of one's life. Once it is over, one takes up one's life plan exactly where one left off and proceeds as if nothing had happened. This is the view of sickness that seems implicit in the ideal Parsonian sick role, illustrating why that theory is so much better suited to acute than to chronic illness. This story about sickness seems to inform Joachim's view of his tuberculosis much of the time: he sees his cure as an unpleasant duty to be gotten over so that he can rejoin his regiment and resume his military career. In *The Cancer Ward,* this is the first view we have of young Asya, who eventually is to have her breast removed. She tells one of the young male patients, Demka, that she is in the hospital for a "checkup"; the entire content of her conversation is of her outside life and activities, which she intends to return to shortly.

To tell this story first about one's sickness, when one has a disease like cancer or tuberculosis, requires denying the severity of the disease, even if one does not deny the disease itself. But the second mode of story (actually, of refusing to tell a story) is full-fledged denial. One refuses to tell any story at all about the sickness, treats it as a nonentity, and proceeds to pursue one's life plan exactly as if nothing is going on. In *The Cancer Ward,* this reaction is typified by Chaly, who goes on arranging black market deals and juggling the visits of his various wives so that they will not meet each other, exactly as he would have had he never been admitted to the ward. (Characteristically, Rusanov takes an instant liking to Chaly.) In an even more extreme case, Siegler and Osmond (1974a) relay the anecdote of a physician who suffered what was obviously, to all his associates, an acute myocardial infarction. The physician refused to acknowledge that anything was the matter with him and waved away all efforts to have him admitted to the hospital; he continued to see patients and work in his office, where he dropped dead twenty hours later.

A third sort of story about sickness is the adoption of sickness as a career, of abandoning one's previous life plan and formulating a new one with the sickness as the centerpiece. This is Siegler and Osmond's impaired role, a role that Hans Castorp adopts through a good deal of *The Magic Mountain* and that his fellow patients have adopted even more firmly and enthusiastically. The story of one's life after the sickness, then, is the story of how one has adopted the various practices associated with the sickness. As our discussion of Hans revealed, this story generally requires that one's previous life plan was highly unsatisfactory and that no attractive alternatives are available. Accordingly we see little of this among the patients in *The Cancer Ward,* since even the Soviet society provides many alternatives more attractive than being treated for cancer. (And, of course, that society would not tolerate an institution like the Berghof, peopled with its capitalist parasites, for five minutes.) One patient who typifies this story is the incurable Sibgatov, whose tumor on his lower back is a smelly, running sore. He is going to die, knows it, and carries out his practice of quiet, polite, uncomplaining existence on the ward because that is all that is left to him consistent with his self-respect.

Fourth, when the sickness is accepted as fatal, one may pursue one's life plan without major modification, only accelerating its pace given the short time remaining. This is the choice of the young geologist Vadim in *The Cancer Ward,* whose goal in life is the discovery of a new geological technique for locating mineral deposits. He frantically searches out purported cancer cures, not out of any hope of cure for himself, but only to buy time to allow him to perfect his discovery before he dies. He self-consciously adopts as his hero the poet Lermontov, who accomplished much of literary note and assured himself a place in Russian history despite the fact that he died very young. Vadim, planning what he is to do with the time that remains to him in accomplishing his life plan, often sounds as if he is prospectively composing his own obituary.[8]

Fifth, sickness may force a modification of one's life plan, so that the story that will be told of one's life includes the previous life plan up until the sickness occurs, followed by a reexamination and a formulation of a new life plan that is rational given the limitations the chronic sickness is expected to impose. The novels suggest that this is a difficult and complex matter.[9] At the same time that one is trying

8. This further reinforces the connection between MacIntyre's (1981) notion of a human life as a connected narrative and Rawls's (1971) concept of a rational plan of life (see chapter 3).

9. From Rawls's (1971) idealistic standpoint, it is sufficient to note that an unforeseen change in circumstances may force an alteration in one's rational life plan. His purposes are philosophical here and not psychological. For other reasons having to do with his overall scheme of justice, he wants to reinforce the idea that envy is irrational and that his hypothetical decision makers will not be motivated by it. Thus he would be forced to ignore the psychological likelihood that the sick person will indeed envy the healthy and will enter upon the process of revising her life plan to take into account the limitations imposed by sickness only with great reluctance and anguish, and not at all with the rational equanimity that Rawls's terminology might suggest. (It is worth repeating that Rawls specifically disavows any attempt to take sickness into account in his scheme and restricts his comments to the healthy population; see Rawls 1980, p. 546.)

to reformulate the new life plan (often having at the same time to submit it to the review of a newly formed group of associates, since the peers who affirmed one's old life plan may no longer be available or may be insufficiently cognizant of the realities of the limitations imposed by illness), one must also undergo the grieving process over the old life plan. This old life, after all, was a major part of oneself, upon which all of one's claim to self-respect was based; one does not lightly undergo its loss. In extreme cases one might even be justified in asserting that the old life plan was such a major part of oneself that to lose it is to lose one's identity, so that the only story that could be told of existence after the sickness is the story of the life of a different individual entirely.[10]

The painful endeavor of formulating new life plans, grieving over the old ones, and looking out for rational and sympathetic associates whom one can trust to affirm one's new life plan on proper grounds unites Kostoglotov and young Demka in a bond of sympathetic friendship. Demka, soon to lose his leg to his cancer, is grief-stricken at his impending loss, but he is still ambitious about his studies and involves his fellows in discussions about what sorts of activities are possible for an amputee. Kostoglotov, as we saw earlier, has less to grieve for in his old life plan, since much of his life has been spent under circumstances where the only rational plan was in effect none at all; but he is determined to wrest whatever simple happiness he can from his life that remains, within the limitations that sickness will impose.

We recall that for Rawls, having one's life plan affirmed by one's close associates was only one of three conditions of self-respect. It is also necessary that the life plan be rational, taking into account one's natural talents and proclivities along with the realities of one's existence (including limitations imposed by illness), and that one be reasonably along the way to fulfilling the dictates of the life plan, in accord with where one is on the expected life trajectory. The last

10. We saw in chapter 3 how such an assertion might be implicit in the play, *Whose Life Is It Anyway?* (Clark 1978), about a sculptor who refuses life-prolonging treatment after he is rendered quadriplegic in an accident.

condition, which demands progress in the fulfillment of one's life plan, envisages a plan that involves the concept of practices and what Rawls calls the Aristotelian Principle; that is, one must in fact be able to demonstrate progress and enhanced expertise over time.[11] The life plan, by this account, cannot therefore be devoted merely to day-to-day existence or the simpleminded enjoyment of passing whims and pleasures. This illustrates the error made by most of Hans Castorp's fellow patients who adopt the bad role and use illness as an excuse for frivolous and loose ("slack") behavior. Because everyone with whom they choose to associate does likewise, they gain the surface appearance of self-respect and do not reflect that true self-respect has been denied them. Rawls's account explains how it might justifiably be said that "no *self-respecting* person would behave that way even if they were really sick."

Sixth, sickness can intrude as a jarring note at the end of one's life story, making a mockery of the life plan that has gone before. This sad outcome is epitomized in *The Cancer Ward* by Shulubin, who has colon cancer that will require an ileostomy. Shulubin describes his state of affairs to Kostoglotov. Shulubin's life plan, in response to the political and social upheavals of the Stalinist purges, was to adopt an attitude of total acquiescence and servility in order to survive and keep his family intact.

> "That's how far they've driven me to the wall. . . . I lectured in several disciplines—and all this in Moscow! But then the great oaks began to topple. . . . They swept out professors by the dozen. Were we expected to confess errors? I confessed errors! Did we have to recant? I recanted . . . They told us to rewrite anatomy, microbiology and neuropathology according to the teachings of an ignorant agronomist. . . . Bravo, I agree, I'm in favor! No, that's not enough, give up your assistantship, too! All right, I won't argue, I'll become an instructor in agricultural methods. No, that wasn't enough of a sacrifice. . . . All right, I agree, I'll become a librarian, a librarian in remote Kokand! How far I had retreated! But never-

---

11. See Rawls (1971, pp. 422–29), and chapter 3 more generally.

theless I was alive, and my children had been graduated from in-
stitutes.'' (Solzhenitsyn 1968, p. 507)

But now, with cancer, has come the final realization that it was
all for nothing:

> "I lived . . . for twenty-five years, maybe twenty-eight . . . and
> saved myself only by cringing and keeping quiet. I kept silent for
> the sake of my wife, for the sake of the children, for my own sinful
> skin. But my wife died. My skin is a bag of manure, and they're
> going to open up a hole in its side. My children grew up so hard-
> hearted that it's beyond comprehension. When my daughter began
> suddenly to write to me . . . it turned out to be because the Party
> organization told her she ought to *normalize* her relationship with
> her father.'' (p. 506)

Something similar occurs to Ivan Ilich in Tolstoy's short story;
and he comes shortly before his death to reject completely all that
he has lived for previously and then to develop a new awareness of
the importance of human relationships. We do not get to see how
or whether Shulubin will resolve the inconsistencies between the life
plan that has served him up till now and his new realizations; at this
point all Shulubin can do is express envy of Kostoglotov's life, both
as political prisoner and as exile: "At least you lied less, do you
understand? At least you cringed less'' (p. 501). We can see, however, that this way of telling a story about sickness could lead easily
to the outcome that Sontag (1978) denounces—the view that cancer
arises from repressed passion or some prior personality trait of the
individual—or to the older view of disease as some sort of divine
punishment.

Shulubin, it should be noted in passing, comes through illness to
learn to regret his life of servility, but there is nothing servile in his
reaction to the illness now. Servility as a reaction to sickness is illustrated rather by another of the inmates of the cancer ward. This
individual, a former university lecturer, is visiting from another ward
when Kostoglotov is telling his fellow patients about a new folk
remedy for cancer he has learned of. Kostoglotov is still operating
under the rules of conduct that governed his survival in prison camp:

in a world where one has so little power, a little knowledge makes a lot of difference; one does not share that kind of power willy-nilly, but only with carefully selected fellows. Kostoglotov himself lacks the money to procure the remedy, a magic root, but he can at least withhold the address of the purveyors except from those few to whom he elects, for his own purposes, to reveal it. This lecturer (who suffers from a tumor of the larynx) importunes him persistently and abjectly for the address. Kostoglotov is first put off by the man's cringing demeanor; he is further disgusted when he finds that the man was a lecturer in philosophy—what good was all the philosophy this man expounded if it cannot help him cope with his illness in a more satisfactory and manly fashion? "It was a shame to laugh at sickness and grief; but sickness and grief too should be borne in such a way as not to provoke laughter" (Solzhenitsyn 1968, p. 173). Here again one encounters the notion that there is a proper way to be sick, a proper way to carry out the role, and that servile behavior will be viewed as self-indulgence rather than as appropriate sickness behavior. In the end, however, Kostoglotov gives the man the address, moved by the irony of the fact that this person, who has depended on his voice for his career and livelihood, should have been struck by a tumor of the larynx.

There is, of course, no guarantee whatever that one could exhaustively enumerate the various ways in which sickness could affect the life plans of individuals and, by that route, affect their self respect. We could probably add indefinitely to the list begun here. But one additional story about sickness notable in its absence from both novels is the story of a fatal illness coming at the close of a long and fruitful life, when one's life plan has been largely fulfilled and one's human relationships fully ripened. Such a story of sickness and death as a capstone to one's life, when no ground for regret or envy exists and self-respect has been fully developed and nurtured in such a way that sickness cannot threaten it, is foreign to the Berghof or the cancer ward, where one meets either denial of death or death's prematurely thwarting the life plans of the young or middle aged. Such a story seems to underlie the notion of a "natural death" as a moral good (Callahan 1977), not disputing the fact that death and sickness remain

fundamentally evil, but still acknowledging that their timing and circumstances can vary in ways that are of great moral importance—
a matter we will discuss further in chapter 9.

A story of death that carries some of this capstone quality, but
with an ironic twist, is the death of the poet Cronshaw in a different
novel, Somerset Maugham's *Of Human Bondage* (1963). Cronshaw
has lived the life of the impoverished, unappreciated, expatriate poet
in Paris, spending his evenings getting drunk in the cafés while ar-
tistically inclined younger men admire his literary conversation. He
finally comes back to London to correct the proofs of the finally-
to-be-published volume of his poetry, but is totally broken down in
health from alcohol, cigarettes, and malnutrition. Philip Carey, formerly one of the young men who gathered around Cronshaw's table
in the café, now a medical student who has undertaken to nurse the
poet in his last days, asks why he will not even at this late date give
up drinking:

> "Because I don't choose. It doesn't matter what a man does if
> he's ready to take the consequences. Well, I'm ready to take the
> consequences. You talk glibly of giving up drinking, but it's the
> only thing I've got left now. What do you think life would be to
> me without it? Can you understand the happiness I get out of my
> absinthe? I yearn for it; and when I drink it I savor every drop. . . .
> I am a man blessed with vivid senses, and I have indulged them
> with all my soul. I have to pay the penalty now, and I am ready
> to pay." (Maugham 1963, p. 405)

Philip asks whether, despite these bold words, the poet is not afraid
of death:

> "Sometimes when I'm alone." He looked at Philip. "You think
> that's a condemnation? You're wrong. I'm not afraid of my
> fear. . . . I know that I shall die struggling for breath, and I know
> that I shall be horribly afraid. I know that I shall not be able to
> keep myself from regretting bitterly the life that has brought me
> to such a pass; but I disown that regret. I now, weak, old, diseased,
> poor, dying, hold still my soul in my hands, and I regret nothing."
> (p. 405)

Cronshaw in fact dies quietly in his sleep, and so never has a chance to alter these final deathbed sentiments. In these statements he presents almost an ideal of rationality in the sense that Rawls used in speaking of a rational life plan—discerning carefully that a particular life plan does in fact have the highest chance (among the alternatives available to one, given accidents of birth, social position, and so on) of yielding the greatest amount of those goods the individual elects to regard as goods worth seeking, and that the life plan develops to the highest degree whatever natural talents and proclivities one possesses. By these standards Cronshaw should be able to die with maximal self-respect, having come as close as could be expected to fulfilling his rational life plan; his denunciation of fear and regret at this final juncture is fully rational even if it strikes the reader as psychologically a bit unrealistic, almost too good to be true.[12]

---

12. For further discussion of Cronshaw's self-respect as related to his role of the bad, or noncompliant patient, see chapter 8.

6

How Sickness Alters Experience

Our focus, so far, has been upon how sickness interrupts and changes the narrative of one's life, and what that in turn does to the individual's self-respect. A narrative of a life has some necessary features. Events within the narrative have to be located somehow within space and time; and for a narrative to flow in the expected fashion, the dimensions of time and space must remain reasonably constant and not undergo unexpected alterations between one portion of the narrative and another. In addition, a narrative of a life assumes a varied cast of characters; the central character, whose life it is, cannot be sufficient unto herself, but rather events take on the meaning that they have in part because of the ways that others are involved.

It follows that one's experience of one's own life is altered appreciably if sickness somehow distorts one's sense of time or space, or one's sense of relationship to others. How sickness can alter experience in these ways will be discussed in this chapter. Later, we will look at a different aspect of altered relationships—how the sick person appears *to others* and how the sickness affects *their* lives.

SICKNESS, TIME, AND SPACE

We may, when sick, reflect upon our life plans and try to determine what modifications would be most rational, given the new and unpleasant fact of sickness. But this activity would assume that we are not unduly burdened with altered perceptions that would render such reflection difficult or impossible. For instance, if the experience of sickness involves a much altered sense of time or space, we might imagine difficulties in the sick person's engaging in such reflection, and indeed in our own ability to communicate meaningfully with that person. In this chapter I will explore how sickness may in fact alter consciousness in this way, basing the discussion both on literary treatments and on case histories.

Time is one of the major themes of *The Magic Mountain,* and the subject of several of its metaphysical discursions. Hans Castorp notes, even very early in his stay when he still regards himself as a temporary visitor to the Berghof, that the mountain has played havoc with his sense of the passage of time, so that he seems both to have only just arrived and also to have been there a long time: "That has nothing whatever to do with reason, or with the ordinary ways of measuring time; it is purely a matter of feeling" (Mann 1944, p. 105). The perception is complicated. On the one hand, each day is full of pre-cisely measured and timed activities—the frequent and sumptuous meals, the periods of rest in between, the prescribed daily walk. On the other hand, during several of those activities, especially the rest cures, it is enjoined that one carefully devote oneself to doing nothing. And from day to day for months on end the routine hardly alters.[1] Settembrini feels obliged to warn Hans that "there is something frightful in the way you fling the months about" (p. 242), and he condemns the prevailing attitude of the Berghof as un-European: "This barbaric lavishness with time is in the Asiatic style" (p. 243), in effect linking disrespect for the passage of time with the "badness" of the "Asiatic" Russian woman, Frau Chauchat. Much later, Hans's final resignation to his apparently eternal stay at the Berghof is marked

---

1. These aspects of time, in the world of the sick, resemble Kermode's (1967) account of the concept of time epitomized by the novel. This he relates, in turn, to the Thomist account of the *aevum,* a third sort of time located in between the temporal mortality of human beings and the eternity of God. Angels occupy the *aevum;* on the one hand, they are immortal and hence outside of time (in the same way that the novel is outside of time); on the other, as they are creatures of free will and choice, their actions have a temporal sequence and thus form a narrative.

by the fact that his watch falls off the nightstand and he fails to have it repaired. (The new brand of cigar that he adopts when he gives up his old flatland brand is, appropriately, called Light of Asia.)

The novelist's sympathies are with Settembrini in this matter. Hans regards this nonchalance over months and years as part of his "freedom," which is ultimately a freedom from any meaningful plan or purpose in life. Mann notes how dependent we are, in our awareness of the passage of time, upon external cues and how quickly we lose any sense of time when those cues vanish. As an image of the total absence of cues, he describes a walk along the beach by a vast ocean. One walks for a long way over seaweed and tiny shells, hearing the never-ceasing surf, feeling the wind, and yet one looks at the distant headland and seems to have come no closer to it. A sail is seen on the horizon, but one cannot gauge the distance, since one cannot be sure whether it is a large craft far away or a smaller craft closer in: "Your eye grows dim with uncertainty, for in yourself you have no sense-organ to help you judge of time or space" (p. 547). "You walk, and walk—never will you come home at the right time, for you are of time, and time is vanished" (p. 546). We may, he argues, dwell in this world without time only in the spirit of the "lawful license of a holiday" (p. 547), or to the extent that this world is useful for reminding us of the proper limits to human reason; but it is within human reason and within the world of time that we are obligated to dwell, for only there can our duty be discerned.

Mann's view here is consonant with MacIntyre's insistence that a human life must be viewed as a narrative and that the notions of personal responsibility and personal identity make sense only within such a narrative framework. Without the passage of time there can be no narration; events cannot take on the meaning that narration gives them if they cannot be located in time. And, by Rawls's notion, one cannot in the world along the oceanfront have self-respect. One cannot determine what would be a rational life plan in the sense of having it fit the expected trajectory of a human life, and one can certainly never determine whether or not one is *on the way to fulfilling* one's life plan if one's sense of time is severely disrupted. And, of course, if one is to confer with one's close associates about life plans and to seek their affirmation for one's own plan, there must be a common currency of time with an agreed-upon social meaning. If one's time sense is seriously distorted by sickness, then sickness threatens self-respect in this very basic fashion.

It has been commonplace for those describing illness to mention the distortions of time sense that accompany it. John Donne, for example, wrote of his sickness of 1624: "*daies* and *nights, so long,* as that *Nature* her selfe shall seeme to be *perverted,* and to have put the *longest day,* and the *longest night,* which should be *six moneths* asunder, into one *naturall, unnaturall day*" (1941, p. 341).

Berger enters into some theorizing about time in the process of describing the work of his English country doctor: "Anguish has its own time-scale. What separates the anguished person from the un-anguished is a barrier of time: a barrier which intimidates the imagination of the latter" (Berger and Mohr 1967, p. 107). Berger suggests that in anguish and sickness, one returns to something like the sense of time as experienced by a young child: "It is a platitude that as we grow older time seems to pass more quickly. The remark is usually made nostalgically. But we seldom consider the contrary effect of the same process—the elongation of time as it must affect the young and very young. . . . If we knew how long a night or a day was to a child, we might understand a good deal more about childhood" (Berger and Mohr 1967, p. 112).

A child not only has a different sense of the passage of time; a child often seems to lack our adult sense of recurring events within a unidirectional time flow. Thus, Berger suggests, the experience of childhood is both that of endless time and that of constant, irretrievable loss. A small child cries at the end of a game. The adult, interpreting the grief according to the adult view of the passage of events and "second chances," seeks to reassure the child: don't cry, you can play again tomorrow. But the child is grieving the loss of *that* game and feels in a way that the adult cannot that the thing that has just gone is unique and irretrievably lost. "When we suffer anguish we return to early childhood because that is the period in which we first learnt to suffer the experience of total loss. . . . It was the period in which we suffered more total losses than in all the rest of our life put together'' (Berger and Mohr 1967, p. 115).

Berger's insight may be rendered in several ways, depending on how strong or how weak an interpretation one seeks. An extremely weak reading would be that sickness is boring, and time seems to pass slowly when we are bored (or, alternatively, when we are chronically bored, a good deal of time may pass while we are scarcely aware of it). This reading, apart from its triviality, seems to do an injustice to the concept of sickness by reducing it to a subtype of boredom; merely being bored hardly approaches the depth of ''anguish'' that Berger is trying to analyze.

In contrast, a very strong reading would hold that we cannot understand any stories told to us by the sick about their experiences, with perhaps the exception of those suffering from totally mundane and clearly non-life-threatening complaints like colds. This reading would spring from the fact that part of what it would mean for young children to have the experience of time that Berger attributes to them is that they have not yet learned to tell at least some sorts of stories in the adult fashion; and once one learns to tell stories in the adult way, one's time sense has irreversibly become ''adult'' and one cannot truly recollect the old, childlike, prelinguistic way of perceiving time, much less describe it. A story told by an adult to an adult about, say, a summer or a Christmas, where the story is built around an unspoken assumption that (in addition to time being limitless) summers and Christmases are the sorts of things that occur only once and then are irrevocably gone, as opposed to their being the sorts of things that recur in cyclic fashion, would in a very important sense be an incomprehensible story. On this strong reading, the sick (at least the anguished sick) cannot communicate to the well what happens to their sense of time and their sense of the sequence of events. Whatever happens to those senses becomes part of the phenomenology of sickness, the unanalyzed and immediate experience of being sick; as soon as one tells a story about it (since stories have their method and structure) one has lost this key feature of the experience. Of course, on this very strong reading, true communication with severely ill persons becomes problematic if not impossible.

A middle reading would provide a warning to listen carefully to stories about sickness, with the reminder that the sick person may perceive some aspects of time differently, but also with the hope that with further questioning we can come to grips with the difference (as Hans Castorp was at pains to explain to Joachim). It is a reminder that a severe illness may be a "gap in the manuscript" of one's life story in an additional sense to the one discussed in the last section—the sickness as temporary interruption in one's ability to pursue one's life plan, after which one again takes up one's usual goals and activities. The sickness may also disrupt the narrative in the sense that the passage of time, during the illness, may have been experienced in a very different way from the usual (especially when the sick person's own account is compared with those of onlookers), and that the connection between events may be construed differently during that portion of the narrative. This altered sense of linkage among events seems, incidentally, to account for some patients who are labeled by physicians as "poor historians" (Coulehan 1984) because they have so much difficulty in answering causal and sequential questions required by the standard medical history; for instance:

"So you say the pain was in the middle of your stomach?"

"Yes, doctor, and it was the worst pain I have ever felt. I hope to God I never feel another pain like that."

"And how long did it last?"

"It seemed like it was never going to end."

"Well, was it ten seconds, or ten minutes, or two hours, or what?"

"All I know is that I was really scared, and the pain was the worst I ever felt."

"Was this after you ate, or on an empty stomach?"

"That pain was really bad. I thought about my aunt who died of cancer, and I wondered if her pain had been anything like that."

Typically, in these exchanges, as hard as the physician tries to restructure the account to arrange the data in what is felt to be a medically meaningful arrangement, the patient persists, as if compelled by a logic internal to the experience of sickness itself, in telling a story that makes clear all the meaningful associations from his own point of view but that is unhelpful for a medical diagnosis.

Although they alert us to the possibility that an altered time sense is a crucial feature of sickness, the works of literature we have reviewed ultimately provide only limited guidance. Even Mann's discourse on time is in the final analysis disappointing in this regard. It seems to tell us how time may be perceived by a very self-conscious, soul-searching late-adolescent in a tuberculosis sanatorium in the Alps, and it tells us about the special personality features of that individual that made seven years at the tuberculosis sanitarium seem like a good thing to do with his life. But beyond that it does not seem generalizable to other sorts of sickness and other persons.

Neurological case studies raise the possibility that disruptions of both space and time, drastically more profound than anything we have yet mentioned, may occur with certain illnesses while preserving almost full consciousness and awareness. Particularly suggestive and poignant in this regard is Oliver Sacks's *Awakenings* (1983). This classic contains case studies of patients who suffered a severe form of Parkinson's disease as a delayed effect of the pandemic of viral encephalitis that occurred between 1916 and 1927. Many of these patients remained almost comatose and unresponsive, "frozen" by the Parkinson's disease, until abruptly "thawed" with the advent of a new anti-Parkinson's drug, L-dopa, in the late 1960s. While fascinating of itself and suggestive of many insights regarding illness, this book serves us especially well here by suggesting the profound disruptions of a sense of time and space experienced by these and other patients with Parkinson's disease. The primary difference between Sacks's reports and the more standard textbook description of Parkinson's disease lies in Sacks's revolutionary, almost antimedical approach to these patients—*he asked them, carefully and consistently, to explain exactly what life was like for them*. The richness of the patients' responses suggests how much we may still be missing with regard to many other diseases, where no careful listener has yet come along to hear the stories of the sufferers.

Sacks learned from the patients that the so-called frozen immobility typical of severe Parkinsonism may be a strange disorder of time rather than a problem of true physical immobility. He described a patient who appeared, for all practical purposes, to be frozen in a wheelchair in the corridor for a space of fifteen hours at a time. The only variation discernible was a slight shift in the location of one hand; early in the day it might be near one knee; later it would be opposite the patient's chest; still later it would be near the patient's nose or glasses. Finally, after L-dopa had successfully rendered this patient communicative, Sacks asked him about these "akinetic poses." The patient's simple and wholly logical reply was, "What do you mean, 'frozen poses'? I was merely wiping my nose!" (Sacks 1983, p. 306). As far as the patient's own perceptions were concerned, these had been purely normal movements occupying a single second; he was disconcerted to learn from Sacks that the movements had in fact taken up the better part of a day.

Sacks notes that there is an uncanny physiological fact about these patients that lends indirect support to their psychological self-reports. If any normal person were to be "deactivated" (pp. 301–02) for even a few weeks, say by enforced bed rest, a very lengthy period of rehabilitation would be necessary for return to full mobility. The human musculoskeletal system does not take kindly to "deactiva tion." Muscles lose their strength, joints freeze rigidly, and bones lose their calcium. Yet Sacks observed that patients rendered immobile by Parkinson's for forty years or more, once given L-dopa, *instantly* were able to walk or run the length of the hospital, and could hardly be restrained in their exuberant (and tragically, in most cases, short-lived) rejuvenation. Their bodies seemed to agree with their perceptions that only hours and not decades had elapsed since they had last exercised. (Sacks further noted that almost all these patients appeared much younger than their chronological ages.)

Other Parkinson's patients characterized their symptoms as primarily linked to spatial incongruity. One patient described her "freezing" as follows: "It's not as simple as it looks. I don't just come to a halt, I am still going, but *I have run out of space to move in.* . . . You see, *my* space, *our* space, is nothing like *your* space: our space gets bigger and smaller, it bounces back on itself, and it loops around itself till it runs into itself" (Sacks 1983, pp. 296–97).

A similar spatial bizarreness was invoked by another patient to explain another textbook symptom of Parkinsonism—the so-called festinant gait in which one careens forward headlong, taking small hurried steps. Sacks observed one patient walking down a hospital corridor, suddenly going from a normal gait into a festinant gait, just managing to pull himself up before running into the nurses' station. His immediate and enraged question was, "Why the hell do they leave the passage like that?" On being reassured that the corridor was quite normal, he roared, "It's got a bloody great hole in it— they been excavating or something? I'm walking along, minding my business, and the ground suddenly falls away from my feet at this crazy angle, without reason. I was thrown into a run, lucky I wasn't thrown flat on my face" (p. 299). On being walked carefully back over the length of the passage,[2] the patient was astonished to admit that the nurse had been right and he had been wrong, that in fact there was no hole. "I could have *sworn* it suddenly dipped" (p. 299).[3]

These few glimpses into ways in which the world of the sick person can be different from the world of the well, even in such basic matters as the perception of time or space, suggest that the social relationships between the sick and the well may have some especially problematic elements. The discussions that follow will take up these matters in more depth.

2. Sacks (1983) observes that a festinant patient will usually display totally normal gait when walking alongside a normal person; it is as if, he states, the Parkinson's patient can still hear the rhythm of human activity but has lost the power to generate the rhythm internally. Similarly, severely "frozen" patients will sometimes become quite mobile when listening to certain kinds of music.

3. It must be emphasized in connection with these self-reports that the textbook description of Parkinson's disease is that of a neurological condition that spares the intellectual and cognitive portions of the brain; illusions, delusions, and disorders of thought form no part whatever of the disease picture. Therefore, the patients' descriptions must (Sacks feels) be taken as honest attempts to report phenomena that are almost outside of the bounds of human language's ability to capture, and not as evidence of delirium or dementia.

SICKNESS AND SOLITUDE

We addressed earlier the matter of how sickness affects the individual's self-respect, which, it was argued in chapter 3, is inherently a social concept. Self-respect and the possession of a rational plan of life presuppose a set of reciprocal relationships among a group of peers. We may then ask how relationships of this sort may be altered as a result of sickness, and in general what sorts of relationships hold between the sick and the well. The sociological theory of a "role" begins to answer this question, but for our purposes we want to get beyond the sorts of abstractions on sick roles that we discussed in earlier chapters into deeper and more detailed stories of particular relationships.

A good place to start would be to review a list, proposed by the philosopher Gorovitz, of four reasons it is bad to be ill: (1) it causes discomfort and dysfunction; (2) it results in an undesirable egocentricity that shrinks a sick person's view of the world; (3) this state of egocentricity and shrunken worldview is in turn boring and constraining; and (4) illness, unless trivial, is an unwelcome, implicit affirmation of human vulnerability and mortality (Gorovitz 1982, pp. 60–61). Each of these characteristics of illness, although explicitly stated in terms of the self, actually presupposes relationships with others. It will be helpful here to expand a little on this point, taking the four posited aspects of illness in turn.

1. Possibly discomfort may be construed in terms of the individual alone. But, as was argued in considering the formal definition of *malady* in chapter 2, *dysfunction* implies a set of norms of one sort or another. There must be expectations of what it means to function properly for a person of one's age, sex, social class, educational background, and so forth. In practice, these are usually social norms. Sickness is often explicitly noted for the first time not by the sick individual but by his or her close associates who observe that function is no longer up to expectations.

2. The relationships that go into making up the practice of reviewing and affirming life plans are reciprocal relationships; and reciprocity is likewise a feature of many other important social ac-

tivities. This reciprocity requires that the individual be willing and able to regard others and the needs and goals of others (at least for purposes of discussion) as one would regard oneself, and that one should take an active interest in how the world appears to those others. But the sick individual is subject to an egocentrism and a shrunken worldview that militates against participation in such reciprocal relationships. The sick individual, until he or she is well again, is not the sort of person one wishes to have as a reviewer for one's life plan; indeed that individual is hardly in the position to be a friend in any of the usual meanings of the word. If it is a serious disvalue to be sick, part of the reason seems to be that it is because one senses and regrets one's unfitness to participate in reciprocal relationships, and not so much because egocentrism is experienced as a disvalued state for its own sake.

3. When one is egocentric and has a shrunken worldview, one constrains and bores oneself as well as others who may be around. The boredom and constraint to oneself may be unpleasant only for its own sake. But there is also the disvalue of appearing boring and constraining to those others upon whom one's self-respect ultimately depends. If they see one as being boring and constraining, they are hardly liable to conclude that one is on the way to fulfilling one's life plan, at least assuming that the life plan is a rational one which they could be expected to affirm. One naturally feels that one's self-respect is in jeopardy when one is at risk for driving away all the people with whom one would choose to associate.

4. Death and mortality mean the loss of one's self and the inability to do anything further to pursue one's life plan. But they also mean the loss of all important human relationships. If one's egocentricity and shrunken worldview, as well as one's inability to function in the way that others expect and value, seem in the present to threaten one's human relationships, this is just an additional foreshadowing of the eventual severing of all human relationships through death, and thus it is doubly terrifying.

It appears from Gorovitz's list that at some times, and in some ways, the badness of sickness can be mitigated by the proper sort of human contact, and yet at other times solitude rather than social contact might appear to be the preferred form of solace. A similar ambivalence on this point is reflected in a set of three literary essays, all by English authors although of different historical periods, on the subject of being ill (Donne 1941; Lamb 1962; Woolf 1948). These essays (representing the seventeenth, nineteenth, and twentieth centuries, respectively) are worthy of study because each places the sick individual, with his or her feelings and perceptions, at center stage throughout; the physicians and others are merely bit players. And (obviously, since each is a first-person narrative) it is taken for granted that recovery, not death, is the final outcome of the sickness. So, whereas the major point of Tolstoy's "The Death of Ivan Ilich" is review of the past life in preparation for death, the narrators of these three essays are free to focus on the illness experience itself, in isolation from the life that precedes and succeeds it. (The extent to which a fear of death enters the account does vary considerably, however, as we shall see below.)

Lamb, in his short piece entitled "The Convalescent," captures particularly well the egocentricity described by Gorovitz: "How sickness enlarges the dimensions of a man's self to himself! he is his own exclusive object. Supreme selfishness is inculcated upon him as his only duty. . . . He has nothing to think of but how to get well. What passes out of doors, or within them, so he hear not the jarring of them, affects him not" (Lamb 1962, p. 215). Lamb notes how the sufferer was, just prior to falling ill, greatly excited about a lawsuit that threatened a good friend with financial catastrophe and bustled about the town on one errand or another in support of his friend's cause; now he lies abed, "as indifferent to the decision, as if it were a question to be tried at Pekin" (p. 215). From an occasional overheard whisper about the house, he finally realizes that the suit has failed and his friend is ruined. "But the word 'friend,' and the word 'ruin,' disturb him no more than so much jargon. He is not to think of any thing but how to get better" (p. 216). Under these circumstances, it is not surprising that solitude appeals to him more than company. "He is his own sympathiser; and instinctively feels that none can so well perform that office for him. He cares for few spectators to his tragedy" (p. 216).

Virginia Woolf, a century later, describes her own bout of influenza in strikingly similar terms. She has resigned herself to not seeking sympathy. All one's illness does, for one's friends, is to remind them of their own past illnesses that went unsympathized by their friends in turn. "Fate" demands that there be no sympathy for the sick, lest the burden be too great and all life stops in its tracks, if to their own pains people had to add the imagined pains of all other people: "one great sigh alone would rise to Heaven, and the only attitudes for men and women would be those of horror and despair" (Woolf 1948, p. 12). In the same note of hyperbole, she admits a passing pleasure from those of her acquaintances who do pay a visit, but does not spare them her irony: "Sympathy nowadays is dispensed chiefly by the laggards and failures, women for the most part . . . , who, having dropped out of the race, have time to spend upon fantastic and unprofitable excursions" (p. 13).

Illness causes us to blurt out truths that in health lie concealed, and one such truth, for Woolf, is that sympathy is really overrated. The idea that all people are inextricably linked (Donne's "no man is an island") "is all an illusion. . . . Human beings do not go hand in hand the whole stretch of the way. There is virgin forest in each; a snowfield where even the print of birds' feet is unknown. Here we go alone, and like it better so. Always to have sympathy, always to be accompanied, always to be understood would be intolerable" (1948, p. 14). In health, we may keep up the pretense that we must always be occupied with the communal and the civilizing; in illness "this make-believe ceases. . . . Directly the bed is called for, . . . we cease to be soldiers in the army of the upright; we become deserters" (p. 14).

Since when sick we turn away from human contact, it surprises Woolf not at all that we have elected to make flowers, "the stillest, the most self-sufficient of all things" (p. 16), our preferred companions of the sickroom. "It is in their indifference that they are comforting" (p. 16). And Lamb similarly finds one sort of visitor to his liking: "Only that punctual face of the old nurse pleases him, that announces his broths, and his cordials. He likes it because it is so unmoved, and because he can pour forth his feverish ejaculations before it as unreservedly as to his bed-post" (Lamb 1962, p. 216).

It is thus an "it" that proves comforting to the sick individual; by offering so little, the "it" gives promise of demanding nothing in return, so that the limited resources of illness will not be taxed further with demands for reciprocity.

But for the third sufferer, John Donne, matters seem different: "As *Sicknes* is the greatest misery, so the greatest misery of sicknes, is *solitude*, . . . *Solitude* is a torment which is not threatned in *hell* it selfe" (Donne 1941, p. 313). The particular occasion of the fear of solitude is the possibility that his disease might have an infectious cause and thus scare away visitors: "A long sicknesse will weary friends at last, but a pestilentiall sicknes averts them from the beginning" (p. 314). His lengthy meditations therefore take him to the connectedness among people. If the final outcome is to be fatal, it comforts him to know that others have passed that way also: "when these hourely *Bells* tell me of so many *funerals* of men like me, it presents, if not a *desire* that it may, yet a *comfort* whensoever mine shall come" (p. 331). The sickness and approaching death of another can benefit, "if by this consideration of anothers danger, I take mine owne into contemplation, and so secure my selfe, by making my recourse to my *God*, who is our onely securitie" (p. 332). Thus for Donne there is comfort in the idea that "no man is an *Iland*" and that one need not "send to know for whom the *bell* tolls; It tolls for *thee*" (p. 332).

But even if the eventual outcome is to be recovery, the thoughts that still appeal most to Donne are those of society and reciprocity: "No man is well, that understands not, that values not his being well; that hath not a cheerefulnesse, and a joy in it; and whosoever hath this *Joy,* hath a desire to communicate, to propagate that, which occasions his happinesse, and his *Joy,* to others; for every man loves witnesses to his happinesse; and the best witnesses, are experimentall witnesses; they who have tasted of that in themselves" (p. 318).

Thus he is certain that upon recuperation he will rejoice to share word of his good fortune with others who likewise have been sick and who have recovered; not only will they through their experience be best able to understand his joy, but the very fact that all of them experience this joy will produce in all of them a desire that it be shared maximally.

Sickness, for Donne, has a theological meaning that is lacking for the other two essayists. Thus, for Virginia Woolf, lying sick abed assures that one will, perhaps for the first time, really look hard at the sky in its ever-changing majesty, whereas Donne can only rail at the "miserable and, (though common to all) inhuman *posture,* where I must practise my lying in the *grave,* by lying still, and not practise my *Resurrection,* by rising any more" (p. 312). But at no time is the purely spiritual aspect of the matter allowed to push the social dimension of sickness entirely out of the picture; so it seems incorrect to speculate that it is Donne's piety alone that leads him to seek solace in human connectedness whereas Lamb and Woolf prefer solitude. The deciding factor, instead, seems to be that Donne genuinely fears for his life throughout most of the time period he describes; Woolf never hints at the possibility of death (after all, the flu is only the flu), and Lamb, although he may have feared for his life at the worst stage of illness, writes about himself specifically from the viewpoint of the convalescent's hindsight. For Donne, the fourth of Gorovitz's aspects of sickness (the threat of vulnerability and mortality) assumes priority; for the other essayists, the second and third seem to hold the most interest. (Donne does have a number of things to say about the first, dysfunction and disability; interestingly enough, Lamb and Woolf largely ignore that aspect of sickness.) When one fears primarily the loss of human relationships, reminders of those relationships can be comforting; when instead one is most aware of one's egocentricity and the resulting constraints upon one's awareness and mental processes, solitude may appear the best solution. Secure in the knowledge that they will soon rejoin the "army of the upright," Lamb and Woolf can join Thomas Mann's walk along the seashore and out of time and space (Woolf: "the whole landscape of life lies remote and fair, like the shore seen from a ship far out at sea"; p. 12), in the spirit of a vacation of sorts. Just like being outside of space and time does not threaten our sense of reason and duty so long as it is kept within the confines of a vacation, solitude does not threaten our basic sense of social reciprocity when it is enjoyed in the same spirit.

7

Sickness and Social Relations

THE EFFECT OF SICKNESS ON OTHERS

To discern how sickness affects one's close associates, we must move away from first-person narratives of the sickness experience in order to hear the stories as told from others' viewpoints. An important description of a sickness experience, told with a focus on the afflicted individual, but from which the stories and experiences of the other characters can be easily reconstructed, is the short story "The Metamorphosis" by Franz Kafka (1979).

"The Metamorphosis" presents a problem opposite that described by Sontag (1978). We are not presented with a story reputedly about sickness and asked to determine whether the sickness is treated realistically or as a metaphor for some more abstract ill. Instead we are presented with an obvious metaphor and challenged to interpret it in terms of sickness. The central character, Gregor Samsa, wakes up one morning to discover that he has turned into a giant insect; the remainder of the story details his sufferings and eventual death in this state and also his family's reactions to his situation. By way of justification for treating the story as a metaphor for sickness, we might note that the state of having become an insect is without doubt a "malady" (Clouser, Culver, and Gert 1981; see chapter 2). Waking up to find that one has turned into an insect is certainly to have something wrong with oneself; one is suffering and is at risk for suffering further the evils of disability, loss of freedom and opportunity, and loss of pleasure; no distinct, sustaining cause can be located for this state of affairs (indeed, in the story, no cause at all can be identified); and the state of affairs is certainly not merely a rational belief or desire.

The story is worthy of a full exploration strictly from Gregor Samsa's point of view. For example, the story reveals compellingly how difficult it is, when one suddenly develops chronic illness, to give up one's original life plan and to grasp the need for developing a modified life plan. When Gregor wakes up to make his horrible discovery, his first thought is that it is later than he had intended to rise—he will miss his train and will be late for an important appointment. The story also reveals a wrinkle in the notion of disability. When Gregor first tries to arise from bed in his new form, he has great difficulty maneuvering his unwieldy body, which lies on its back with its six stubby legs flailing in the air; he injures himself significantly in the effort. Later, as he heals and learns slowly how his new parts work, he is able to run around the room quite comfortably, even on the walls and ceiling, and takes some pleasure in this form of exercise. Still later, an apple is thrown at him by his father to chase him back into his room; it lodges in his back and slowly festers there, so that he becomes unable to run about with any facility. Now, from the standpoint of Gregor-as-former-human-being, he is almost totally disabled from his malady and remains in this same state throughout. But from the standpoint of Gregor-as-insect, he is clearly more and less disabled at different points in the course of his malady (because of maladies—the injury, the apple—on top of the basic malady). This example serves as a further reminder of the essentially relative nature of the term *disability*.

For our present purposes, however, the story is most compelling as an account of the Samsa family's reaction. An extremely important feature of that reaction occurs at once and is never modified by later events. When members of his family try to enter the room to see why he has not come out and then flee in shock and disbelief at the sight of him, Gregor attempts to speak to them; his brain forms the appropriate words, but his insect mouth cannot utter them. They see that Gregor cannot speak to them and immediately conclude (incorrectly) that he cannot hear them either. From that time on they converse in front of him or in the next room exactly as if he did not exist or as if he were an uncomprehending object. This, of course, adds greatly to Gregor's anguish. The suggestion is that an immediate barrier to communication is established between the sick individual and his friends and family; that barrier is created in part by the human reaction to illness, over and above the barrier that is inherent in the facts of the illness itself.

Overall, the Samsas' reactions to Gregor's metamorphosis pass through four stages. First, there is the initial shock and disbelief. There are no family traditions, no cultural rituals, to assist them in knowing how one is supposed to respond to an event of this type. Next comes a dutiful stage. The family does not think of sending for an exterminator, for someone from the zoo, or for anyone from outside who could approach the task of removing the giant insect. Perhaps letting the outside world know of this would be too embarrassing and stigmatizing; but at any rate, at this stage, the insect is still their son and brother, Gregor. They supply him with food, watching carefully to see what sorts of foods he favors and what he rejects; they rearrange the furniture to allow him space to run around. His sister outdoes the other family members in these attentions: she feels privileged in her own mind because she imagines that she has a special ability to discern what Gregor wants and becomes jealous if other family members take over one of her self-appointed tasks in Gregor's care. But the other family members still cannot stand the sight of him; they are very gratified, when they enter the room, if he manages to hide under the sofa and pull a sheet over its edge to further conceal himself. (At this point, Gregor is occupying the good sick role, and he is gratified that they are gratified at this accomplishment of his.)

The dutiful stage gradually deteriorates as no hope for any change arises and gives way to a resentful stage. The room, formerly kept clean, is allowed to become dusty and neglected and eventually is used by the family as a storage dump for refuse from other parts of the house. The food offered to him is inadequate. But this neglect corresponds with the growth of the family in several new directions. Previously he had been the family breadwinner; his father has been pensioned off for a disability, and his mother and sister have never worked. His insect state initially worries him considerably because he wonders what will become of them without his support. But over time they adapt in ways he had not anticipated. The father gets a new job; the mother starts to make some money by performing domestic tasks for others; they take in boarders; and the sister embarks on a career of her own. They are proud of these new accomplishments; the fact that Gregor persists as an insect makes them more resentful because confrontation with him reminds them of their former state, detracting from their new progress. (His insect state also creates problems with the boarders, leading to the hurling of the apple at his back.) Finally, his sister, formerly the most dutiful, states openly that they should stop kidding themselves; this insect is not Gregor at all but a foreign presence to which they owe no obligations and with which they have no kinship ties. Their growth in new and different directions has sped up the process of disengagement.

The final stage of the process, once Gregor dies, is grief, which lasts for a few minutes of solemn leave-taking. The grief is followed immediately by a deeply felt sense of relief, of a newfound freedom, and of new possibilities in life that now lie open to all of them, the sister especially. The reader sympathizes with this stage of the reaction despite the fact that the family has actually killed Gregor in a very real sense; he has died as a result of their poor feeding and of the ultimate consequences of the rotten apple.

Trautmann, in commenting on the medical significance of this story, notes that the family members regard Gregor's malady as something that happens to them, not as something that has happened to Gregor, the effects of which they must share (Trautmann and Pollard 1982). In an important sense they are sicker than Gregor is. To return to the language of Parsons, Gregor has a sick role he can occupy; this involves his taking on some relatively minor new responsibilities (such as hiding under the sofa to spare his family's feelings) at the same time that he gives up almost all his old responsibilities. But society provides no family sick role that his mother, father, and sister may occupy; indeed there is no way that society provides for their predicament to be recognized at all. Instead of a trade-off of responsibilities, each family member is presented with a dual burden; they must take care of Gregor, distasteful as that is, and simultaneously take over all the breadwinner functions that Gregor's transformation has left undone. Duty gives way to resentment, and that death brings much more relief than grief seems understandable under these circumstances.

The Samsas' range of reactions to Gregor's affliction is limited by the fact that they have so little choice (or think they have); they see themselves as being trapped and victimized. What is the reaction to malady on the part of those who have some choice, and who can go home at night to settings of nonsickness? Preston (1979) has used the Kafka analogy (he refers to the impact on others of serious illness or bodily deformity as the "Gregor effect") to study the reactions of nurses caring for the chronically ill and aged. He is interested specifically in reactions to people whom he labels "acutely ambiguous" in that they are like us and yet not like us (pp. 37–46). In participant-observer studies on hospital wards, Preston observed the following distinguishable reactions to the acutely ambiguous:

1. Impulsive reactions (startle, flight).
2. Prejudiced reactions. These resemble impulsive reactions in part, but whereas impulsive reactions are purely emotional, prejudiced reactions partake of preconceived social values and are partly ritualized. They include taboo reactions and aversion reactions.
3. Obscenity reactions, in which the individual tries to resolve the ambiguity by excessively identifying with the deformed or disabled, almost wallowing in their freakishness.
4. Ritual separation, of which death is the ultimate form, but which, short of death, can consist of banishment or sequestration of the sick.
5. Humanitarianism, which occurs via a broadening of perspective. The ambiguous are restored in the observer's mind to a fully human status because the observer has expanded his or her concept

of what it is to be human. This seems to be an ideal reaction but is hard to adhere to in practice; it tends to degenerate easily into a superficial do-gooderism.

6. Spiritual transcendence, often tied to religion; in practice it often works better than humanitarianism because it searches for an extra-human reference point for resolving the ambiguity.

7. Normalization, in which one tries to resolve the ambiguity by making the sick or disabled "just like us." This can serve as an attractive "power trip" for those who can protect threats to their identity only by enthusiastic activity directed outward.

8. Diversionary tactics, such as the use of black humor.

9. Induration, which may develop gradually and result in diminished perception of the ambiguity (Preston 1979, pp. 47–84).

Preston's list is helpful as a reminder that people can respond to others' sickness with as full a variety of reactions as the individual responds to his own sickness. These reactions are reactions to perceived ambiguity and are themselves ambiguous. This is not surprising; just as to be sick is to sense an unpleasant disruption of the self-body unity ("ontological assault") (see chapter 2), to perceive sickness or disability in others is to be reminded of one's own vulnerability and mortality in an equally unpleasant and threatening way. Thus much reaction to sickness that superficially appears to be solely outward-directed (that is, toward meeting the needs of the sick person) is in reality also inner-directed as an attempt to remove, resolve, or transcend this inner threat to integrity. Such reactions to sickness defy the efforts of those who would wish to tidily label all human behaviors as "healthy" or "pathological." For instance, Gregor's sister's attentiveness to his needs during her dutiful stage might be seen at first as a positive and altruistic reaction to illness in the family; but her obsessiveness and jealousy in this role signal the fact that the behavior pattern serves to mask a deeper turmoil.

THE SUFFERING OF THE FAMILY

Chapter 2 addressed the question of how sickness and suffering is immediately experienced by the sufferer; and the major themes that emerged, primarily from the analyses of Gadow (1980) and Cassell

(1982), indicated that suffering and sickness at bottom represent disconnectedness and disruption, in which the self is cut off from social meaning and social support, and in which the self experiences itself as divided from the body. We also encountered, in chapter 1, Berger's account in which healing was linked to "recognizing," to a restoring of the social connection (Berger and Mohr 1967). Now, if one adopts the perspective of the hierarchy of natural systems, the "biopsychosocial model" described in chapter 2, one sees that this disruption need not appear only at the level of the individual person, or between the person and the higher-level social systems. The family, consisting as it does of a tightly knit group of individuals such that the behavior and attitudes of any one family member are very likely to affect all the other members and vice versa, could readily experience an analogous disruption, to the extent that one could speak of the suffering of the family unit in a reasonably concrete rather than in a strictly metaphorical fashion.

The possibilities for family suffering have already been noted in the situation of the Samsa family. They are at high risk for a feeling of meaninglessness, a feeling of being cut off from their community and their culture, because there is no well-defined family sick role they can fill. Had Gregor simply dropped dead, they could fill the well-defined social role of the grieving family and go through the accepted, comforting social rituals of wake and funeral; these roles and rituals would not only lend social meaning to their sadness and loss but would also serve to mobilize supportive and caring reactions from the community. But the roles and rituals relating to chronic illness of a family member are either very poorly defined or nonexistent, and if anything tend to instill avoidance reactions in one's neighbors and associates. One aspect of this problem is the Samsa family's inability to make any sort of public declaration of their plight. Had there been a death or marriage in the family, there would be a clear mechanism for making this known to the community at large in a way that links the family's situation clearly to the larger network of cultural expectations and values. But the Samsa family clearly perceives that there is no way that they can announce publicly that their son has become a six-foot insect without bringing down upon their heads social ostracism and social repugnance at the least. The fact that this would inevitably be the social reaction to their announcement cannot but affect their private image of themselves; and thus a deep sense of shame must be added to their shock and grief. The experience is different only in degree, not in kind, for the families of many with chronic illness, especially children.[1]

In literature, one of the most extreme portrayals of family suffering in reaction to sickness is Ernest Hemingway's short story "Indian Camp" (1930). The story is a grim portrayal of the outcome that Cassell (1982) most fears in modern technological medicine—the physician cures the disease but in the process increases suffering. The story is an ironic twist on the black humor of "The operation was a success but the patient died." A doctor in an Indian camp in the northern Michigan backwoods performs a virtuoso cesarean section with jackknife and fishing line and no anesthesia on a woman who has been in labor for two days. Mother and baby survive, but the husband, who has been lying silently in an upper bunk, is discovered to have cut his own throat.

The narrative is told in the taut, almost clinical Hemingway style, which is especially effective because it gives the reader no hint whatever of the nature of the relationship between husband and wife; the reader must fill this in from the imagination. As the doctor, his young son, Nick, and his brother approach the Indian camp, they find the men sitting and smoking in a circle, out of earshot of the cries of the pregnant woman. In this society the men acknowledge the event of birth by withdrawal into their own circle; it is the women who gather around the laboring mother. But an axe wound in the foot

---

1. Recent research has shown that in our present society, parents of chronically ill and congenitally handicapped children frequently encounter blaming responses on the part of social peers, with thinly disguised assertions that if only the family had done everything right, the handicap would somehow have been prevented, so the outcome must be the family's own fault. This seems to arise from a widespread fear of sickness and handicap, such that one can psychologically defend oneself against the fear of such an event only by pretending that it could never happen to "good people like us." This, of course, significantly increases the suffering of these families and pushes them for solace into organized groups of similar families. I am indebted for these unpublished findings to Johanna Shapiro, in her presentation before the conference Working with Families, Society of Teachers of Family Medicine, Newport Beach, Calif., March 1984.

has ripped the husband out of this comforting and meaningful social pattern; he must lie in the upper bunk, hearing every scream and yet unable physically and socially to participate in any useful way or to come to his wife's aid. He cannot form a part of the social support group that is helping his wife; and he is unable to join his own social support group of the men outside. No role or ritual that his culture has taught him equips him to deal meaningfully with this predicament. We do not know whether he was able to comprehend the intent of the doctor's surgical intervention; the story makes it clear that no attempt was made to explain it to him or to include him in any way in the medical encounter. It seems quite likely that the husband was able to interpret the surgery only as a bloody and painful assault upon his wife's body, which he was powerless to prevent, and that the only way in which he could give any ultimate meaning to this event—the only way he could reestablish any meaningful social and cultural connection with his wife in her suffering—was to mimic the bloody incision upon his own throat.

A short story portraying deep-seated family suffering but with a more positive outcome is Tillie Olsen's "Tell Me a Riddle" (1961). The story opens by showing the deep-seated quarrel between a husband and wife married forty-seven years, who have emigrated to the United States, produced children and grandchildren, and lived the American life of the middle twentieth century. The quarrel, at this time, seems to be the main cement that holds them together as a couple. Each has stored up a litany of grievances of forty-seven years, to be dragged out at a moment's notice in order to hurt the other. He has been a jovial and fun-loving man in company, popular with his children and friends, hardly ever helping her with the children or household tasks, and always able to get a laugh in company by making fun of her. She, during her girlhood, was a political prisoner in Russia, a passionate believer in ideals and causes, a lover of books and music; the drudgery of child rearing through poverty was experienced by her primarily as a wedge driven between her and the activities (reading, singing) she craved.

The current content of the quarrel has to do with where they will live in retirement. He wants to sell their house and move to a retirement village run by his lodge, where financial security, companionship, and activities will be assured. She wants to remain in her own home; now that the children are gone she can clean the house without it being messed again and can have time for her own pursuits. There are bitter arguments about whether the house will be sold:

> "Leave on the television. I am watching."
> "Like . . . a four-year-old. Staring at shadows. *You cannot sell the house.*"
> . . . "The television is shadows. Mrs. Enlightened! Mrs. Cultured! . . . Yes, Mrs. Unpleasant, I will sell the house, for there better can we be rid of each other than here." (pp. 69–70)

She begins to feel ill and weak. One evening, as he is about to go out, she uncharacteristically asks him to stay home with her:

> "Hah, Mrs. Live Alone and Like It wants company all of a sudden. It doesn't seem so good the time of solitary when she was a girl exile in Siberia. 'Do not go. Stay with me.' A new song for Mrs. Free As a Bird. Yes, I am going out, and while I am gone chew this aloneness good, and think how you keep us both from where if you want people, you do not need to be alone."
> "Go, go. All your life you have gone without me." (p. 74)

The first impression of her sickness is that it is "a psychological thing" (p. 73); finally metastatic cancer is diagnosed. The husband and children agree among themselves to conceal the truth from her—not a hard thing for him to do, as concealing true feelings seems to have become their mode of married life. Just as she wishes only to return home, he starts to take her on a round of visits to the homes of the children. (The depth of her sense of disconnectedness, even before she knows her prognosis, is suggested by her refusal, all during one of these visits, to hold her newest grandchild.) As she gets worse, he takes her to Los Angeles, presumably for the climate; and gradually it becomes clear that she will die there—an exile again, with her husband having succeeded in taking her away from the home she has craved, but ironically without being able to enjoy for himself any of the hoped-for benefits. The moment that she finally realizes she is dying is the moment she looks into his face and reads there an undisguised fear and pity for *her*, not for himself alone.

Into this apparently irretrievable tangle of regrets and lost opportunities comes an unexpected savior, in the person of a granddaughter with nurse's training, Jeannie, who arrives to cheerfully take over the care of the invalid and the emotional support of the husband. She allows Jeannie to approach her and to be with her in a way that she has not allowed any other family member. When she is bedbound and wracked with vomiting, he wants to take her to the hospital; she refuses. Jeannie interposes: "She needs you, Grandaddy. . . . Isn't that what they call love?" (p. 104). Jeannie succeeds in reestablishing a connection between them that they have been powerless to establish on their own. The wife becomes delirious, rambling in the night of childhood memories, memories of books she has read. He is tormented—does she have no pleasant memories of their shared life together, of the children?

> [He] went to press the buzzer to wake Jeannie, looked down, saw on Jeannie's sketch pad the hospital bed, with *her;* the double bed alongside, with him; the tall pillar feeding into her veins, and their hands, his and hers, clasped, feeding each other. And as if he had been instructed he went to his bed, lay down, holding the sketch (as if it could shield against the monstrous shapes of loss, of betrayal, of death) and with his free hand took hers back into his. (p. 115)

The last day before she dies she is wracked with pain; he cannot bear it and must leave the room:

> Jeannie came to comfort him. In her light voice she said: Grandaddy, Grandaddy don't cry. She is not there, she promised me. On the last day, she said she would go back to when she first heard music, a little girl on the road of the village where she was born. She promised me. It was a wedding and they dance, while the flutes so joyous and vibrant tremble in the air. Leave her there, Grandaddy, it is all right. She promised me. Come back, come back and help her poor body to die. (pp. 115–16)

In death the individual must ultimately disconnect from the family. The wife's last day is disconnected, her memory one of solitude. And yet there is a final reconnection as well. Her promise, a message for her husband, is meant to be comforting; the granddaughter, as bearer of the message, brings the husband and wife together even as the wife is past communicating.

Although the last day of bodily suffering recalls "The Death of Ivan Ilich," especially in the fact that the bodily anguish disguises an inner peace, there is the chance of the final connection that relieves suffering and makes events emotionally meaningful in Tillie Olsen's couple that is not present in Tolstoy's story. In Ivan Ilich's case there is no motive to send the comforting message and no sympathetic yet perceptive family member to whom to entrust it. Ivan Ilich's family have throughout perceived his sickness and impending death only selfishly, as inconvenience for themselves. Their suffering, such as it is, is individual only; there is no real family unit to suffer from being rent asunder by sickness and death.[2]

THE SOCIAL POWER OF THE SICK

To look only at the experience of the sick individual is to be struck by a sense of disability and powerlessness—it is to have something wrong with oneself, for which one is not morally responsible, and which therefore by implication one is powerless to remove or alter by one's own will. But if, as argued above, the sick affect the healthy in deep and powerful ways, and if, as the sociologists argue, to be sick is to occupy a well-defined social role that creates reciprocal

2. If the family, conceptualized as an organic unit, can suffer, what of larger social units? In *The Plague* Camus (1972) invites us to imagine an entire city as undergoing sickness and suffering. His treatment, ultimately, seems solely metaphorical. To imagine a city suffering, in the sense that the term is being used here, we would have to imagine a city so closely knit that the fate of each individual citizen could be predicted to affect every other citizen in a fairly intimate manner; and this strains credibility. Ultimately Camus's vision carries conviction because he paints the picture of a city that is less an organic unity in its own right and more a composite of the doings and the lives of each individual within it, almost as if the city is simultaneously a projection of the individual life of each citizen.

role responsibilities in others, then the sick person is ironically also in a position of great power. We saw little evidence of this in *The Magic Mountain* and *The Cancer Ward,* since the sick, by being placed together within a community of sick people, had little opportunity to exercise the power they might have had over the healthy. (One healthy person who felt this power was the uncle of Hans Castorp, during his ill-fated mission to return the prodigal to the world of the flatlands.) Other literary works reveal this aspect of sickness more clearly.

A brief short story by D. H. Lawrence, "A Sick Collier" (1955), describes the marital relationship between a collier (of the British Midlands, one presumes) and his new wife. At the beginning it might seem that she has considerable power to exercise over him: "She was too good for him, everybody said" are the words that open the story (p. 267). She is a year older, better educated, of a more respectable class, and good-looking. But in the coal-town society he soon indicates her place in the household—he sets her to learn how to lay out his miner's outfit at night for him to have ready for his half-past-five awakening, and he disdains to wash off his grime when he returns home for supper. "They were nevertheless very happy" (p. 268).

Then things begin to go poorly. There is a long strike; later his bladder is injured in a mine accident. In bed, at home, he is in continual pain and finds it very hard to bear.[3] In the sixth week of his confinement, the miners go out on a national strike; the streets are now full of idle and angry men, who are ready to become violent with little provocation. Outside, someone asks who will go to see a football match nine miles away; the husband shouts that he will and starts up from his bed. The wife restrains him; he cannot possibly

---

3. This story also makes important statements about the effect of sickness on the sick person: "He had never been ill in his life. When he had smashed a finger, he could look at the wound. But this pain came from inside, and terrified him" (Lawrence 1955, pp. 269–70). Sadly we do not have one of Trautmann's pithy and excellent commentaries on the medical implications of this story, since it is one of the few that has escaped her attention (Trautmann and Pollard 1975, 1983). I am indebted to Martin Benjamin for calling my attention to this story.

walk the distance in his state. He begins shouting at her in a delirium—it's she that is causing the pain to come on: "It's 'er, it's 'er.
Kill her!" (p. 272). With difficulty and with the assistance of a
neighbor woman she gets him back in bed and calmed down; he
breaks into tears when he realizes what he has been saying. "You
didn't know what you was sayin', Willy. . . . It doesn't matter,
Willy. Only don't do it again" (p. 273). But the wife remains terrified. Did anyone overhear? "If it gets about as he's out of his
mind, they'll stop his compensation. . . . whatever shall we do?"
(p. 273).

This delirious miner, unable to move without pain, has threatened
his wife with loss of livelihood and (had his screams produced a
reaction among the milling men outside) with the possibility of violence. Her powerlessness in the face of the threat he poses is a complex matter. Part of it is an outgrowth of his status as a sick person,
but a good deal of it reflects the economy of a mining town and the
role of women in the society.

Another, longer work illustrating the powers of the sick is Anton
Chekhov's play *Uncle Vanya* (1967). This will be worth explicating
in some detail because it has to do in part with a clash between
incompatible life plans.

The elderly Professor Serebryakov has devoted his life to study,
to writing about art, and to making his way in the academic world.
He is supported by the income of the estate that was the property
of his late wife; the estate is managed by the wife's brother Vanya
and Serebryakov's plain daughter Sonya. With retirement, Serebryakov finds that this income will not support his accustomed life in
the city, and so he decides to move back to the estate in the company
of his second wife, Yelena, who is practically the same age as Sonya.
In effect, Serebryakov's preferred life plan has been sidetracked for
lack of funds. In the country, away from the society he craves and
the fame his reputation has earned him, he slips into what is in effect
a modified, fallback life plan—if he cannot accomplish anything of
worth in his own eyes, at least he can dominate and manipulate those
around him and make sure their thoughts are not turned too far away
from himself. For this he finds his gout and rheumatism a useful

device, allowing him, for instance, to send for the rural physician, Dr. Astrov, at odd hours, and then disdain to follow any of his medical advice. An ally in this new life plan is Vanya's mother, to whom her son-in-law is still the great academician; she will allow nothing to be said against him.

Meanwhile, Vanya and Sonya have been dutifully working the estate for years, following what is, for sensitive people in rural Russia in the late nineteenth century, the only life plan that is practicable—hard work, mixed with a simple-minded and therefore unquestioned faith. (For Dr. Astrov, a simpleminded cynicism seems to work about as well as faith, without estranging him from his friends.) Into this stable household Serebryakov brings an infectious leisure, and Yelena brings an equally disruptive sexuality to which Vanya soon falls victim. The old servant bemoans the intrusion of these variant life plans, with both Serebryakov and Yelena committed each in their own way to doing as little as possible—tea at eight! dinner at one! not rising until eleven in the morning and then staying up half the night! Dr. Astrov confronts Yelena: "The moment you and your husband arrived here, everyone whom you found busy and engaged in active, creative work felt compelled to drop it and to give himself up to you and your husband's gout for the entire summer" (p. 218). Thus sickness and sexuality are put on a par, as excuses for a sort of leisure that is totally disruptive of the rural life-style of the estate. After a crisis occasioned by Serebryakov's contemplating selling the estate so that he can live off the profits, the incompatible life plans are finally separated; Serebryakov and his wife return to the city while Vanya and Sonya go back to their neglected work on the estate.

The sick can exercise this sort of power over the well only at the cost of resentment or fear in the long run. Here Parsons's sick role seems pertinent—one allows the sick to be let off from their usual obligations only in exchange for a commitment to disvalue the state of being sick and to comply with all efforts for healing. A suggestion that the sick person is enjoying special advantages as a result of the sickness will be resented as a violation of his reciprocal part of the bargain. Thus a life plan for dealing with sickness by using the sickness to manipulate others is an inherently unstable life plan, which ideally would not lead to self-respect, if articulated, since it would not be affirmed by those others. Such life plans, of course, in practice remain unarticulated and succeed for a greater or lesser time depending on the manipulative skills of the sick person and the nature of the preexisting family relationships.

SICKNESS AND SOCIAL JUDGMENT

The stories so far in this chapter have illustrated an irony in the power of the sick person: the person's power to manipulate and even devastate the lives of the healthy does not extend to the power to heal his or her own sickness. The stories do not, however, indicate any serious, articulate social reaction to the way the sick choose to exercise their power. The families and close associates may feel resentful, but they seldom feel comfortable passing judgment on how the sick person behaves. And yet, as argued previously, a sick person may wish self-respect, and this self-respect will in turn hinge upon the judgments that close associates pass upon the sick person's way of living. These issues are compellingly captured in the myth of Philoctetes, the subject of a play by Sophocles (1979).

A bit of background narration is necessary to place the action of the play in perspective. The story of Philoctetes and his wound actually begins with the suffering of another, Heracles.[4] Heracles, in agony after having put on the coat secretly impregnated with the blood of the centaur Nessus, cannot cure his affliction and yet, because of his great strength, he cannot die of it either. He decides to immolate himself upon a funeral pyre. Philoctetes, alone among all the followers of Heracles, is willing to come forward to perform the last request of the great hero and set the pyre alight. The last act of the dying Heracles is to bestow in gratitude upon Philoctetes his magic bow and arrows, which never miss their mark.

Philoctetes later joins the Greek expedition on the way to the war

---

4. Following the dramatist, this discussion employs the Greek names for all characters—hence, Heracles instead of Hercules, Odysseus for Ulysses, and so on.

with Troy; but on a small island, at which the Greeks had stopped to sacrifice to the local deity, Philoctetes accidentally strays into a portion of the shrine that is off limits for mortals. The shrine's guardian, a serpent, bites his foot. He does not die of the bite, but it develops into a virulent infection that periodically causes him excruciating pain before the abscess bursts and drains. Philoctetes' moans and the horrible stench of the wound are so disturbing to the Greeks they cannot tolerate his presence on the expedition. The crafty Odysseus takes the lead in concocting a plot to get rid of Philoctetes. The plot succeeds, and Philoctetes is abandoned on the nearby isle of Lemnos while the rest of the Greeks proceed on to Troy.

Ten years pass; Philoctetes ekes out a hermit's existence, limping about the island and living in a cave, avoiding starvation only through his ability to secure game by means of the magic bow. The Greeks, meanwhile, fare poorly at Troy. Their heroes Achilles and Ajax are both killed. Finally a soothsayer reveals that they can win the war only if two conditions are fulfilled—Achilles' son Neoptolemus must be brought to Troy and given his father's armor; and Philoctetes and his bow must be returned to the Greek forces.

Sophocles takes over the story at a point where Odysseus is approaching Lemnos in the company of Neoptolemus, whom he has fetched from Greece. Odysseus fears that Philoctetes will still resent his abandonment ten years previously and will never come willingly if it is Odysseus who approaches him. So he prompts Neoptolemus to gain Philoctetes' confidence by pretending to have his own grievance against the Greeks—Neoptolemus will claim that his father's armor was wrongfully denied him and given to Odysseus instead. Then, at the first opportunity, Neoptolemus will steal the bow and thereby force Philoctetes to be brought on board the ship. In the end, it is expected that this will be to Philoctetes' advantage; for among the Greek host at Troy is the son of the physician-god Aesclepius, who will probably have the power to heal the wound.

Neoptolemus reluctantly plays this false role with success; Philoctetes accepts him as a sympathizer, pours out his spleen against Odysseus and the Greeks, and begs Neoptolemus to take him on board ship back to his native Greece. As they are about to board, Philoctetes is seized by one of his paroxysms; he writhes on the ground in his agony, and screams:

> Be kind . . . pick me up, and burn me
> To ashes . . . a funeral pyre. . . .
> Please, Neoptolemos! Once I, too,
> Did that kindness for Heracles, son of Zeus. . .
> A kindness, a favour . . . he gave me the bow. . .
> He gave me the bow for it . . . it's in your hands. (Sophocles 1979, p. 135)

Philoctetes swoons, and sleeps. On awaking, he finds Neoptolemus still at his side with the bow in hand, and congratulates him for his compassion in not abandoning the sufferer. Finally Neoptolemus can tolerate his own duplicity no longer, and he admits the ruse to Philoctetes. Seeing that the secret is out, Odysseus appears from hiding to lay claim to the bow. Philoctetes berates Neoptolemus for his treachery; he sees himself robbed of his bow and left to starve on the island by his enemies; he attacks Odysseus for hypocrisy in coming to fetch him only now that the gods have commanded it. Finally, Neoptolemus defies Odysseus, throws in his sympathy with Philoctetes, and hands him back his bow.

There follows a dramatic dialogue in which Neoptolemus tries to persuade Philoctetes to come willingly to Troy, now that Neoptolemus has demonstrated his sympathy and his unwillingness to engage in coercion. He appeals to Philoctetes' patriotism as well as to the possibility of a cure for his wound. Philoctetes at first withstands all these blandishments and insists that Neoptolemus honor his original agreement to take him back to Greece. Finally the standoff is resolved by the appearance of Heracles from the skies; the god tells Philoctetes to follow Neoptolemus to Troy, where they will both find glory, and not to let hatred and resentment keep him in exile. Philoctetes does as his former patron commands. On arrival at Troy (which occurs at a point in the myth after the conclusion of Sophocles' play), his wound is healed by the great physician; and he and Neoptolemus are the heroes of the Greeks' final victory over the Trojans.

In a classic analysis of this story, Edmund Wilson (1947) lays special stress on the irony of the incurable wound wedded to the invincible bow, and sees this as a metaphor for the frequent link between power and genius with infirmity and madness.[5] But this aspect of the myth seems to miss slightly the essential dramatic tension that Sophocles exploited in his play. The tension is a psychological one, causing the audience to experience a split in sympathy. The audience find themselves agreeing with Philoctetes that, after suffering and patiently enduring his exile for ten years, he is under no obligation to help the Greek cause and has every right to refuse his aid. But the audience also find themselves agreeing with Neoptolemus that everyone would be better off if Philoctetes were to put aside his bitterness and come to Troy where his exile would be ended, his wound would be healed, and his bow could aid his country's cause. In this regard Neoptolemus' crucial speech to Philoctetes is:

All men must bear whatever fate the gods
Allot them, good or bad—but when a man
Brings suffering on himself, and clings to it
As you do, no one forgives or pities him. (Sophocles 1979, p. 153)

The sudden appearance of Heracles can be reinterpreted psychologically as representing Philoctetes' coming to his senses and suddenly realizing the force of Neoptolemus' arguments. (The tension is further reflected in the ambiguity in the soothsayer's prediction. It is not clear whether, to win the war, the Greeks must possess merely Philoctetes' bow without the man himself; or whether they must have them both, by whatever means; or whether it will suffice only if Philoctetes brings his bow as an act of free consent. As already noted, the first option would be especially cruel, since Philoctetes left on Lemnos without the magic bow would starve.)

---

5. This linkage of genius and madness or sickness is itself a popular literary theme, well represented in the play *Equus* (Shaffer 1973). It is a theme, however, that I expect few physicians to support; it represents most often a romanticizing of illness of precisely the sort that Sontag (1978) appropriately condemns. For that reason I do not explore the theme in any depth in this inquiry.

What is it that justifies the resolution of the dramatic tension in the direction of Heracles' injunction? It could be argued, in the terms of our previous analysis, that the tension is fundamentally between two differing concepts of self-respect. To Philoctetes, self-respect is gained when one demonstrates steadfastness in commitment to the course that one has chosen; hence he is obligated to cling to his bitterness and refuse to aid the Greeks, even if by so doing he gives up his chance for a cure. Neoptolemus is arguing for a view of self-respect that demands taking the broader picture into account and altering one's life plans and commitments in response to changed circumstances. This view of self-respect entails a social dimension, an admission of social relatedness, that is absent in Philoctetes' more individualistic view. Sophocles, through Heracles, determines that the second view of self-respect is the more sophisticated and satisfactory.

The reason Philoctetes eventually gives in to Neoptolemus' conception of self-respect and accepts Heracles' resolution to the impasse can be analyzed on either a psychological or a philosophical level. Psychologically, Wilson (1947) notes how important it is that the person who makes the argument is the single individual who has humanly sympathized with Philoctetes' plight. The other Greeks, represented by Odysseus, have without exception treated Philoctetes as a nonperson, an object—first abandoning him on the island when his presence became too much of a burden and then seeking him out again when it became apparent he could fulfill an essential function on their behalf. This underlines the significance of Heracles' appearance in the divine vision. It is not simply that Heracles was Philoctetes' former patron and could be expected to command obedience from him. Rather, the very fact that Philoctetes has the magic bow is a reminder of how he himself had sympathized with Heracles in his mortal agony; Philoctetes cannot ignore the fact that Neoptolemus now stands in the same relationship to him as he in bygone days had to Heracles. Psychologically, Philoctetes cannot have it both ways; he cannot remember with pride his own past services to his demigod-patron, for which he was rewarded with the bow, and at the same time spurn Neoptolemus' advances which are based on a genuine, proven sympathy for his sufferings.

In the terminology of Berger (Berger and Mohr 1967; see chapter 1), Neoptolemus has performed the vital function of *recognizing* Philoctetes in his suffering and anguish, and thus has engaged in the crucial social role of restoring Philoctetes to a sense of full personhood. Now that Neoptolemus has stood in this relationship to Philoctetes, the latter cannot dismiss his arguments in the same way that he could reject the wiles of Odysseus.

There is also a philosophical analysis of why Neoptolemus' arguments are destined to win the day. By his previous behavior, Philoctetes has acknowledged that he indeed values Neoptolemus' sympathy. The "recognition" has been a genuinely meaningful and gratifying event, coming at the end of ten years of a hermit's exile, and Philoctetes cannot deny the importance of it without willful self-deception. But if his own view of self-respect were the correct one— if his self-respect consists solely in steadfast adherence to his previously chosen course—none of this ought to matter; he should be happy to go on limping about the island and cursing the Greeks even if it costs him the sympathy and understanding of all other mortals. Since Philoctetes has recognized the force in Neoptolemus' rejoinder ("when a man brings suffering on himself, and clings to it as you do, no one forgives or pities him"), he cannot go on insisting that self-respect is solely an individual matter, and that it has nothing to do with what others think of him, and whether others are ready to extend their sympathies. And so Philoctetes cannot go on rejecting the view of self-respect that Neoptolemus holds out to him without self-contradiction; Heracles in the vision merely points this out.

As with so many other literary characters we have reviewed above, Philoctetes, to maintain self-respect in the face of sickness and suffering, must modify his life plan. The dramatic irony of his case, which also allows a "happy ending" atypical of Sophocles' plays, is that the life-plan modification must be in the direction of a cure and return to full and normal function, whereas most of the chronically sick must modify their life plans in the direction of accepting continued disability.

Sophocles shows great psychological insight in the play's brief final scene. Philoctetes has heard Heracles' predictions that in Troy he will find healing for his wound and glory in battle. But his final thoughts are of a wistful farewell to Lemnos and its cave that sheltered him and brooks that bathed him during his ten years of solitude. One cannot without a sense of grief and loss lay aside a life plan, a major piece of one's life story, even if that life plan held only suffering and solitude and the new life plan promises health and success.

In chapter 6 we discussed the sick person's ambivalent love for solitude, and earlier in this chapter we glimpsed the sick person's great social power. Odysseus has a healthy respect for the power of the sick, and this does not simply mean that he fears what will happen to him once Philoctetes gets a clear shot at him with the magic bow. He adopts a course of wiles and lies, instead of a course that will recognize Philoctetes as a person, partly because he fears, rightly, that he and Neoptolemus would be totally disarmed once they allow themselves to feel the human emotions of sympathy and pity. He fears, in effect, what Virginia Woolf (1948) warned against, that if we paused to truly pity the sick, our workaday world would stop in its tracks. Odysseus realizes that we rob the sick of their social power over us if we somehow suppress the human reaction to their plight.

But Neoptolemus (speaking for Sophocles) realizes that there is another way to turn aside the power of the sick person, when that power is directed toward continued suffering and bitterness instead of toward healing; and that is the route of reestablishing fully human contact so as to graphically remind the sick person of the importance of social connectedness. The sick person may indeed have accepted solitude as preferable to being rebuffed in his search for sympathy, and may have tried hard to forget about the importance of social relationships in maintaining identity and self-respect. But Sophocles argues that these are only temporary barriers that cannot withstand the concerted efforts of the reaching out of human sympathy. Here Thomas Mann (seconded by Talcott Parsons and by Siegler and Osmond) might add a qualification—we must assume that the person has not adopted the bad sick role and decided to be sick as a way of licensing irresponsibility. But if the person, like Philoctetes, has accepted a good sick role and has genuinely sought patience and fortitude in the face of sickness, then we may assume that the person's underlying values are the same ones shared by the healthy—the values that claim that the sickness is an undesired state of affairs and that the sick person is an unwilling victim of that state. Once those shared values are recognized in a socially and humanly supportive atmosphere, the way is cleared to return the sick person to an awareness of full membership in the society.

8

Maladaptive Ways
of Being Sick

In the previous chapter, we discussed the appropriateness of passing judgment upon the way a sick person is choosing to live his life. The notion of a sick role or roles, and our comments in chapter 5 regarding the good and bad sick roles (Siegler and Osmond 1974a), further lay the groundwork for an exploration of how one *ought* to be sick in various situations. True, the origin of these concepts is within medical sociology, and sociologists would presumably look askance on any efforts to confer moralistic overtones upon their neutral descriptions. And their skepticism would be appropriate if we had no grounds for condemning a particular sick role except personal distaste or the conviction that we would never want to act that way if we were ill. But we need not leave it at that level of subjectivism. Our discussions of self-respect and of rational plans of life give us reasonable grounds to view some ways of responding to illness as maladaptive—that is, as likely to lead to trouble, no matter where along the range of possible human conceptions of the good one's personal values lie.

In this chapter I wish to look at three examples. First, I will glance at noncompliant behavior and suggest that this mode of coping with illness, although clearly maladaptive from the biased viewpoint of the health professional, may indeed be reasonably adaptive from the standpoint of the patient. Next, I will discuss what I will call "dogmatic coping," illustrated by a recent publicized case, as an example of what seems clearly maladaptive. Finally I will summarize the controlling approach to sickness found in *Heartsounds* (Lear 1980) and suggest that this mode is ambiguous, having strongly maladaptive elements and yet perhaps in the end serving the needs of the sufferer.

NONCOMPLIANCE

We can begin by returning to the case of the poet Cronshaw (Maugham 1963), whom we met first in chapter 5. In that context we described Cronshaw's reaction to sickness as almost too good to be true. Having lived a life of alcoholic indulgence, he was at the end fully prepared to pay the price with equanimity. He was not in the least disposed to whine or make excuses or bargain for an eleventh-hour reprieve, and he showed no interest whatever in giving up his alcohol even as it was poisoning him. He admitted freely that, being only human, he was likely to have pangs of regret; but he then proceeded to disown those regrets, attributing them to his baser nature and not to any fundamental refusal to accept responsibility for how he had chosen to live his life.

In one way it might seem perverse to celebrate Cronshaw's self-respect. He is, after all, the quintessential "noncompliant patient."[1] By his behavior he rejects the value system of those care givers who

1. There is a voluminous literature on noncompliance. Very little of it (as the very term *compliance* would suggest) is willing to consider even for a minute the possibility that a patient might have *good reasons* for not following the prescribed medical regimen. For some less offensive summaries of the topic, see Stimson 1974; Eraker, Kirscht, and Becker 1984. A frequently cited authority is Haynes, Taylor and Sackett 1979. Arthur Kohrman has reminded me that the popularity of the term *compliance* within the medical profession indicates the predominance of the standard Parsonian (acute) sick role and the lack of tolerance of chronic illness. The idea of passive compliance fits the acute case nicely, as putting oneself under the healer's authority in that setting is expected to lead to a prompt return to normal function. In chronic illness, by contrast, talk of compliance can speedily degenerate into a form of victim-blaming—you are supposed to follow doctor's orders so that you will get well; therefore, if a long time has elapsed and you haven't gotten well, it must be your own fault because you failed to follow orders (presentation at conference, The Child with Chronic Illness, Lansing, Mich., April 18, 1986).

seek his restoration to health (slim as that chance might be) and thus might be thought to occupy the bad sick role, using sickness as an excuse for self-indulgence. But to see Cronshaw in this fashion (as, indeed, many physicians and nurses would without hesitation) is as inappropriate as the Soviet physicians' criticism of Kostoglotov as a bad and ungrateful patient because he wanted more information about his disease than they wished to share with him. The badness of the Berghof patients, who acted on the mountain in licentious ways that they would never have dared to act in their responsible roles on the flatland, must be distinguished from the badness that is simply part of the individual's accepted life plan and that has been customary for this person, sick or well. This latter form of behavior appears as badness when there is a conflict between the pursuance of the patient's more basic life plan and adherence to the standards that others (who may understand that life plan very imperfectly) expect from the good sick person. So long as close adherence to the good sick role will actually pay off, in the form of increased chances that one will be able to go on and fulfill one's life plan, then self-respect demands compliance; but where compliance and the life plan are fundamentally in conflict, the wise person sees that his self-respect is more closely linked to the life plan than to any role expectations.

This latter appreciation of badness lends some sympathy to James Dickey as he seems to celebrate noncompliance in his poem "Diabetes." He goes into the woods in the warm summer: "I will shoot my veins / Full of insulin. . . . My blood is clear / For a time. . . . But something is gone from me, / Friend. This is too sensible" (Dickey 1970, p. 9). "Companion, open that beer," he orders:

> How the body works   how hard it works
> For its medical books is not
> Everything: everything is how
> Much glory is in it: heavy summer is right
> For a long drink of beer. (p. 9)

Or, in the poem, "The Cancer Match," Dickey portrays a terminal cancer patient going home from the hospital to get drunk, picturing the bourbon as his good self, the "Basic Life Force," doing battle inside him with the tumor, "that turgid hulk, the worst / Of me" (p. 32). "Tonight," he tells himself as the battle between the two rages, "we are going / To win, and not only win but win / Big, win big" (p. 32):

> . . . I have been told   and told
> That medicine has no hope, or anything
> More to give,
> But they have no idea
> What hope is, or how it comes. (p. 31)

DOGMATIC COPING WITH SICKNESS

People in our society struggling to cope with handicapping conditions or chronic illness commonly turn to various lay self-help groups that lobby for the interests of persons with specific diseases or disabilities. These groups accomplish a great deal of good. Although sometimes privately derided as "disease-of-the-month clubs" by physicians who are aware of how these lobbies promote a piecemeal, uncoordinated approach to the funding of medical research, these groups are seldom criticized in any serious way, since such criticism would imply disregard for the sufferings of the victims of the disease in question. We might wish, however, to explore the connection between the need of the handicapped or sick individual to build and maintain a sense of self-respect and the dogmatic posture toward disease and handicaps that frequently emanates from these groups. For purposes of this exploration it will be useful to turn to the case of Elizabeth Bouvia, whose request that she be hospitalized while hastening her own death by refusing tube feedings was rejected by a court in Riverside, California, in 1983.[2] My focus will be less on Bouvia herself and her difficulties stemming from her cerebral palsy, and more on

---

2. A useful summary of the case with pertinent commentary is Kane (1985). (See also Annas 1984; Steinbrook and Lo 1986.) The subsequent history of the case is convoluted. Eventually a higher court overruled the district court and stated that she did indeed have the right to refuse tube feeding in the hospital, even if that resulted in her death. As of this writing, it has been reported that Bouvia is suing the hospital ethics committee at Riverside for their complicity in her force-feeding.

the handicapped citizens' groups that participated in and reacted to the trial court's decision.[3]

One might expect such groups to defend the right of the handicapped citizen to carry out functions or to have access to services precisely to the extent that the nonhandicapped (the "temporarily able-bodied") have the same rights and privileges. It could readily have been argued that Bouvia was simply seeking the right to end her life such as would be open to any nonhandicapped person, and simply wished to do so in maximum comfort and security with the aid of services that could be provided by a hospital setting. All the hospital was being asked to do in maintaining her while tube feedings were withheld was to provide the same sorts of services a nonhandicapped person would be able to dispense with because of intact motor skills. It could coherently be argued that respect for Bouvia's equal rights as a citizen demanded that she be given every facility in carrying out her free choice, without us having the arrogance to second-guess the rationality of her decision. But the attitude taken by the court, and by various handicapped citizens' groups that reacted to the trial, was exactly the opposite.

This attitude might be restated as follows. The nonhandicapped in our society are quite capable of deciding on their own that their life has meaning and that they have an interest in continued existence. The state has no special need to provide this service on their behalf. Handicapped citizens, however, are profoundly different. Their self-respect and self-esteem are so tenuous that they need a very strong and repetitive symbolic reassurance from the state that their lives are viewed by their fellow citizens as being worth living. If handicapped citizens did not receive this constant external reinforcement, they

---

3. I will here provide a reaction to one particular point of view that occurred frequently in public press accounts of the trial and of reactions to it. I cannot document the extent to which other, divergent viewpoints may have been present within organizations for the handicapped. I will also, for purposes of this discussion, put to one side all the ethical questions raised by the case, and withhold judgment on what was the proper way to respond to Bouvia's requests. Although the interpretation I will provide is only one of several possible, nothing in the more scholarly analyses of the case (see n. 2 above) appears to contradict it.

might become depressed or even commit suicide in large numbers. Given the severe and unequal psychological and physical vulnerability of the handicapped, Bouvia cannot be allowed to end her life because of the important symbolic message this would represent for the handicapped community.

If one accepts this as a possible interpretation of a portion of the judge's ruling, it is somewhat disturbing that the judge found it proper to rule in this fashion. But it is even more upsetting to note that this decision was received with approval and satisfaction by the handicapped groups themselves.

Since Bouvia was clearly a handicapped person and clearly was trying to exercise her options of free choice (whether rightly or wrongly, rational or irrational), we might ask what led other handicapped citizens to reject so quickly and completely any position of sympathy with her, to the extent that they would be more willing to accept implied social paternalism rather than take Bouvia's side in the dispute. It seems plausible that Bouvia forfeited the sympathy and support of her handicapped fellows by virtue of the fact that she was choosing to be handicapped in the wrong way. She violated very deeply held expectations within handicapped circles of the right way to live one's life when one suffers from cerebral palsy. If she were a "good handicapped person," she would try as hard as possible to carve a career and a life for herself, ideally occupying some position that one would normally expect a paralyzed person to be unable to occupy. She would avoid any attitudes that suggested self-pity or a dwelling upon her disability. She would also avoid any attitude suggestive of passive acquiescence or resignation to life with her handicap. Instead her life would be devoted to an enthusiastic and diligent struggle against her handicapping condition, in which she sought to wrest for herself every opportunity for normal function, achievement, and happiness. In particular, she would avoid any suggestion of using her handicap as an excuse for failure to achieve some goal she had previously sought. The handicapped citizens' groups that took public stands on the Bouvia case seemed to be saying that this good handicap role is the only legitimate way of living life with a handicap, and that they would respect the rights of their fellow handicapped citizens only so long as they tried as hard as they could to adhere to this one way of living life with a handicap.

In this approach they are not alone and deserve no special criticism for their dogmatic posture. For it seems to be the case more generally in our present society that wherever one finds a group of persons suffering from some chronic disease or condition who have banded together to offer each other support, to contract mutually for health services, and to lobby for greater scientific efforts to ameliorate the disease in question, one is very likely to find a similar degree of dogmatism, a similar insistence that there is one and only one right way to cope with the disease. Whenever anyone advocates publicly that one should handle the disease in a way that deviates significantly from the established doctrine of the group, the reaction of the group is likely to resemble that of religious zealots attacking a heresy.[4]

The importance of the disease self-help group for the individual sufferer can be elaborated in terms of our model of self-respect. When a person who previously was functioning in a fairly normal way in our society becomes afflicted with a chronic illness, it is likely that important features of the previously acceptable life plan will no longer be realistic, given the new constraints imposed by the illness. For purposes of maintaining self-respect, it is crucial that the inability to carry out one's former life plan because of circumstances beyond one's control be distinguished from failing to make reasonable progress toward one's life plan because of mere laziness or lack of discipline. Furthermore, in the difficult process of giving up one's former life plan and developing a new modified plan that takes the limitations imposed by chronic disease into account, one may very well find that one's previous associates, to whom one looked for approval of the old plan, understand the realities of the disease insufficiently to be rational judges of the new plan. Those who suffer from the same disease and have to some extent overcome its limitations, however, seem much better able to offer advice and

---

4. Witness, to take just one example, the reaction of Alcoholics Anonymous to the Rand Corporation study several years ago that argued that at least some recovered alcoholics could resume moderate social drinking (cf. Fingarette 1985).

counsel in the difficult task of developing a new plan. Viewed in this way, the self-help group is a very important social structure for helping the chronically ill person maintain self-respect. Denigrating the contribution of the group is a disguised way of minimizing the importance of self-respect for the ill person and failing to recognize the potential threat to self-respect that chronic disease imposes.

But our model also raises important questions about a self-help group that is able to provide self-respect for its members only at the cost of doctrinaire rigidity in prescribing a formula for coping with the disease. In order for a life plan to be rational for an individual, it must take into account that person's peculiar talents, proclivities, and desires. This means that the group of close associates, if they take their job of life-plan approval seriously, must investigate very closely the individual qualities of the person and cannot impose on that person some life plan produced ready-made as if in a factory. If one is dogmatically committed to a particular form of life plan, and willing to urge it on one's close associates without taking the time to discern their uniqueness, one has shown oneself to be a poor judge of others' life plans.

As previous chapters have shown, sickness frequently renders one's own sense of self-respect tenuous and insecure. If one lacks confidence in one's ability to choose a rational life plan and is afraid that if this plan is submitted for frank examination and criticism by close associates it may be rejected, one has an alternative means of maintaining a semblance of self-respect without the real article. This semblance requires simply that one choose to associate only with those whose outward activities conform completely with one's own behavior. In this way one can be reasonably sure that no one will ever raise uncomfortable questions about one's life plan, how well it suits one's talents and desires, or how well it fits with the ideas of a well-ordered society. This, basically, is the Berghof bad-patient method of maintaining an outward semblance of self-respect.

It is even better if this association can be solidified into a formal organization, and the common behavior pattern embodied in the form of a doctrinaire belief system. When someone is bold enough to raise unpleasant questions about the basic belief system or to behave in a markedly deviant manner (as Bouvia did), the group as a whole can define this individual as threatening the most basic values shared by the group; so that the deviant behavior becomes rejected as a matter of heresy and need never be dealt with by a rational analysis of the needs and desires of that particular individual.

It is one thing to sympathize with an ill or disabled person whose self-respect is tenuous, and who therefore seeks external reassurances about the worthiness of his life and his life plans. It is another, however, to allow groups of such individuals to dictate public policy in such a way as to foreclose the free choices of others. It is only a slight extension from the Bouvia controversy to consider the support by handicapped citizen's groups of the original and restrictive versions of the "Baby Doe" guidelines requiring treatment of severely deformed infants.[5] The position of these groups appeared to be: I have a handicap, but I am glad that I'm alive and I would never want anyone to kill me. If, however, the government states it is permissible for some parents to elect medical nontreatment of some severely handicapped infants, then that is the same as the government's saying that my life is not worth living, and that it would be all right for somebody to kill me. Therefore I must favor stringent restrictions to oppose any nontreatment of handicapped infants. Issues of differences among families and their ability to raise a handicapped child, and indeed differences between types and degrees of handicap, are irrelevant.

If our model contains any psychological insight, the Berghof strategy will ultimately be unsatisfactory as a substitute for true and robust self-respect, even if it were acceptable in society for an insecure individual to maintain his self-respect by using political power to force everyone else to act just like him. The trials of chronic sickness and the problems of self-respect and life-plan review among the handicapped therefore deserve our close attention; and one may hope that inquiries like ours, and a greater sensitivity to the unique stories of such persons, may point the way toward social policies that provide

5. For more extended discussion of the Baby Doe controversy, see chapter 9.

maximum opportunities for true self-respect without interfering with the liberties of others.

SICKNESS AND CONTROL

A final way of responding to illness that may appear maladaptive is laid out in great detail in *Heartsounds* (Lear 1980), a journalist's account of the prolonged illness and eventual death of her physician-husband. The story is one of great suffering, both physical and emotional.[6] The book, generally, is very difficult for physicians to read.[7] The frustration and rage of the bereaved wife are directed in large part at the physicians who failed to halt the disease and save her husband. The primary redeeming feature of Martha Lear's diatribe is the relentless honesty with which she handles all characters in the story; hence she is willing to turn upon herself and her own motives the same pitiless searchlight with which she exposes the physicians. This searching honesty allows us to use the book to assess the adequacy of the coping style she and her husband Harold adopted to deal with his myocardial infarction and later complications.

Basically the Lears coped by seeking control and by having faith that control was ultimately possible and desirable. To this extent there is nothing maladaptive in their approach. We saw reasons, in chapter 1, to regard the seeking of mastery and control by attaching a positive meaning to the experience of sickness as one of the primary means by which people assuage suffering. It is a universal human reaction. Therefore, if we are going to regard the Lears' coping as

6. Since Dr. Lear suffered almost every known complication of myocardial infarction and open heart surgery, I have myself used *Heartsounds* as the study text for a small group of medical students studying the clinical problem of chest pain.

7. Borgenicht (1983) was surprised at the very negative reactions of a group of first-year medical students in sharp contrast to the generally positive reviews in the lay press. Another jaundiced medical reaction to the book is that of Stephens (1981). My own final reaction on finishing the book was "Thank heaven they were not patients of mine," although I am sometimes regarded as enjoying challenging, highly educated patients generally.

maladaptive, we must seek a way to distinguish a good search for control with an overly obsessive search for control.

The events leading up to Harold Lear's heart attack are important in understanding what came later. A professor of urology in a New York medical school, Dr. Lear had pioneered in the as-yet-undeveloped field of sex therapy and had originated a course for medical students in sexual issues. He then had to witness the political infighting that resulted in the course being taken away from him and given to the department of psychiatry, which had neither the interest nor the ability to teach the material as well as he could, but which felt the need to protect its academic turf from upstart surgeons. For Lear, the message might have been that he lacked control, and this allowed others to take over and ruin his most cherished projects. He would have to get more control if he was to prevent something like this from happening again. And the best way to get more control was to understand the academic-medicine power structure, and to make sure that he was well placed within it.

It was in this setting that he suffered his first heart attack; and the setting in turn may have stimulated the way he chose to respond to it. For Martha Lear, it also laid the groundwork for her own later reactions. Those evil men who robbed her husband of his course at the medical school, she ultimately felt sure, were to blame for his heart attack. Thus, if he later got worse or if he died, one of her questions was bound to be: who is to blame? In effect, she was setting up precisely the situation that Siegler and Osmond (1974a) had hoped that the Aesculapian authority of the physician would prevent—the hunt for a scapegoat when things do not go well.

The answer thus seemed clear when it came to recovering from a heart attack. The first part of control was for Dr. Lear to turn himself into his own patient. He took voluminous and frequent notes regarding every aspect of his case. He was not stupid, however, and realized that a urologist ought not treat myocardial infarction; and so he also placed himself in the care of cardiologists. His earlier lessons dictated that these ought to be the "best" cardiologists, that is, the ones highest up on the appropriate academic ladder. And, if he had any doubts about his ability to get their fullest attention and energy, he could rely further on his status as a fellow academic and physician. In this, Martha apparently copied him. They were two highly rational, upwardly mobile Manhattanites. The idea that there was anything one could not get, if only one had the right connections and talked to the best people, seemed never to occur to them. (In this respect the Lears seemed little different from the Rusanovs in *The Cancer Ward*).

The result of all this (as unfortunately often seems to happen when a physician is the patient) was that everything that could conceivably go wrong went wrong. Dr. Lear suffered almost every known complication of his condition, both natural and iatrogenic. The Lears pestered the physicians mercilessly with trivial details and thus almost assured that the physicians would miss the complaints that portended serious trouble. They were so demanding that the physicians withdrew, and then the Lears mercilessly condemned them for withdrawing. All their energies were devoted to finding the rational answer to every trivial or random event, in the hopes that the rationality would guarantee control and cure. No energy at all was devoted to coming to terms with sickness, disability, mortality, or loss.

The psychic suffering experienced by Dr. Lear fits one category discussed by Gadow (1980) in her analysis of the various ways body and self can be split apart by sickness and rejoined by healing. A particularly radical body-self split occurs when one's reaction to sickness is to totally distance oneself from one's body, to the extent that the body becomes simply a scientific specimen rather than a part of oneself. This, however, is tempting as a means to cope with some illnesses because the very distance seems to promise safety of the self from the ills that afflict the body. (The pathologist, after all, does not expect to suffer from the symptoms of the cadaver that she dissects.) This apparent safety is spurious, however, both because it *is* after all one's own body and not somebody else's and because suffering arises precisely as a result of the distance between body and self, with the loss of perceived wholeness. Gadow suggests that this reaction (which she terms seeing the body as the "abstract object body") is almost of necessity short-lived, but Dr. Lear appears to have engaged in it for a substantial portion of his illness. And yet the way he reacted to both his physicians and his wife shows clearly in retrospect that an underlying terror was never fully exorcised by his efforts, and was never openly dealt with either.

A clue to the underlying ambivalence of the Lears, and the ultimate failure of the rational-control coping strategy for them, is found in Martha's reaction to truth. Several passages in *Heartsounds* are among the most poignant counterpoints to the contemporary ethical dictum that physicians should almost always be frank with patients. Martha characterizes this truth-telling, however, as an ill-thought-out, passing fad that is ultimately destructive to the patient or the family who seeks to maintain hope. Since the physicians are not omniscient, the fact that Harold had outlived some of their survival predictions was proof to her that the medical "truths" were useless. Yet, she cannot quite shed the appropriate "modern educated patient" role. She feels obliged to ask the physicians to be frank with her— silently saying to herself all the while, will this doctor be smart enough to see I'm asking a trick question? Will he figure out that I don't really want to know? The doctor, of course, is not smart enough and proceeds to tell her more bad news about Harold; and then she rages against the doctor for telling her and against herself for bringing more agony upon herself.

It is tempting to see this as simply one more example of physician insensitivity, treating patients by formula or protocol instead of as unique individuals with unique needs. But a deeper question is both why Martha felt compelled to go through this charade and, more specifically, why it was that the truth, when it came, was so devastating. It seems that, although a policy of coping by rational control would necessarily require full disclosure of all pertinent information, Martha is more desirous of good news only. She wants, in the end, a magic shield to ward off mortality; the quest for rationality is only a superficial manifestation and is thus marked as a failure.

The extreme proof of this is Martha's complicity, along with the cardiologists, in withholding from Harold himself a crucial piece of information—that he did as poorly as he did following open heart surgery because (as could be diagnosed only in retrospect) he suffered a second heart attack postoperatively and, along with it, some brain damage. Harold rages against his problems with memory and concentration, and (as he continues writing up his voluminous notes about his own case) seeks vainly for the explanation. Martha keeps silent, after she has learned the truth, for the old and trite reasons—it would be too depressing for him; it would take away his hope and slow his recovery. Ultimately Harold does find out the truth and berates her. And she answers with all the old and trite statements—I did it for you; I acted only for the best. At this point he seems sadly aware—although the point seems to escape her—that this manipulation of the truth between them, this betrayal of the trust he had had in her, shows the failure of the rational-control coping approach for them.

All the foregoing has tended toward the conclusion that this rational-control strategy, or at least the facade of rationality as employed by the Lears (probably more by Martha than by Harold), was highly maladaptive. But the story, the full story, will not permit this facile conclusion. It still remains the case that Harold lived for several years, considerably beyond what the most sanguine physicians had predicted, and that for much of that time he was able to carry out at least some of his favorite activities and to be with and to enjoy the relationship with his wife and family. An argument could be framed that it was only his "fighting spirit," his refusal to resign himself or to seek a reflective acceptance of his sickness, that could have accounted for his survival.[8] It may simply be that Harold chose the coping style that was most functional for him. Martha tried to copy his style, but was able to do so only superficially and halfheartedly; because it is her book, we see more clearly its maladaptive features. In the end, at the very end, Harold found both an acceptance of his imminent death and a young, nonprestigious family internist who was able to comfort the two of them and not draw out the inevitable with useless technological exercises. But Harold, perhaps, had to take his own good time to get to that point. It was not simply

8. There is a similarity between this aspect of Harold Lear's story and the coping strategy of author Cornelius Ryan in dealing with his cancer. On the latter, see the extended treatment by Hawkins (1984).

that this young internist was kindly and humane, and the cardiologists were cold and self-important; had the former appeared at an earlier phase of the illness, when Harold's needs were different, the Lears could not possibly have accepted either him or his advice.

The notion of a maladaptive way of coping with sickness suggests a ground for a moral judgment. The discussion of Bouvia and dogmatic coping, I hope, illustrated that an analysis in terms of life plans and self-respect can provide at least a quasi-objective basis for such moral judgments. But the case of Harold Lear also shows that these moral judgments are questionable unless one is willing to take into account the full particulars of the story of the sickness, even those features that do not tidily fit one's favorite theory. These observations lay the groundwork for the questions of the next two chapters—how might ethical decisions, and ethical principles, in medicine be altered or modified if we had a better and deeper sense of stories and of the narrative organization of human existence?

9

Medical Ethics and
the Life-span Narrative

THEORY OR CASES?

This book is primarily addressed to philosophy of medicine, not to medical ethics. But if, as argued in chapter 2, medicine is a practical craft rather than a theoretical science, the most compelling reason we would have for seeking better to understand the impact of sickness on the person is a belief that this understanding will make a difference in the way medicine is practiced—that insight will translate into better performance. And, according to the methodology of wide reflective equilibrium (Rawls 1971; Daniels 1979), ethical considerations are part of the overall fit against which theoretical constructs must ultimately be tested.[1] And so it is appropriate to draw some tentative ethical implications from the foregoing discussions. These implications will only be sketched in a preliminary way; full development

1. Wide reflective equilibrium, as I understand it, is an approach to philosophy consistent with that advocated by Rorty (1979, 1982); see chapter 2, n. 1. In wide reflective equilibrium one gains confidence in one's conclusions, not because they have been deduced from indubitable or "foundational" first principles, but because they cohere within a system of mutually supporting and mutually illuminating theories and judgments. Instead of viewing the use of, say, ontological or empirical considerations to support ethical conclusions as threatening to violate the naturalistic fallacy, the method of wide reflective equilibrium sees such an overall fit as evidence for the strength and coherence of the inquiry. See also Rawls 1980; Daniels 1979, 1980.

of them would require much more space and more detailed arguments. They should be read as promising lines for further inquiry rather than as conclusions or ethical principles.

Some statements in the medical ethics literature suggest that there is basically one way to be sick, that sickness affects all sick individuals in this one way, and that therefore one can usefully generalize, for ethical purposes, among all such cases without inquiring too finely into the details. The extreme form of such a statement is something like *"All illness represents a state of diminished autonomy"* (Komrad 1983). I have tried to show the fallacy of any such facile generalization by showing how important the specific details (the story of the sickness) are to any meaningful comprehension of the impact of the sickness on the person.

Medical ethics has been subject to some of the same tensions as medicine itself in dealing with the idea of stories (chapter 1). The analytic tradition has been powerful in condemning anecdotal or ad hoc reasoning as hopelessly subjective or intuitionistic and in insisting that reason in ethics requires that conclusions be logically deduced from more general principles. And yet, when philosophers concerned with medical ethics have looked at their own day-to-day activities, a different picture emerges. First, both the literature and the conversation of such people reveals a central role for a set of leading cases, well known to all "ethics insiders" by abbreviated titles ("the Johns Hopkins case," "the Quinlan case," "the Galveston burn case"), the repetitive mention of which tends to contradict the purported reliance on principle and devaluation of anecdote. Further, the success stories (if any) accumulated by philosophers who have taken up the post of "in-house ethicist" in medical centers tend to illustrate a high level of creative, situational, ad hoc thinking. They tend not to illustrate the utility of having a sophisticated understanding of the *Critique of Practical Reason* at one's fingertips, or the importance of a rigorous and formal explication of logical fallacies (Caplan 1983). Success for the philosopher on the wards may in fact hinge upon a ready familiarity with what counts as good reasons to support a claim (Morreim 1986); but this reasoning is commonly revealed through the manner in which it addresses specific cases, not by the elegance with which it draws deductions from theory.

This dichotomy between the theory and practice of the ethicists can be partially resolved if (in a move that MacIntyre, 1981, would approve) one looks back beyond the Enlightenment period for the historical and methodological roots of present-day medical ethics. Jonsen (1982, 1986) has suggested that the medieval tradition of casuistry is a more congenial explication of the activity of modern medical ethics than is the deductive or applied ethics model suggested by the analytic tradition. Jonsen reminds us that the term *casuistry* acquired a negative connotation in the later Renaissance, which it still possesses today. But during earlier times casuistry was a logically rigorous and fully respectable method of approaching ethics by means of case studies. Instead of looking for a few ethical principles, casuists identified a multiplicity of moral maxims or rules of thumb (such as "tell the truth"). They then selected for each a paradigm case that seemed to illustrate the maxim in its most perfect form and with the fewest special circumstances that detracted from the understanding of its application. For many Americans, for instance, the apocryphal story of George Washington and the cherry tree has fulfilled this function of paradigm case with regard to the maxim "tell the truth." The casuist then proceeded to consider a variety of cases and to lay them out in orderly fashion around this paradigm case. A case that differed only in a few minor details from the paradigm case would be shown as still illustrating the maxim clearly, whereas a case that had a number of novel circumstances, causing less of a clean fit between the case and the maxim, would be described as being farther out on the periphery, as it were. Eventually the casuist would come to the fuzzy or borderline cases where the application of the maxim was very questionable or where there was a serious doubt as to whether to apply either of two contradictory maxims. For instance, the casuist might describe Kant's famous case "Do you tell the truth to a homicidal maniac who comes to the door brandishing a weapon and asks which way your friend has fled?" as occupying the borderline between the two maxims "tell the truth" and "preserve others from harm."

Today, medical ethics is assumed to derive from philosophy. Jonsen therefore takes pains to note that, although the classical casuists made free use of philosophical concepts when this suited their purposes and helped illuminate cases, they did not see their activity as fundamentally grounded in philosophy. (They made equally facile use of legal and theological concepts or arguments when that seemed to suit better.) Instead they appealed to the discipline of rhetoric, which (within the Aristotelian framework) dealt with sound and persuasive reasoning in those realms of human activity where only probability and not certainty could be obtained. But even this much of a claim for "disciplinary grounding" may provide a misleading impression of casuist activity; actually the casuists "may not have thought much about method, as we understand the idea" (Jonsen 1986, p. 68). There was, indeed, rigor and skill in their work, but it was the "skill of *interpreting the case*" (p. 68).

If the case study of modern medical ethics is, as Jonsen submits, more closely allied with casuistry than with the applied ethics model, the role of stories and storytelling becomes clearer, and the importance of telling a patient's story with a richness of contextual detail becomes more apparent. For modern use, however, we must provide an alternative to the casuist's reliance on medieval natural law concepts. To the casuist, the maxims were given and could not be altered by the case-study method. If we were simply to add the idea that one might eventually come to revise the maxims, or add new maxims, as a result of testing the fit between the maxims and a wide variety of cases—so that the reasoning would be bidirectional—we would modify the casuist approach so as to make it more applicable to a secular pluralist culture like our own.[2] This model of ethics allows the ethicist to utilize case studies without embarrassment as a central research tool, instead of having to pretend that these are simply teaching devices necessary to get the attention of physicians who are unschooled in ethical theory.

ETHICS AND THE TIME DIMENSION OF NARRATIVES

The time dimension and the historical sequence are crucial features of a narrative. An event gains its meaning in part because of the

---

2. With this modification there is, insofar as medical ethics is concerned, a congruence between the casuist method and Rawls's Kantian constructivism (Rawls 1980).

place it occupies in the narrative sequence and its relationship to events that precede and follow; a single event, taken out of the narrative context and analyzed in terms of its intrinsic characteristics only, is likely to be misunderstood. Physicians know this; they are trained to ask as part of a routine medical history questions such as "Have you ever had a symptom like this before?" and "What does this symptom remind you of?" Writers in medical ethics are sometimes inclined to deemphasize this feature of the sickness experience, and this has led to a variety of problems in contemporary medical ethics. I will address two general problem areas. In this chapter I will consider the narrative form of the typical human life span, looking first at the newborn and next at the elderly. In chapter 10 I will take up the relationship between doctor and patient viewed as a narrative.

I will suggest a visual metaphor to aid in considering the human life span as a narrative. Let us picture a parabolic curve with both ends resting upon a base ("gravity's rainbow," to steal the title of a novel by Thomas Pyncheon). The left-hand base represents a life getting started, from birth through childhood, and establishing the trajectory that will mark it as a particular and unique life. The peak of that trajectory marks the prime years, in which one's rational plan of life comes as close to fruition as it is going to, and when one has developed one's powers and talents to the fullest extent. The right-hand base then reflects the gradual decline, ending in death. This visual image might be supplemented by the observation that, although there are many different ways of being a young child and many different ways of getting old and dying, there will (I will submit) be much greater variation at the peak of the parabola. The uniqueness of the individual and of the life plan are most prominent there. Nevertheless, one's life is not over until the "rainbow" falls back to earth; and, as noted earlier, a life plan cannot consider only the peak but must also in part take into account the manner in which one's narrative is wrapped up at the end. The story of one's life will develop its full meaning, and reveal itself as a tragedy, a comedy, or whatever, only when it is the story of a complete life.

This sketch has importance for medical ethics if some ethical constructs that are highly relevant along the arc of the trajectory of the life story turn out to have limited applicability at one or either end. Consider, for example, the discussion of personhood in chapter 3. To be a person is to be a bearer of rights and interests, which is to say, to be an autonomous, fully functioning moral agent; and as Rorty (1979) has it, the philosophical question of personhood is fundamentally a question of who is to count as ''one of us.'' Now the first picture that comes to mind when we seek a typical sketch of ''one of us'' is that of a fully functioning adult with a fairly definite life plan whose daily activity is a matter of trying to further that life plan. We do not, in seeking such a mental picture, ordinarily think of an infant or young child, or of the elderly person who is awaiting death. So it is quite possible that the ethical principles that seem most useful in describing ''respect for personhood'' in medical care—such as the moral tension between paternalism and autonomy (Veatch 1981; Beauchamp and McCullough 1984)—may turn out to have much less applicability at the ends of the life parabola. If we then try to solve ethical problems peculiar to the infancy and predeath life stages with an uncritical application of these principles, we may gain little ethical insight.[3]

This suggestion, naturally, is unlikely to prove persuasive in the abstract. I will therefore consider first some of the ethical problems now encountered with the very young to see if any of the ethical confusion is lessened by applying the lesson of the parabola.

3. After completing the final manuscript draft of the body of this chapter, I read James Rachels's *The End of Life* and encountered a sort of endorsement of this approach. Anxious to break down the classic objection to euthanasia—that it is wrong because it violates the time-honored rule against intentionally taking an innocent human life—Rachels argues persuasively that the rule is itself suspect on further analysis because it confuses *being alive* with *having a life*. ''Being alive'' is primarily a biological attribute, whereas ''having a life'' ought to be construed biographically—as having a story or a life plan. For Rachels, biographical lives are what primarily deserve strong moral protection; the rule against taking biological life should be seen as derivative, since depriving a being of its biological life is generally a way of depriving it of its life construed biographically. But when one's biographical life is over or when, because of severe birth defects, one has no chance for a biographical life, then a prohibition against taking merely biological life loses its point. On this, see Rachels (1986, pp. 18–38).

NEWBORNS AND THE BEGINNING OF THE NARRATIVE

Since decisions around handicapped newborns figure prominently in the ethics debates of the past several years, the infant end of the trajectory is an obvious place to look for such problems. There is considerable disagreement over whether infants with severe birth defects such as meningomyelocele (spina bifida) should be allowed to die if the parents request this or should be kept alive to the maximum allowed by modern technology even over the parents' objections. But there is less disagreement over the moral principle that is proposed to guide the entire debate—that any treatment decision should be made according to the best interests of the newborn, with other moral considerations being regarded as extraneous and dangerous (Fost 1981; President's Commission 1983; Weir 1984). This infant's-best-interests argument has almost totally supplanted arguments in favor of recognizing legitimate interests of the parents (Strong 1983) and arguments urging physician tolerance for parental choice (Duff and Campbell 1976).

However, this attractive notion of the infant's best interests has received much less critical attention than it deserves. We certainly have a good idea of what it means for something to be in the best interests of the average adult. We have an idea of the sorts of life plans and goals that characterize adult existence, and we have a good idea of which acts by other parties further those plans and which acts hamper them. This same reasoning, by analogy, often seems legitimately applicable to newborns. It thus makes sense, apparently, to claim that an infant with Down's syndrome and intestinal obstruction requiring surgery would be better off having the surgery and then being placed in an institution or foster home than not having the surgery and being allowed to die simply because the parents cannot face raising a child with mental retardation. And it similarly makes sense to argue that if we put an infant to death because of Tay-Sachs disease, in which it faces a brief life of pain and misery followed by inevitable death, we might be doing so at least in part for the infant's own sake.

But, in some of the problematic cases, it still seems on critical reflection that to speak easily about the infant's best interests is to treat the infant as fundamentally a different sort of being than it really is. The infant at and near birth is a human being with much more potentiality than actuality. It is born into an existing network of family and community relationships, but presently represents much more of a place-holder than a participant in such relationships, and to a large extent it is incapable of any truly reciprocal role in those relationships.[4] It has before it a wide variety of possible life plans; and yet the specific range of life plans it will eventually choose or have thrust upon it can only be guessed at. Its values, desires, and goals largely represent unknown quantities. We know only that some things will almost certainly be good for it—it will want food, shelter, and loving nurturance and it will want to avoid pain; and respect for the autonomy that it will develop later in the normal course of events (assuming here a newborn without severe mental handicap) seems to require that we avoid unnecessarily and unreasonably acting in such a way today as to limit this infant's options for free choice tomorrow.

If this infant is quite a different sort of being from the average adult, we might then ask how, in the normal course of events, it will develop into the adult person for whom the notion of "best interests" is relatively unproblematic. The normal infant develops in this manner as a result of being raised and guided by adult parents who make a number of choices on the infant's behalf—unilaterally for a long time, and then gradually allowing the child a greater and greater role in the decisions as the child's capacity for autonomous behavior develops. And these decisions, in sum, while leaving a

4. Engelhardt, who follows Tooley (1973) and Feinberg (1976) in regarding a newborn infant as not yet a person (see chap. 3, this book), yet deserving of receiving the protection of personhood by social convention, notes that an infant is in an important sense *not yet anybody*, and simply a promise of a future somebody to appear later (Englehardt 1986, chap. 6). Bemporad (1978) discusses the "essential incompleteness of the neonate" (p. 82) and cites biologist Adolf Portmann on the significance of the human infant's continued neural development through the first year of life, whereas other mammals undergo the corresponding stages of neural maturation in utero. It appears as if social interaction is essential to the full creation and finishing off of the basic biological apparatus of a member of the human species.

number of decisions still open for the adult-to-be, nevertheless by their nature severely limit the range of life plans that will eventually be available. The small child is sent to one church out of many possible ones or is not sent to church at all; some talents receive early recognition and nurturance while others are ignored; some behavior is rewarded while other behavior is effectively extinguished. These decisions might seem to be a violation of the parents' presumed duty to respect the options of the adult-to-be (Blustein 1978), were it not for the fact that refusing to make these sorts of decisions is tantamount to refusing to raise a child. In practice, the roles of child and parent require that the parent acts so as to limit the possible future options for the child.

One might claim that the parent, in making all these decisions, is duty bound to respect the child's best interests. When dealing with very basic interests, of the sort Rawls (1971) calls "primary goods," we have a clear picture of what this means, to the point that we are satisfied in taking legal action against parents who violate infants' interests in this way. But when we get beyond the provision of food, shelter, basic medical care, and avoidance of inflicting pain and injury, the best interests notion requires that something already be in existence that in actuality is still in the process of formation. Given the sort of being that an infant is, and the role relationship between an infant and its parents, it seems much more accurate to say that an infant's actual best interests *follow in the wake* of parental decisions, and not that these best interests preexist and thus can guide those parental decisions (B. L. Miller 1984).

It thus develops that the idea of the infant's best interests, accepted so readily by participants in the deformed-newborn debate, is a much more problematic concept that is subject to attack at many levels.[5] The most basic argument, consistent with criteria for personhood discussed in chapter 3, is that a newborn infant (at least up to three to six months of age or so) is not a person because it lacks the capacity

5. For an excellent summary of the evolution of the "Baby Doe" debate in recent years, along with the shifts in moral presuppositions underlying the public policy positions, see Rhoden and Arras (1985).

for a minimal level of cognitive awareness and consciousness of self
(Feinberg 1976; Tooley 1973). If this is the case, then it is meaningless to attribute to this infant an interest in its own continued
existence (Benjamin 1983). An infant is a sentient being and has an
interest, therefore, in not experiencing pain. But for a being to have
an interest in its own continued existence requires that it be able to
have a concept of itself and to project that concept into the future.
This seems far beyond the mental capacities of infants as best as
can be determined on both behavioral and neurophysiological
grounds. *If* this infant continues to exist, it will develop more sophisticated mental capacities and with them, additional interests.
Some neglectful or hurtful actions that could be taken now would
violate those *contingent future* interests. But *that* this infant continue
to exist cannot now be said to be in its own best interests, nor contrary
to them.

Another level of argument, likely to be perceived as less radical
than denying personhood to the infant, is that the best interests of
the infant may exist in principle but must for practical purposes be
considered to be largely indeterminate. Consider the debate over
whether to urge surgical treatment for an infant with high meningomyelocele and hydrocephalus. One physician may argue that surgery is in the infant's best interests and point to the high probability
of death without surgery, the occasional success story of a child who
does well despite an equal level of initial handicap, and so forth.
Another physician may argue that nontreatment and an early death
serves this infant's best interests better, citing the very high probability of severe physical and mental handicap, the miserable level
of existence of children in the state institutions where most severe,
multiply-handicapped children end up, and the fact that children who
have the first surgery typically have to have additional, painful procedures to treat later sequelae. Now it may be that these physicians
disagree over the facts (for example, is the probability of the success
story occurring 1 percent or 40 percent?) and that their clarification
could end the dispute. But if, as is equally likely, the facts and the
probability estimates are not in dispute, there seems no practical way

to resolve this debate of what is and isn't in the best interests of the infant. Each physician could say—instead of "This is in the infant's best interests"—"This is what I think we ought to do"; and the clarity of the debate would not suffer one bit for the failure to bring the notion of best interests into the matter at all.

Finally, there is yet a third objection, that of Strong (1983), that the best interests of the parents deserve at least some mention, and it is evidence of oversimplification and an ethical blind spot to refuse to give those interests any consideration.

All the above objections to the notion of the best interests of the infant may be derived from Kantian concepts of rights, interests, and the necessary capacities for personhood. They do not depend on adopting a narrative concept of human life. But, coming from another direction, they buttress the importance of a narrative concept. They help to support the idea that the life of a newborn is a story just getting started—a story even more closely intertwined, and dependent in a different way on the life stories of other actors, than the story of an adult. They illustrate the intuitions that may, over the centuries, have supported the widespread notion that infanticide is not the same as the killing of an older child or an adult, and that, in many cultures, full personal identity (in the form of a name, for instance) is not bestowed until some time has elapsed since birth.

Now, clearly a narrative approach can make too much of tradition. It can be argued that the entire traditional way of conceiving of persons, nations, and cultures was radically altered in the nineteenth century with the acceptance of the idea that it is wrong to hold other human beings in slavery; yet no one would urge us to go back and recapture the traditional mode of understanding. Similarly, the acceptance of the rights and interests of the newborn is the twentieth-century equivalent, and it is an equally important advance in human civilization. As already noted, this argument works well in supporting the advances in the reporting and prevention of child abuse and neglect, and in the existence of enhanced (although often still inadequate) prenatal care and newborn intensive care. But there might well come a point at which the limits are reached and one begins to view an infant as if it were not an infant.[6] Those limits may be reached when one argues that a very strong obligation exists to support the start of a life that is destined to be marked by a very low parabolic arc—a life in which even very minimal concepts of a life plan and of self-respect may never come to apply and in which instead considerable suffering and disability may be the norm. And the limits seem clearly to be reached when one argues that others, whose life stories are intimately bound up with the new life story that will either run its truncated course or be stopped in its inception, ought to have little or nothing to say about the moral choices.

If accepting the narrative structure may lessen the protection we are inclined to offer infants with the most severe birth defects, it also enhances the protection we are likely to offer normal infants and those with very mild handicaps (or, indeed, infants who have severe handicaps but also a high potential for evolving and being able to pursue a rational life plan). Viewing the infant within a Kantian framework simply as a being abstracted from its life story inevitably leads to the observation that adult mammals of many species have significantly greater mental capacities for self-awareness, and hence much more fully developed interests, than a human newborn (Singer 1983; Engelhardt 1986). If interests may give rise to rights, many animals thus seem to have more claim on our sympathy and protection than do our infants. But clearly the life story that is begun with the appearance of this infant is a totally different thing from the life story of a horse or pig. Seeing the infant as the start of a life narrative, and not as an isolated entity frozen in time, is crucial in seeing what the moral stakes are.

To supplement these suggestions I will now offer narrative analyses of two general lines of argument that might be encountered in the

---

6. I am here paraphrasing Paul Ramsey, who claimed that using children as the subjects of nontherapeutic research would be to treat the child as if it were not a child. He had in mind the child's inability to offer any true consent to the participation. McCormick, in replying first that parents routinely place their children at slight risk without censure and second that parents have the right to try to teach their children altruistic behavior (accepting some slight risk and inconvenience in order to help others), seems closer to the position I am arguing than does Ramsey. (See Ramsey 1976; McCormick 1974b.)

newborn arena. I will try to show that both make some sense from an analytic, nonnarrative perspective but fail when subjected to narrative scrutiny, thus showing why they are unhelpful to the ethical debate. I will end with an anecdote to illustrate how a narrative perspective may change the way one approaches a case, even if the ultimate conclusions do not alter.

The first unhelpful argument is the possible conflict of interest between parents and infant.[7] Fost (1981) notes this in perhaps the strongest form by observing that, if there exists some person who will be terribly burdened both emotionally and financially by your own continued existence, that person is probably not the one you would choose to be your own proxy decision maker when it comes to issues of life-prolonging medical treatment.[8] When one has bought into the approach suggested by the best interests of the infant, this point makes perfectly good sense, even if the average parent will take considerable umbrage when it is uttered. What may then be lost sight of is the extent to which this statement implies a precise analogy between the infant case and the adult case. We are led to imagine an infant somehow choosing who is to be its proxy to speak on its behalf. We are led to the idea that the dependency of the infant on its parents, and the financial and emotional burdens of parenting, somehow disqualify the parent as the appropriate person to make decisions for the infant that will shape the future of its life story. We are led to see infants as readily transferable, so that if one set of parents wishes not to raise a child with a severe handicap, the problem is solved without turmoil or trauma by carting the infant

7. I must again emphasize that I am addressing cases where it is most defensible to hold the infant's future best interests to be practically indeterminate. I do not want to apply these comments to obvious cases of child abuse and neglect; and I would agree with the President's Commission (1983) that it is difficult to deny that a child born with a mild or moderate defect like Down's syndrome has an interest (construed somehow or other) in having life-saving surgery for an easily curable alimentary obstruction.

8. Another possible set of objections to Fost will not be pursued—first, that the very intimacy that produces the grave burdens simultaneously makes that other party the *best possible* proxy decision maker, and second, that even if this were not the case, the imposition of those grave burdens gives that other party a right to decide, regardless of the interests of the principal. See also Churchill 1983.

off to another set of parents who would like to raise it. And we are led to imagine the future life story of an infant as being not only the sort of thing in which the society has a stake (which is undoubtedly true on any reading) but also as something that is negotiable in the social marketplace, so that parents must make a bid for the privilege of shaping it. When we look at these implications of the conflict of interest argument, it must seem much less pertinent and persuasive, except in the most extreme cases of child abuse and neglect. It seems to ignore totally the normal human manner in which one's life story (like Henry Adams's) comes to have its first chapters, as well as to deny the very nature of family interconnectedness and interdependence.

The next unhelpful notion is one condition Engelhardt offers as necessary to justify a woman's giving birth to a child when she knows, through prenatal diagnosis, that it is at significant risk for a congenital handicap—or to justify the woman's continuing to carry a fetus to term when she also wishes to engage in some behavior, like smoking, that places such a risk on the child. This condition is that, if later on life with the handicap proves insufferable for the child, nothing will be done to foreclose the option of committing suicide as a release from that life of intolerable burden.[9] Once again, the moral force of this condition relies on an analogy to a more usual adult case. For instance, a terminally ill cancer patient, who is skeptical about the benefits of proffered medical treatment, might be persuaded by family or friends to try the treatment for a specified period, with a promise that suicide is always an out if the pain or suffering prove to be intolerable. (I will leave aside all discussion on the morality of suicide or assisting suicide in such circumstances, since Engelhardt regards it as unproblematic.) But once again, when this is applied to the birth and newborn setting, considerable gaps and difficulties make themselves apparent.

9. The other two conditions Engelhardt would impose is, first, that the mother's intentions toward the child be nonmalevolent, and second, that the reasonably predictable prognosis is that the benefits of living a life with such a handicap will outweigh the harms (1986, p. 223). Obviously, Engelhardt feels comfortable with the morality of abortion of any such fetus.

First, this argument seems to treat life as a good or commodity, not as a narrative or a story that unfolds over time. If you don't like your life (on this account) you simply return it for a refund before the warranty expires. Second, and at a deeper level, this argument fails to place accurately the relevant decisions and events within the parabolic arcs of the life stories of the individuals involved. The mother's decision to bear a child under conditions of risk is a part of her carrying out of her adult life plan and is open to review by her self-respect peer review network both on grounds of its rationality for her and on grounds of its morality in putting another at a disadvantage so that her life plan can be pursued. A decision to commit suicide is also a decision that belongs to the adult or peak phase of the parabola and that, if decided in one way, collapses that part of the curve into the downslope and end of the curve. It is a decision about whether to write one's own abrupt end to one's own life story or to await further events to see how the story will turn out later; and it is simultaneously a decision to accept or reject a network of ongoing relationships and commitments to family and friends.

Clearly, these two decisions (the mother's to bear the child, and the child's later on to commit suicide) are linked in an intimate fashion. The child as an independent decision maker comes into existence only if the mother decides the question of bringing the pregnancy to term in a positive way; and the child's decision to consider suicide as a later option becomes relevant only if the risk of possible suffering translates into later, actual suffering.[10] But, looked at in a narrative mode, it seems incomprehensible how the possible existence of the second decision speaks even partially to the moral rightness or wrongness of the first decision.

"Knowing the risks in advance, I gave birth to a child who suffered so much from her afflictions that she ended up committing suicide" is a coherent and meaningful telling of a part of a mother's life story.

---

10. This point, by itself, seems to me sufficient to call radically into question the Kantian presupposition of the individual and her free moral agency, that is necessary for Engelhardt's (1986) entire ''foundation'' to be constructed (cf. MacIntyre 1981).

What is difficult to see is how the fact of the suicide makes the story a better one or a less tragic one.[11]

I have argued that the two concepts reviewed above (conflict of interest between infant and parents, and later right to suicide as necessary moral justification for bringing a child to term despite known or imposed risks) prove ultimately unhelpful to ethical inquiry when viewed from the narrative perspective that I am advocating. I close this section with an anecdotal report that may illustrate how adopting a narrative perspective may give one a different viewpoint and prompt one to ask a new set of questions, even in a case where the traditional, analytic principles and concepts are not necessarily unhelpful or misleading.

I was one of several people knowledgeable in medical ethics who were asked by a pediatric hematology team to attend a case discussion. The child being discussed had been diagnosed as having acute lymphocytic leukemia, was treated with the appropriate chemotherapy according to an experimental protocol (including preventive treatment for possible central nervous system spread of the disease), and had successfully achieved a remission. But, in the process, the child suffered from leucoencephalopathy, a rare toxic effect of one chemotherapeutic drug. (The technological up-to-dateness of these unfortunate events was driven home by the fact that the toxic reaction was first diagnosed by the medical center's new, experimental magnetic resonance imaging device.) As a result of the brain damage induced by the leucoencephalopathy, what had originally been a bright, vibrant eight-year-old girl had suddenly changed back into the functional equivalent of a two-year-old. According to all available literature, this toxic process is irreversible, and no improvement had been seen in the child's condition over several months. The con-

---

11. Engelhardt is justified in objecting here that I have misrepresented his meaning. He would want only to insist that, if the child decided rationally upon suicide as the only escape from intolerable suffering, no authority or coercion should be employed in stopping the free exercise of that wish. I would agree that the story as above altered to ". . . who suffered so much from her afflictions that she was determined to commit suicide, only she was forcibly prevented from doing so,'' *would* under some circumstances be a more tragic story than the story related in the text. I do not, however, feel this alters my principal point.

ference was called to discuss future treatment options and how aggressively the team ought to try to extend the patient's life if the leukemia relapsed.

The discussion that followed took the form of a standard inquiry into medical ethics, utilizing the ethical concepts and principles generally recommended for discussion of such cases; and afterward the hematology team unanimously reported that they had found the discussion useful and enlightening. For example, further discussion elicited the fact that being a two-year-old did not seem to constitute a state of suffering or perceived loss for the child herself, who could not remember or appreciate the eight-year-old state from which she had been reduced. Therefore, the physicians' basic duty to prolong life did not seem altered by any quality-of-life considerations. "It's as wrong to allow a functioning two-year-old to die as it would be for an eight-year-old" was one statement made. But the duty not to inflict further harm, or to cause even further deterioration in the child's mental functioning, was also recognized; and the question then turned to possible courses of chemotherapy that would be effective in preventing or treating relapse and yet at the same time would be unlikely to produce a worsening of the leucoencephalopathy. The major conclusion of the discussion was that possible efficacy was so closely linked to possible toxicity that no practical course of treatment could be recommended.

All of this was a scholarly as well as a practical discussion of what to do for a child, chronologically an eight-year-old but functionally a two-year-old, who had been reduced to that state by an unintended iatrogenic complication. But what was effectively left out of the discussion was the full sense of the narrative account of what this meant for the life of an individual, and the possible ethical ramifications of the social context in which this narrative had occurred. There was an analogy to Fost's (1981) ready assumption about the replaceability and transferability of children. That is, the discussion of the case, and the application of concepts like beneficence, nonmaleficence, quality of life, and so forth, had to take into account that this was no longer a fairly normal eight-year-old with a life-threatening disease, but a functional two-year-old with both a life-threatening disease and a major toxic complication. But the fact that the parents had, in effect, had one child taken away from them and a different child substituted was somehow to be pushed into the background as being of no moral relevance, since the analytic philosophical framework offers no principle or concept that comfortably handles it.

If a human life basically assumes a narrative form, it is pertinent to note two basic ways in which one can demolish a narrative. One is to leave out a portion (as anyone has discovered who has become engrossed in reading a magazine fiction article only to discover one of the back pages ripped out). The other is to reverse the narrative, to get the events out of sequence. These assaults effectively render the narrative meaningless and destroy the power of the narrative itself to offer meaning to other events. And this was precisely the cruel joke that fate, aided by benevolent medical technology, had played on this family. The life of this child had been turned into a movie film that was put into a projector and played backward, but with no chance of it ever being played forward again. From a narrative perspective, this seemed to be the most basic and horrible fact about the case; and yet the analytic, ethical discussion was somehow supposed to proceed as if this fact were irrelevant.

All this is not to say that the team members had exhibited insensitivity to the plight of the parents. Indeed a good deal of time was spent with them and a great deal of emotional support was offered. There was still a firm bond between the parents and the team—not surprisingly, even given the tragic complication, since this was the team that had in effect promised to save the life of their daughter and had then done so. In saving the daughter, the team had also, in a sense, killed her; but they were clearly not to blame for this Hawthornesque outcome and were clearly as anguished as the parents. If, in the final analysis, they were not grappling with the fundamental fact of narrative reversal and meaninglessness, it was probably because both the team and the parents found it too bewildering.

It is not at all clear that the casuist, as described earlier in this chapter, would necessarily have decided the moral obligations in this case differently. I would merely submit that the casuist, in trying to get a handle on the "facts of the case," would have been more open to the unique horror of the reversal of a life narrative and would have been much slower in trotting out principles and maxims from other cases of sick or retarded children to apply to the present circumstances.

THE ELDERLY AND THE END OF THE NARRATIVE

I have used the parabola image to suggest that the beginning portion of the life-span narrative tends to display a level of uniformity different from the wide variations possible at the peak. The same may be true at the other end of the "rainbow." There is a great difference between the promise of a future life plan that characterizes the infant and the life plan near completion, coupled with a firmly enmeshed set of family and social relationships, that characterizes the older person. The latter is a person in the full sense and has already lived a life in the full sense. But we can imagine the person living to the point at which most of his life goals have either been realized or have been set aside as unrealistic; his children are grown and are largely independent; many friends may already be dead; and possibly some chronic illness or infirmity has already made its appearance to limit even further his future prospects. If we imagine the individual falling ill and eventually dying at this point in life, we have a reasonable picture of what can be called a "natural death" (Callahan 1977). And it is equally questionable whether all the concepts that apply to ethical decisions at the peak of the parabolic arc necessarily apply equally to this end of the life span. In the case of the infant, concepts related to rights, interests, and autonomy were particularly called into question. The elderly person near death may still be fully autonomous and may have rights and interests that demand respect in a manner not true for the infant. But those rights and interests must be tempered, in a way not applicable to the peak of the parabola, with an awareness that it is inevitable that the story must end soon and that some endings are more desirable than others from a standpoint of narrative coherence and not necessarily of life prolongation.

Clearly, the situation of an elderly individual with a terminal illness is very different from that of an infant. The elderly person is frequently capable of a fully autonomous choice, and even if not, has had ample opportunity to make desires and values known to the other parties that may make choices on his behalf. The elderly person has a long history of fully reciprocating participation in a wide network of relationships, and the loss of such a person is a different manner of loss than the death of a newborn infant.[12] It is therefore much easier to judge on an individual basis what the best interests of an elderly person with respect to medical care might consist of. Increasingly, however, the ethical issue with regard to care of the elderly has to do not with individual decisions but with allocation of social resources, as cost containment becomes a dominant factor in U.S. decision making around health and aging policy.

Observations that about one-third of all money spent on health care is spent for people who have less than one year to live have been taken as evidence of irrationality in our resource allocation scheme. It is readily assumed that this money is spent on futile efforts to prolong biological existence instead of "quality" life, and that in general it makes little sense to allocate such a large portion of medical dollars to the aged and/or severely ill when there is likely to be so little payoff in terms of survival. But this same reasoning leads to countercharges of discrimination against the elderly and arguments that the elderly, as a politically less powerful group, are being set up to bear the brunt of our newly found enthusiasm for cutting costs (Avorn 1984).

A comment that may be used to support Avorn's position is the suggestion by Daniels (1982) that we ask what would count as a rational distribution of health resources if we assumed that each person on reaching adulthood is given some lump sum to be spent on all future medical care and has to make arrangements to allocate it

---

12. This is not to say that the parents of a dead infant will not experience a full-fledged and genuine grief; but, as noted above (see especially n. 4), the parents' grief is in some ways for the loss of the promise of a future individual—for the "anybody" who is not yet. Indeed this may make their grief much more overwhelming, to the extent that they grieve for a range of possible children rather than for a single individual.

over the expected life span (say, by purchasing one or more insurance policies with the money). By this approach, it might not seem irrational at all if an individual elected to bank one-third of the sum specifically for use during the last year of life (or whenever it seemed likely that the last year of life was at hand); but if this is so, we cannot charge irrationality if our collective system adopts precisely this mode of distribution.

The major point to notice is that Daniels's way of approaching the problem specifically takes account of the trajectory notion of a human life span and regards life in narrative form, whether or not one agrees with a specific scheme for the rational distribution of health resources over a life span (and regardless of whether the last year of life is a meaningful unit of time with which to discuss such matters). At any rate, it might be suggested that some form of narrative life-span approach will be more useful in resolving such ethical disputes than some approach that attempts to apply the same concepts of just distribution across all age groups. To the extent that an elderly patient near death is capable of autonomous choice, respect for persons dictates that many or most health care decisions will be made by the individual on his own behalf. But to the extent that autonomous individual choice is not feasible (and it is not at the macroallocation levels), then it would seem to make some difference whether medical treatment is being used to prolong a life in which some crucial features of a rational life plan have not yet been fulfilled, or whether medical treatment is being used to prolong a life when a life plan has been completed and no outstanding projects of importance are left undone from that individual's perspective. Such discriminations, in the political realm, are bound to raise charges of discrimination against the elderly, just as proposals around handicapped infants raise charges of violation of the civil rights of the handicapped; in both cases a defense lies in showing that there are morally relevant differences that apply to the portion of the life span in question (cf. Arras 1984).

A government policy to give or withhold medical treatment based on the extent to which one's life plan and life projects have been completed is almost sure to be either tyrannical or ham-handed or both.[13] The safest policy, as is now most generally advocated, is to try whenever possible to allow the individual to make these choices, either at the time the choice must be made or prospectively if the choice can be anticipated (President's Commission 1983; Bayer et al. 1983). In those cases, however, where a first-party decision cannot be made, some social group who has more intimate knowledge of the individual's life than a government agency may ideally be called upon to make a decision. The fundamental ethical question, here as elsewhere, is: what is the right thing to do in this situation, all things considered (Benjamin and Curtis 1981)? Along with possible harm or suffering of the patient, level of daily function with and without aggressive treatment, and possible alternative uses of scarce medical resources, I would submit that among those things to be considered are the elements of the life narrative that is drawing to a close, and which sorts of endings *make the most sense* within the context of that narrative. When the individual cannot help in framing her own end to her own story, a small group of individuals bound to that person by some ties of sympathy and community may ultimately have to decide what sorts of medical care and support *seem most reasonable for that particular case*. And what seems reasonable will hinge not only on standard ethical principles but also on an awareness of how that individual's life story has unfolded, and on what makes that life story unique.[14]

13. One might note that it is not at all clear that, having completed one's major life projects and plans, one does not if possible deserve a little time to simply sit back and savor the feeling of a well-lived life about to close. A narrative that halts too abruptly has its own aspect of meaninglessness and unsatisfactoriness.

14. The mechanism currently being advocated for these sorts of decisions at a social microlevel is the hospital ethics committee, which holds out promise despite being untested on any wide scale; see, for example, Cranford and Doudera (1984). At any rate, a hospital ethics committee is a forum in which a patient's life story can be briefly reviewed as part of the process of deciding upon the appropriate form and level of care, if the participants see the relevance of this exercise. Slightly related to this need is a suggestion emanating from geriatric medicine—that good care of the aged patient includes asking him to bring in a photograph of himself when he was "in his prime," whatever that means to him, and giving that photo a prominent place in the medical chart. The idea, I take it, is that one is reminded that one is treating a person who has a life story, and that one is now seeing only a small part of that life story as one "gets to know" the geriatric patient.

The idea that either individual autonomy or substituted judgments by family or friends will lead to reasonable end-of-life-span decisions, however, assumes that the concept of a narrative form of a human life exists in the general public awareness, even if forgotten by medical ethics "experts." MacIntyre's critique of the fundamental incoherence of ethics in a modern pluralist society (1981) would suggest that this assumption is flawed. Elsewhere MacIntyre suggests that "the lady with the blue rinse in Florida who behaves as if she were twenty, but who knows all too well that she is seventy-five, is as frenetic as she is because she does not know what kinds of experiences she is undergoing" (1977, p. 210; quoted in Long 1986). That is, in order to attach meaning to her experiences, she would have to place them in the context of a connected and coherent narrative, but that is precisely what she is unable to do. It is therefore important to know how much this problem is the lady's as an individual and how much the problem is that of a culture (like Hans Castorp's pre–World War I Germany) that is unable to provide for the lady a sense of who she is and of what activities could make her life meaningful.

These observations raise, in turn, some questions about how to pursue appropriate cost containment in the care of the elderly without unduly limiting individual freedoms and options. A major dilemma now facing geriatric medicine, as a relatively new area of specialization, is how to weave a middle course between two unacceptable extremes. One is the view that the elderly patient is basically a broken-down piece of machinery who cannot be helped by medical means; the error of this fatalistic view has been shown by much recent research, such as studies showing that those earlier felt to be "too old to stand" coronary bypass surgery, organ transplants, and so on, in fact do quite well once the procedure is actually tried. The other extreme is the view that medicine can somehow confer immortality, so that one is obligated to try every possible aggressive intervention in a dying ninety-year-old exactly as if she were a twenty-year-old. Clearly *appropriate* geriatric care seeks a comfortable middle ground; but where that middle course lies may require delicate clinical judgment in individual cases. And the way to avoid expensive and wasteful medical interventions at the end of life—the second unacceptable extreme—might in the final analysis be less a matter

of setting up strict rules and limits to entitlements under Medicare
and other insurance schemes. It may be more a matter of assisting
both patients individually and our culture more generally to remember
what it means to live a complete and a completed life according to
a narrative conception. If physicians were to help patients and their
families answer the question "What do you take to have been the
story of your life up till now? How would you like to see that story
draw to its inevitable conclusion?" then we might experience fewer
demands for futile and wasteful "heroics" from the "lady with the
blue rinse" and her relatives. On the other hand, we might encourage
demands for genuinely helpful medical services, including rehabilitation, chronic care, and in-home care, for those who have good
reason to insist that their lives and life projects are not yet nearing
their end.[15]

If the entitlement approach and the narrative conception represent
two contrasting ways to discuss appropriate care for the elderly and
terminally ill, some further implications suggest themselves. Using
an entitlement conception, the debate over care for the elderly turns
into the question of what is a fair slice of a pie of a given size that
ought to be allocated to a particular interest group within society.
And that sparks replies from competing interest groups that they
have a higher level of need or entitlement and hence ought to receive
a larger slice at the elderly's expense. In particular, some defenders
of health services for pregnant women and children have been drawn
into the debate by insisting that those just beginning life are a more
vulnerable (both politically and biomedically) and a needier group
than those at the end of their life span, and hence deserve more
funding to be diverted from Medicare and other sources.

The narrative conception tends to oppose a debate over what is a
fair slice of the pie for each of the two competing interest groups,
the young and the old. Instead, it encourages asking the question of
what sort of society we are if we have come to view our task as that
of refereeing a battle between the young and the old members of

15. I am indebted for some of these ideas to conversations with Robert Butler and
Christine Cassel, although they may not agree with the use to which I have put their
suggestions.

our community over a fixed stock of provisions—particularly when our society appears to be one of the wealthiest in the world. Further, the division of the old and the young into two warring factions, instead of two transition phases abstracted from the entire life span of an individual person, seems suspicious if not incomprehensible. And so, faced with the compelling public policy debate of today— "To what fair share of total health resources are the elderly entitled?''—the narrative conception will not resolve the debate, but will instead call into question the very terms in which the debate is framed.[16]

If the narrative conception undermines discussion of entitlement and fairness in terminal care, it reinforces another notion that has received relatively little attention in the medical ethics literature— the medical management of death.[17] With the shifting of the site of death from home to hospital, and with technological intervention more the norm than the exception during the dying process, the way in which one dies becomes increasingly a matter of medical control and medical choice. By contrast, in former times, one died the way one did because no control was possible, or else one took matters into one's own hands through deliberate suicide—but in either case no medical choice or medical involvement was evident. And so today one who wishes to exercise some control over the end of one's own life story must usually deal with an array of medical options.

Physicians who believe that cure or life prolongation is the only legitimate medical function will shrink from accepting any such responsibility or from openly assisting the patient in examining this array of choices. Physicians with humbler and more compassionate views will find themselves, whether or not they wish it, confronting

16. I have relied for these ideas on talks given by W. Andrew Achenbaum, at a conference on ethical and legal issues in care for the elderly in Lansing, Mich., on June 14, 1985, and by Robert Butler at an Anglo-American conference on health care needs and resources in London, December 2–4, 1986.

17. An exception to this lack of discussion is Battin (1983). Malcolm, in a newspaper article (1984), speaks alternately of "arranged death" and "negotiated death." Battin (1983) tends to downplay the actual difficulty both in predicting how easy or how difficult for any particular patient a specific mode of death will be and in using medical means (other than direct killing) to ensure that a patient dies in one way and not in another.

the fact that for many terminally ill patients, they cannot avoid or even much postpone death, but that they can envision several alternative modes or scenarios of death that may have very different implications for the patient's own choices and values. For example, a patient with widespread colon cancer and threatened intestinal obstruction may die of perforation with peritonitis, of hemorrhage, or of dehydration; and these different modes of death portend very different outcomes in terms of amount of pain, ability to remain lucid, and other features likely to be important to the patient. And the physicians may have the power to nudge the patient toward one of these modes of death. The choice among them need not be unduly glorified by speaking of a ''natural death'' or ''death with dignity''; it will suffice to discuss the physician's duty to aid the patient toward the ''least worst death'' (Battin 1983).

Medical ethics has generally approached such decisions by focusing upon the right of the autonomous patient to refuse life-prolonging treatment (President's Commission 1983) or by debating whether or not there is a compelling moral distinction between active and passive euthanasia (Rachels 1975; Trammell 1979; Menzel 1979). What has been little discussed is the possibility that the circumstantial realities of the nudging process, assuming the physician has both the requisite technique and prescience to assist the patient in selecting one from among several possible modes of death, will be such as to defy any simple distinctions between active and passive means, or between accepting treatment and refusing treatment.

A case study may illustrate this point. A forty-two-year-old psychologist, almost totally paralyzed and respirator dependent as a result of amyotrophic lateral sclerosis, and able to communicate only by laboriously typing out messages on a special device by means of head motions, informed her husband that she had become tired of fighting her irreversible condition and wished to die. The hospital refused requests to disconnect the respirator or to discontinue tube feedings, but noted that the patient visited home one day each month with the aid of a portable respirator, and that if something were to occur during one of those home visits, they would have no special obligation to inquire too closely into the matter. With the aid of a supportive lawyer, the husband located two physicians willing to help. In a plan fully approved of by the woman herself, one physician came to the home and administered an injection of a tranquilizer, after which the husband himself disconnected the respirator. (Without the sedative, the patient would have experienced air hunger and involuntary gasping when the respirator was disconnected.) The husband then contacted the second physician, who filled out a death certificate saying that she had, to his knowledge, died from natural causes with no suspicious circumstances (Malcolm 1984).

Had this case occurred in the Netherlands in 1987, instead of in New York City in 1984, a physician could have been found who would have been willing to kill this patient openly and directly by means of a lethal injection. But, given the options the patient, husband, physicians, and lawyer felt they had open to them at the time, the best description of events appears to be that this patient chose one possible mode of death as being superior to the alternatives (remaining helplessly attached to the respirator until an unpredictable future time when she would succumb to infection or some complication of therapy), and that her physicians used the available medical technology to assist in implementing her choice. It seems inaccurate to say that she died as a result of refusing further treatment—the administration of the tranquilizer was, after all, crucial to making this mode of death superior to the alternatives. It seems inaccurate to say that she died as a result of either passive or active interventions—the withdrawal of the respirator, by itself, could be viewed as passive, but the overall plan was actively implemented, and the action of injecting a tranquilizer was a crucial part of it. It seems only partially accurate to say that this patient committed suicide or that the physicians assisted a suicide—a choice for death is one thing when a long and healthy life exists as a live option, and quite another when all available options are essentially death options. It seems inaccurate to discuss this case as an example of the patient's ''right to die''—this right would have been meaningless without the physicians' willingness to cooperate actively and without the information they offered regarding her choices and their implications for her. In the end, the only useful language seems to me to be that of ''medical management of death,'' which is to say the use of medical means to allow the patient to write an end to her life story in the best possible way.

The discussions in this chapter have provided only a preliminary glance at how taking seriously the idea of a narrative life span might change some modes of making ethical decisions in medicine. In the next chapter I will address the narrative perspective as applied to the physician-patient relationship.

10

The Physician-Patient Relationship
as a Narrative

RELATIONAL AND DECISIONAL ETHICS

In this chapter I will discuss how the ethical aspects of the physician-patient relationship may be viewed from the same sort of narrative perspective that was employed, in the last chapter, to characterize the normal human life span. First, I will address the different settings in which medical decisions are made to see if the applicability of the narrative perspective varies among them. In a later section, I will address a particular problem—informed consent—at somewhat greater length.

A commonly voiced criticism of the body of medical ethics literature of the past fifteen years or so is its focus on the unusual, hospital-based, life-and-death case to the exclusion of commonplace, office-based, ambulatory-patient cases of the sort that make up the vast majority of medical encounters (Geyman 1980; Dickman 1980). The question "Should I tell this patient for whom I'm recommending flu vaccine about the association between Guillain-Barre syndrome and the swine flu shots several years ago?" arises much more often in practice than "Should I tell this patient that we have just confirmed a diagnosis of metastatic cancer?"; yet the literature exhaustively analyzes the latter with hardly a nod to the former.

One possibility is that the very same ethical principles apply to both sorts of cases; we study the rare, dramatic cases simply because the issues are raised in clearer and more compelling fashion. But a second possibility is starting to receive some tentative attention in the newer literature, and that is that the "ethic" of the tertiary care referral hospital and the intensive care unit is somehow fundamentally different from the "ethic" of primary care medicine, administered by the generalist physician in the office setting.[1] At one level of abstraction, this proposal of two ethics seems nonsensical—it can hardly be the case, for instance, that the cardiologist should routinely tell patients the truth in the coronary care unit while the family physician routinely lies to patients in the office. But if we look at more subtle nuances rather than at central principles, this proposal has some initially attractive features.

Let us assume, for purposes of argument, that the tertiary care setting is characterized more by a *decisional ethic,* whereas the primary care setting is characterized more by a *relational ethic.* This means that the approach to ethics in the intensive care unit tends to be that among people who have no prior history with each other, who have to carry out discrete and generally predictable actions over a limited time span, and who then will part company for the future. In contrast, the approach to ethics in the office of the primary care physician tends to be that of two or more parties who plan to engage in a long-term relationship, the possibilities of which for the future can only be guessed at vaguely, and for whom most particular behaviors will be much less important than the maintenance of that relationship. Thus, in the decisional ethic, the question regarding truthful disclosure of diagnosis is likely to be "Should I disclose this particular piece of information to this patient at this time?" In the relational ethic, it is more likely to be a series of questions: "What can I assume this patient already knows, judging from past discussions? On the basis of those same past discussions, what can I assume he wants to know? What should I say now? How will I judge how what I have said has affected the patient? What will be

---

1. The most ambitious statement of these two ethics of primary as opposed to tertiary care that I have read appears in an unpublished paper by Larry Churchill and Alan Cross, for which I am indebted to them.

my next opportunity to add to or modify what I will say, in light of that reaction?''

Another difference can be seen with regard to patients who display only partial autonomy or lack motivation to engage in fully autonomous choice (B. L. Miller 1981). In the decisional ethic, such a stance must be taken as a given. Informed consent requires that the patient who is capable of autonomy be given an opportunity for full information and free consent, regardless of whether that opportunity is fully taken advantage of. Alternatively, if the patient is not capable of autonomous choice, some other means, such as proxy consent, must be found to deal with the case. Judgments of patient autonomy, within the decisional ethic, are thus likely to assume an all-or-none character.

In the relational ethic, diminished autonomy much more often represents one point along a time continuum, and a number of maneuvers on the physician's part may effectively alter this state of affairs (Ackerman 1982). If the patient lacks information, additional education regarding the illness and treatment may be indicated. If the patient is limited by emotional reactions such as anger or denial, counseling may be effective. If the patient has assumed a passive stance because he assumes that this is what the physician expects and values, further experience in this relationship may dispel these false expectations. Thus, the question "What can I do to enhance this patient's autonomy for the future?" becomes as important as "What degree of autonomous choice is this patient capable of with regard to this immediately pressing medical decision?" The moral principle of "respect for autonomy" may require the tertiary care physician to ask only the latter question; the primary care physician who takes the moral principle seriously will have to ask both questions.

A weakness of many approaches to autonomy that characterized medical ethics about ten or fifteen years ago was the assumption that the greatest enemy of patient autonomy was the paternalistic physician who would, if not strictly reined in, take all effective decision-making opportunities away from the patient (Brody 1985). This assumption fit well with some historical origins of the renewed interest in medical ethics as a discipline, which grew out of the civil rights and consumers' rights movements of the 1960s.[2] It did, however, tend to ignore the possibility that the illness was itself often a source of diminished autonomy, and that the physician might actively join forces with the patient to protect the latter's autonomy against the vulnerability imposed by illness (Ackerman 1982). The consumers' rights approach to patient autonomy often seemed to require the physician to assume the passive role of technician plus neutral purveyor of information—since anything more involved than that was likely to overly sway a vulnerable patient into agreeing with the physician. A more sophisticated approach (although equally intolerant of physician paternalism in the form of deception, manipulation, or coercion of patients) in contrast requires a much more active role for the physician. The physician must work with the patient to identify factors that could reduce autonomy and try over time to modify or eliminate them.

Indeed, Tomlinson (1986) points out that restricting the physician to a passive role of informing the patient in value-neutral terms without expressing any preference actually tends to produce an anemic and inadequate conception of autonomy. The person with a robust sense of autonomy realizes that we can best take full responsibility for our decisions, and recognize them as truly our own, when decision making is preceded by a process of social dialogue in which we try out various possibilities and bounce the ideas off those most likely to aid us. We can be helped both by those who know us well as individuals and recognize our core values and projects and also by those who have technical expertise relating to the decision at hand. Within the relational ethic, the primary care physician can offer at least one and sometimes both of these types of assistance.

INFORMED CONSENT AND CONVERSATION

The difference between a decisional and a relational ethic can be further illustrated by considering informed consent as a specific aspect

---

2. I am indebted for this historical observation to Gerald Osborn and to his 1985 master's dissertation at Cambridge University.

of respect for patient autonomy. In the decisional ethic, informed consent is a fairly routine matter of disclosure of information, the answering of questions, processing of information by the patient, and consent or refusal of the offered treatment. In the relational ethic, informed consent assumes much more the character of an ongoing relational attitude than a discrete set of explicit procedures.

This has led some observers to suggest that informed consent is absent in the usual office visit and that the primary care ethic is fundamentally paternalistic and ignores patient autonomy (Beauchamp and McCullough 1984). If this *were* true, it would be disconcerting, since the office patient, suffering only from minor illness if any at all and capable of being up and about his affairs, seems much more capable of autonomous choice than does the seriously ill patient flat in bed in the strange environment of the hospital (Lidz et al. 1983).

I would argue that it is *not* true. It is simply the case that the exercise of autonomy in the outpatient setting is almost always at the implicit rather than the explicit level. The primary care physician who wishes to respect and enhance patient autonomy generally does so not by taking up time with an explicit, routine process of disclosure and consent but rather by establishing a tone and an attitude that runs through every patient encounter, with each encounter building sequentially on the previous ones. She will, for instance, take care to explain diagnoses and treatment in understandable language and encourage questions from the patient. She will frankly admit uncertainties, and when two or more treatments are equally feasible, she will describe all of them and invite the patient to participate in the final choice. She will come to know a lot about the patient's family, employment, and community ties, and so be able to make shrewd guesses about how this patient will act when presented with various medical options in the future; but whenever possible these shrewd guesses will be checked out with the patient first and not acted upon as if they were certainties. Over time she will try to encourage the patient to be an advocate for his own views—to ask questions and to indicate his doubts or fears regarding a proposed treatment without waiting for her to raise these questions first.

When all this has transpired in the relationship, this physician might tell a patient on one office visit, "That greenish nasal discharge sounds like sinusitis, and the physical exam tends to confirm it. I think you need a course of amoxicillin." The patient might reply, "Whatever you say," and await the writing of the prescription. The decisional analysis would indicate total absence of any semblance of informed consent and would mark down this physician as paternalistic. The relational account, however, might focus on prior visits in which it has been made clear to this patient that questions are encouraged and that uncertainties will be frankly shared. Furthermore, it might be noted that on a previous office visit, when this physician suggested an antibiotic, the patient objected and demanded to know the precise reasons an antibiotic was needed. Thus there is evidence that the patient has genuinely accepted the relationship on the doctor's terms and is not simply making a show of participation while inwardly maintaining a totally passive role. When this relational history is described, it can then be claimed with some conviction that the fact that this patient asked no questions and accepted the amoxicillin was an implicit acknowledgment that he had been sufficiently informed for his purposes and had freely consented.

One important implication of the relational ethic concept for informed consent in both primary care and tertiary care settings is the possibility of a "training effect." We could hypothesize that the patient who is actively involved in therapeutic decisions of lesser consequence in the office around episodes of minor illness—such as whether to try an antibiotic now or wait two more days to see if symptoms clear spontaneously—will, if later stricken with a major illness that requires treatment in an intensive care setting, be better able and more willing to participate in major medical decisions, compared to a patient who had had no previous training in the notion of informed participation in medical care decisions. This hypothesis, of course, could not be accepted without empirical study, but the study seems worth carrying out.

Katz (1984) has offered an analysis of informed consent that squares in important ways with the relational-ethic model developed above. Most pertinent is the characterization of informed consent as a type of *conversation,* a metaphor that accomplishes several things. First, it delegalizes and demystifies the concept of informed consent, which is important for physicians who have gradually come to regard informed consent as a legal requirement artificially grafted onto medical practice instead of having arisen within medical practice as a manifestation of its fundamentally moral nature. Second, it emphasizes the concept's narrative and historical quality. A conversation is the sort of thing that occurs over time, and although it may occur as a discrete event, it can also be laid aside for now and picked up again later. It is assumed that participants to the conversation have memories, so that things discussed earlier can be taken for granted and need not be repeated unless a disagreement or misunderstanding arises. Third, it suggests a much more meaningful sharing of responsibility. The physician may be the one who must start the conversation, indicate that a conversation is in order, and explain technical matters in understandable terms. But the patient also has a responsibility: he has an equal power with the physician to terminate the conversation or to keep it going. So he has the responsibility to decide when the conversation has gone on long enough for his purposes, or whether there are still pertinent considerations that must be addressed before he can make a choice. Neither participant in a true conversation can properly be viewed as totally passive or totally lacking in responsibility for the outcome.

If the notion of conversation as capturing an important aspect of informed consent could be elaborated in sufficient detail and then grasped both by physicians and by courts involved in medical issues, important improvements might occur. For instance, it seems clear that physicians are disturbed by the idea of informed consent to a degree out of proportion to the frequency with which medical negligence lawsuits hinge on informed consent.[3] I hazard the guess that

---

3. I base this judgment upon experience gained in presenting medical-ethics conferences frequently before audiences of physicians. As Katz (1984) notes, the current legal standards of informed consent actually provide considerable protection for physicians. To win a suit on these grounds, a patient must prove that the physician's failure to inform adequately *directly caused* the harm suffered by the patient. Generally this means that the patient must convince a jury that she would have refused the medical treatment had she only

this rests, in part, on the apparently open-ended nature of the physician's duty to disclose information. If you tell a physician that she has a duty to treat a particular infection with antibiotics, she knows exactly how to go about it. She knows, in particular, when she is *done* with treatment—when the antibiotic has been given in a large enough dose for enough time, when the fever and white blood count have returned to normal, and so on. This same physician, reading that she is obligated to disclose "all the information that the average reasonable person would want to know" about some medical treatment, has much less sense of when enough is enough. If she is particularly fastidious, she will want to go beyond providing what some hypothetical reasonable person would want to know and address herself to what *this patient* wants to know (Katz 1984). But she also knows that how much this patient wants to know may be directly related to how much she tells him. If, for instance, she fails to mention that the pill she is prescribing for tennis elbow has as a possible but rare side effect the suppression of bone marrow or the alteration of kidney function, the patient will not have the chance to say that he wants to know more about these risks or that he does not want to know about them. And she also knows that there may be several reasons the patient might say, "I don't have any more questions," besides the reason that he has received all the information he needs to make his choice. He might say it because it is getting late and he is fatigued. He might say it because he knows the doctor has a lot of other patients waiting. Or he might say it because of a fear, which, if explored in more depth, might be put aside to the ultimate enhancement of patient autonomy. She sees, therefore, an open-ended duty that she can never be sure, *at the time*, she has adequately discharged. Instead, she can always foresee the possibility of being

---

known that the toxic effect (which she ended up suffering) was one possible risk of the treatment. In a case in which the patient was severely ill, the treatment offered considerable hope of benefit, and the probability of the toxic effect was low, it will be hard to convince the jury of that. Thus the wailing and gnashing of teeth among physicians about the requirements imposed by informed consent seem to be at odds with legal realities. I am grateful to Dan Bronstein and Tracy Dobson for further insights into relevant legal matters.

shown, *in retrospect* at a later time in a court of law, that she should have said something that was not said.[4]

So long as informed consent is viewed as a legalistic concept smuggled into medical practice at the behest of attorneys, our physician is most likely to respond by demanding a set of rules or an algorithm to deal with this uncertainty. And yet she is too smart to see this as the answer, for after all her concern is with the individual patient and his unique needs, and that is precisely what any algorithm is bound to leave out. And so her view of informed consent leads to a sense of unfulfilled duty and unresolved anxiety.

To the extent that physicians are uncomfortable with uncertainty generally, switching from a legalistic view to a conversation view will not improve matters and may indeed worsen them. But at least the conversation metaphor may indicate the reasons no algorithm can be given—even physicians are likely to accept the idea that a conversation takes off and comes to an end in a way that can't be predicted or regulated by rules stated in advance. If successful, the conversation metaphor will help primary care physicians remove the focus from the information being disclosed and refocus on the *attitude of openness and sharing* that is the necessary precondition for a conversation of the sort Katz advocates to occur.

4. These considerations reveal an unresolved ambiguity in Katz's largely insightful commentary (1984). In most places Katz seems to wish to drive a wedge between informed consent and the idea of clinical judgment or standards of medical practice. This is natural, since under the older court standards, the standard of care in the medical community could be used as justification for not informing patients at all. Katz, at times, would rather insist that informed consent is a moral and legal right of patients, independent of whatever physicians may decide is good practice. And yet, if Katz is ultimately to be successful in reforming medical practice in the direction he advocates, he must show how informed consent can be *integrated into* medical practice and clinical judgment. In the example just given in the text, it is clearly a matter of *clinical judgment* on the part of the physician when the conversation has gone on long enough and over the right topics. No legal standard for informed consent, in the final analysis, will be able to come into the examining room with the patient and alter the physician's behavior. For this reason, the conversation metaphor may actually justify the physician's failure to disclose a serious but extremely unlikely risk of a commonly employed procedure. (See Allen, 1976, on advocating a refusal by radiologists to mention the 1-in-40,000 risk of a fatal reaction to urography.) It could be said with some justice, if the risk is remote enough, "How could you have expected *that* to come up in any *reasonable* conversation?"

If legal standards of informed consent were then altered to focus not on precisely what was said but on how the patient was encouraged to state his concerns and to participate in the decision, it is possible that some patients might lose some legal protections they now enjoy. Failure to disclose some items of crucial information might, under the hypothetical new system, go unpunished. But the net effect would, one hopes, be a much more positive alteration in how physicians approach patients, in contrast to the adversarial attitude that today's tort system often prompts physicians to adopt. Overall, patients would be given much more information, would be involved more in decisions to the extent that they wish, and would feel more comfortable in indicating their needs and desires for information and participation.[5] The fear of decent physicians—that they might practice high-quality medicine and indicate respect for their patients as persons and still end up being sued—might be materially lessened.

Two provisos should be offered. First, if patients generally desire information, and yet any reasonable conversation will be limited in terms both of how much information can be included and of how much the average person will retain, then the physician is clearly obligated to supplement the conversation with readily available written material going into more detail. Second, with similar logic, the more the physician-patient relationship model moves toward the decisional ethic, the more a legalistic view of informed consent may be useful in place of a conversation model. For instance, the specialist who frequently carries out a small number of procedures may well want to invest in a set of videotapes describing these along with their risks and benefits, which patients may watch prior to offering consent. This, however, would simply be unrealistic in a primary care setting.

I have been arguing, in effect, that viewing informed consent as a type of conversation supports the concept of at least some physician-

---

5. It should be noted that several empirical studies indicate the nonlinkage between a desire to be informed and a desire to participate in decision making (Lidz et al. 1983). One study of hypertensive outpatients suggested that physicians systematically underestimate the first desire and overestimate the latter (Strull, Lo, and Charles 1984).

patient relationships assuming an overall narrative or historical structure that ought to be taken into account when exploring the ethics of the relationship.[6] In the next chapter I will have some additional observations on the physician-patient relationship, in light of the earlier material on stories of sickness.

6. In this discussion I have restricted the conversation metaphor, following Katz (1984), to the subject of informed consent. Elsewhere I have explored the notion of conversation as it might apply to inquiry in medical ethics generally (paper presented at Conference on Applied Ethics in Medicine, University of Western Ontario, April 1986). In addition to works like Rorty (1982) and Bernstein (1980), I am indebted to Martin Benjamin for many of these ideas.

11

Concluding Remarks

We are, in an important sense, the stories of our lives. How sickness affects us depends on how sickness alters those stories. Both sick persons and physicians make the experience of sickness more meaningful (thereby reducing suffering) by placing it within the context of a meaningful story. Physicians, because of their special knowledge and their social role, have special powers to construct stories and to persuade others that these stories are the *true* stories of the illness. The emphasis, in the previous two chapters, has been that physicians can properly exercise that power only when they attend carefully to the stories their patients tell them and engage them in meaningful conversation, within the broader context of the range of life stories made available to all of us by our society and our culture. In concluding, I wish to address briefly some further features of the physician's power to tell a story of the sickness, particularly as it may pertain to the training of physicians.

The interest in research and teaching of medical ethics in the last two decades has been prompted in large part by a conviction that medical care has become too technologically focused, and that if proper attention were paid to its human and interpersonal dimensions, it could regain a level of care and compassion that it was judged (correctly or incorrectly) to have had in the past. This concern, generally regarded by teachers of medical ethics as legitimate, has nevertheless put them in something of a bind. It is all very well to stress the compassion element and the need to humanize future physicians, especially when one is trying to convince a medical school dean to put some curriculum time and dollars into a medical ethics program. But there is unfortunately little evidence to support the notion that the teaching of ethics, as is currently done in "respectable" academic circles, produces a more humane or compassionate product. It is not generally felt to be the case, for example, that philosophers who study and teach ethical theory are more compassionate or kindly as a group compared to their colleagues who teach formal logic. It is extremely hard to relate compassionate behavior, or lack of it, among newly graduated physicians to the presence or absence of a course in medical ethics in their curriculum.[1] Moreover, this justification for the teaching of ethics is hardly likely to endear the ethicist to the practicing physician, whose (presumed) inhumanity toward his patients provides the ethicist with a raison d'être.

The material in the central portion of this book might persuade one that the way to produce more compassionate physicians is to abolish all courses in medical ethics and replace them with courses in medicine and literature. Although not prepared to go quite so far, I would still submit that an openness to and acceptance of the story that captures the patient's individualized response to an illness episode must be one of the key ingredients of the compassion we seek. We could do much worse than to graduate physicians who resemble Berger's English country doctor in having always about them *the air of one trying to recognize*—trying to make a link between their own humanity and the humanity of the anguished individual before them

---

1. The experience of the medical ethics teaching project in the Medical Humanities Program, Michigan State University, has been that we can evaluate and document the strengthening of specific reasoning skills after a short exposure to ethics, but that it is very difficult to document any longitudinal and long-term changes in basic attitudes. On the first point, see Howe and Jones (1984). For one study that claims to be able to measure and compare the humanism of newly graduated physicians, see Abbott (1983). On the need for teaching in medical ethics to address behavior as well as cognitive concepts, see Culver et al. (1985).

(Berger and Mohr 1967). And it seems to me that doing so involves skills and attitudes that can be taught and reinforced as part of medical education and that the investigations in this book can help identify and highlight.

Kleinman, Eisenberg, and Good (1978) have suggested, as part of their analysis of what medical social science ought to consist of, that every medical history should include a description of what the illness means to the patient—what the patient thinks has caused it, what he thinks will happen to him in the future as a result, and what he thinks the best treatment ought to be. This suggestion could be viewed in purely technical terms (for example, identifying atypical folk medical beliefs that might interfere with compliance with standard therapy). But properly interpreted, it has a deep ethical dimension as well. It recognizes how impoverished the routine medical history is by comparison with the patient's own story of the illness. And it promotes respect for persons by insisting that the patient's own "unscientific" way of organizing and giving meaning to events is equally worthy of being recorded and studied alongside the physician's diagnosis (Burnum 1984). We saw, in chapter 2, that being sick includes experiencing a special and generally very frightening sort of disruption in the unity of body and self, and it also includes undergoing an alteration in one's social role and in the way one relates to others and vice versa. It is unlikely that these essential features of the sickness story will be elicited by the standard medical history, but they may be better understood if the patient is asked to relate the meaning he attaches to the illness.[2]

Once the patient's story is elicited in sufficient detail, the physician must, in the view of Pellegrino and Thomasma (1981), proceed to bring all available scientific knowledge to bear upon that story, with

2. A valuable teaching exercise along these lines was presented by Rita Charon, M.D., of Columbia University (workshop, Society for Health and Human Values annual meeting, Washington, D.C., October 1985). She has asked classes of second-year medical students to interview various patients so as to be able not to produce a standard medical history but to write a first-person story of the illness episode as the patient herself might tell it. Sample stories written by these students reflect considerable insight and sensitivity, once the restricting features of the standard history and physical have been put to one side temporarily.

the concluding product of this inquiry being a right and good healing action which the physician can administer on behalf of the patient (or recommend to the patient to do on his own behalf). The mind-body dualism that continues to infect most medical thinking would distinguish sharply between this healing action—automatically assumed to be primarily physical or chemical in nature—and the words the physician might use to describe this action to the patient. But the observations of the various authors cited in this book, most notably those of Cassell, Gadow, and Freidson, all go to show that this sharp distinction is mistaken, and that the physician's words to the patient—the revised, medicalized, and professionalized version of the story of the illness—are a part of the healing process itself. The therapeutic impact of the physician's story upon the patient is most easily perceived in psychotherapy, where the story constitutes virtually the whole of the therapy (Hillman 1975; E. B. Brody and Tormey 1980). But, as we saw in chapter 1, the story plays a therapeutic role, for better or for worse, in every physician-patient encounter in which the patient is capable of symbolic communication. Cassell (1982) emphasizes how the meaning attributed to the illness could have the power either to ameliorate or to increase suffering, depending on the decrease or increase in the perceived disruption of one's personhood produced by the story. It may reasonably be hypothesized that the placebo effect, well known to be ubiquitous in medicine, works precisely by way of this meaning route—a story that makes sense, implies enhanced social support and caring, and tends to lead toward mastery and control of the illness will maximize the perceived (and objective) relief of the sickness episode; a story that promotes meaninglessness, social isolation, and helplessness will do the opposite (Brody 1980).

The ethical implications of the power of the physician's story as told back to the patient are somewhat more complex than may first appear. Freidson (1970) has emphasized the social authority that lies behind this power. To be a professional simply is, in large part, to have been granted the authority to create by one's own pronouncements what counts as true and what counts as false about a certain subject. On this analysis, the patient's version of the story can hardly stand up against the social power of the physician's version, even where the patient thinks the physician must be mistaken, or where the patient, given the chance, would construct a much richer and more meaningful story of the illness event than is forthcoming from the physician. Such a view of the physician's power seems to lie behind a good deal of the history of the truth-telling issue in medical ethics (Reiser 1980). For centuries, during which physicians routinely withheld bad news from patients and thought this practice fully justified, the reasons given had to do with the presumed power of the physician's gloomy prognosis to drive the patient immediately into a fit of depression and despair that might itself hasten death. It was similarly presumed that the patient, along with the family and lay support group, would be totally unable to counteract the power of the physician's symbolism in such cases. But, within the past twenty years, there has been a significant reversal in accepted medical wisdom, so that truthful disclosure of diagnosis and prognosis appears to be the current standard of practice.

One would like to think that this might represent at least a partial rejection of the power role formerly attributed to the physician. And, to the extent that this change in physician behavior was prompted by new research on the psychological response to death and loss, this seems partly to be the case. For example, a powerful finding of thanatology research was that the majority of patients came to know their terminal status despite the supposed power of the physician's pronouncements to the contrary. And the positive reading of the most popular of this research (Kubler-Ross 1969) stresses the willingness of the care giver to be comfortable spending time with and listening to the dying patient—which is to say that the care giver is now more open to the patient's own story of his dying process. And yet this same research has given rise to an attitude that treats the "stages of dying" as dogma and closes the ears of the care giver to the individual nuances of the patient's dying experience (Churchill 1979). And to the extent that the duty to disclose truthfully is enshrined as "clinical judgment" whose philosophical and ethical justification is ignored or poorly understood (Novack et al. 1979), physicians may go through the motions of telling the "truth" without achieving any of the basic values that are at stake in the process. The physician, for example, may mouth words that fit with his understanding of the case, but may fail to assess what these words mean to the patient and what image of reality is being created in her mind. In sum, it is striking that a 180-degree turnaround in physician behavior regarding truthful disclosure should have been accompanied by a striking unwillingness to give up the central assumption of the almost absolute power of the physician's spoken word, and the helplessness and passivity of the patient in response to that word.

And so this one line of argument, which emphasizes the physician's social power to create truth and meaning, gives rise to one set of ethical obligations regarding the stories physicians might tell to patients.[3] By this approach, the physician must be extremely conscious of this power to do good and harm and must weigh every word told to the patient in the same way that we would want the surgeon to take hold of the scalpel before making the incision. Depending on what set of assumptions one starts with—whether words are seen more often as helpful or as harmful—the policy proposed may be one of rather full disclosure or of quite limited disclosure in the sorts of stories the physician tells the patient. But what remains constant is the presumed fragility of the patient, the fear that the patient will shatter into pieces if one so much as adopts the wrong tone of voice in telling the story.

This ethical view, I think, holds power over the mind of the physician for two major reasons. One is that it is not clearly inappropriate. There are compelling examples of cases in which the physician's story greatly increased the suffering and distress of the patient. Such cases seem not to be simply mythical, in the way that the idea that cancer patients would, on being told the diagnosis, immediately commit suicide turned out to be mythical as soon as a valid epidemiological survey was conducted. The second reason is that physicians, if the above account is true, can use their discussions with

---

3. It should be noted, since I have attributed the "first view" to Freidson, that this sociologist is fully aware of the limitations of the physician's power and the many other social forces that shape the individual reaction to illness. See generally the discussion in chapter 2, "Sickness, Social Roles, and Cultural Beliefs."

patients, their storytelling, as important tools of their trade. And the careful and committed craftsman is more likely to do a good job if he believes implicitly in the power of his tools than if he does not.

Yet the presumed power of the physician and the corresponding fragility of the patient still represents only a part of the true picture. This is the part of the picture that leads to facile generalizations, such as "sickness is a state of diminished or absent autonomy," of which we have found so many reasons to be suspicious. The stories of reaction to sickness that we reviewed in earlier chapters are not, by and large, the stories of people being blown to pieces by one story told by one person, regardless of that person's social authority. As soon as we shift our focus to recall the multiple examples of human resilience in reaction to sickness, this idea of fragility disappears to be replaced by a profound respect for the power of individuals to shape their own stories, to give meaning to their illnesses, and to ameliorate their own suffering.

An anecdote that illustrates this second approach concerns an investigator doing research on families of American soldiers missing in action in Vietnam. At the time the research was being conducted, it was highly probable that most of these soldiers were in fact dead, and yet the families adopted very different stances on this issue as they sought ways to cope with their suffering. One boy of about twelve years of age particularly caught the attention of the investigator. This boy clung fiercely to the belief that his father must be alive, and this seemed part of a generally angry and unhappy state of existence, accompanied by multiple behavioral and emotional problems in family relationships and in school. The investigator feared that this boy had an especially bad prognosis for future emotional adjustment.

Some time later, the families were gathered together in a retreat setting as part of the ongoing research effort. The investigator found an opportunity to get this boy alone and go for a walk in the woods. At first little was said, and the boy appeared to be his usual sullen and withdrawn self. Then they came upon a large dead tree, at the base of which a sapling was growing. The boy stopped and stared at that tree for a while, and the investigator was considerably surprised when the boy said, "That tree makes me think of my father. You know, I realize now that my father is dead. I think he's that big tree and I'm the sapling. As it dies, the big tree loses its leaves, and that lets the sunlight through so that the sapling can grow."[4]

There are a number of points worth noting about this anecdote, which shows a striking case of a new story giving meaning to an event that was bewildering and inexplicable according to the old story, such that the new story ushers in a striking decrease in suffering.[5] First, there is the ingenuity of the story constructed by this twelve-year-old with no special talent or proclivity for storytelling in the literary sense and certainly with very limited knowledge of medical and psychological theories of grief and recovery. This boy managed in one brief parable to accept the fact of his father's death, to establish a meaningful connection between his father's death and his own continuing life and growth, and to place a positive connotation upon the connection so that the death was no longer an unmitigated evil (without, however, taking upon himself any inappropriate guilt for doing so).

Second, this story, for its therapeutic effect, could have been told only by the boy to himself. It is hard to imagine the investigator having the combination of creativity and arrogance necessary to have seen the two trees and then to say to the boy, "Now look at those two trees over there. Imagine that the big tree is your father and you are the sapling . . . . " But if he had been so bold as to have said such a thing to the boy, we suspect that it could not possibly have had any useful effect. At best, it would simply have created a deeper rift between them.

Third, and partly explaining the second point, this story depends on its therapeutic effect for being told (or thought of) at a very specific and limited time in the history of the boy's reaction to the loss of

4. I am indebted for this example to a paper presented by Hamilton McCubbin, "Critical Family Factors in Health Research and Intervention," presented at the conference, Working with Families IV, Society of Teachers of Family Medicine, Newport Beach, Calif., March 1984.

5. For a contrasting instance of a story that increases and perpetuates suffering, see chap. 1, n. 4, above.

his father. The reason the investigator could probably never have told this story to the boy was mostly his inability to judge the boy's readiness to give up his denial defense and open himself up to this more creative and growth-oriented way of coping. It could be argued that the old, denial-anger-acting-out story was a "bad" story from a therapeutic point of view, that this new story is a "better" story, and that the boy's best interests would have been served had someone come along with the "better" story a year ago. But it is at least as likely that the boy was not ready for the new story a year or even a month ago, and that it would have had no impact or could even have been hurtful. It may even be argued that the denial, anger, and acting out was somehow necessary to lay the groundwork, to set the stage, for the better story. It would take a particularly self-confident professional to argue that he knows better than this boy does what counts as the "right time" for any therapeutic intervention, or what the "right" intervention is for any given time—the sort of professional who would declare with full assurance to anyone, "I know your story better than you do."

Another reason the professional ought not to have told this story to the boy is that the message would be different in that case, compared to the boy being allowed to fashion this story on his own. The message in the latter instance (as actually occurred) is not *simply* that death must be accepted and life goes on but *also* that the boy was a powerful enough agent in control of his own destiny to divine and formulate this meaning *for himself*. In contrast, the investigator's telling the story to and for the boy would have inevitably contained a message of the boy's own relative powerlessness. Thus, considerable skill in psychotherapy is needed to assist patients in getting ready to tell their own story without inappropriately completing the task for them prematurely.

This second approach to the ethical issues agrees with the great power to be attributed to stories, but casts doubt on the physician's ability unilaterally to construct stories and impose them on the patient. It suggests that physicians may add to or detract from the quality of the story of the illness event; but this is much more likely to result from the continued give-and-take between physician and patient over time (as part of the relational ethic) and much less likely to result from one magic word dropped at the psychologically critical moment.[6]

What is the ethical obligation of the physician who wishes to relieve the patient's suffering, who realizes the power of words and stories to give effect to this, and yet who has no illusions as to the ease or power with which he can accomplish his ends? Obviously he needs to view this task as an interactive process with the patient over time. And it seems he will be more likely to succeed if he explicitly recognizes the relationship between sickness and self-respect, and carefully looks for clues as to the link between various aspects of the illness, the reaction of the social peer group to the illness, and the patient's previous and future life plans. It will be a relatively unusual case in which the relationship between the physician and the patient is so close over a long period that the physician becomes a full-fledged member of what we earlier called the life-plan peer review group, and has direct input into the regaining of self-respect by the reformulation of a life plan that is realistic given the facts of the illness but that maximizes the patient's chances of achieving what he takes to be the good in human life. The physician, however, can at least ask himself what he would do, what he would say to the patient, if he were an optimally rational and informed member of that peer review group. And, based on this picture of how the ideal peer review group would operate, the physician might assess, first, whether there is a real-life group operating with and around the patient in something like this fashion, and second, whether there is anything

6. When I had just begun my residency training, a senior resident, Henry Willner, reported a case of an immediate cure effected by one sentence. A patient had had repeated visits for a pruritic dermatitis for which no organic etiology could be found. Finally, when asked for additional information about sources of emotional stress in his life, the patient launched into an increasingly bitter discussion of his relationship with his boss. The resident said, "It sounds like he really gets under your skin." This sentence triggered a sudden insight on the patient's part into the connection between this relationship and his dermatological symptoms, and the itching was later reported to have ceased completely after that interview. In the nine years since then I have discussed stress-and-illness connections with many patients and have eagerly awaited a similar "cure" of my own. Alas, it has yet to happen with any such dramatic immediacy.

the physician can do to facilitate that process (such as referring the patient to a lay self-help group with a similar disease problem, to cite a mundane example).

What counts as a "right and good healing action" is easy to see when a sickness can be cured, or when no sickness exists and the patient simply requires reassurance that this is so. But, when sickness is more or less chronic, we cannot understand a right and good healing action without understanding what the sickness is doing to the person's self-respect, to his life plan, and to the narrative account of his life. One characteristic of a story is that it clearly makes sense and hangs together once it has been told, but can seldom be anticipated before it has been told. There is unlikely to emerge any scientific or philosophical truth that will allow the physician to predict accurately what the impact of any given sickness will be on the life plan of any given patient. But it is another characteristic of stories that certain similarities do emerge when one has been told a number of them. We hope that as physicians pay more attention to the stories of the patients, their ethical quest to enhance personal autonomy and self-respect in the wake of sickness will be aided by an increased awareness of the richness of the human response to illness and anguish.

References

Abbott, L. C. 1983. A study of humanism in family physicians. *Journal of Family Practice* 16:1141–46.

Ackerman, T. F. 1982. Why doctors should intervene. *Hastings Center Report* 12(4):14–17.

Adams, H. 1961. *The education of Henry Adams.* Boston: Houghton Mifflin.

Akiskal, H. S., and W. T. McKinney. 1973. Depressive disorders: Toward a unified hypothesis. *Science* 182:20–29.

Allen, R. W. 1976. Informed consent: A medical decision. *Radiology* 119:233–34.

Altman, L. K. 1983. Patients' privacy is being invaded. *Detroit Free Press,* October 4, p. 1C.

Annas, G. J. 1984. When suicide prevention becomes brutality: The case of Elizabeth Bouvia. *Hastings Center Report* 14(2):20–21.

Aranow, H. 1979. Commentary on Bernard E. Rollin. *Man and Medicine* 4:173–75.

Arras, J. D. 1984. Toward an ethic of ambiguity. *Hastings Center Report* 14(2):25–33.

Avorn, J. 1984. Benefit and cost analysis in geriatric care: Turning age discrimination into health policy. *New England Journal of Medicine* 310:1294–1301.

Bakan, D. 1968. *Disease, pain, and sacrifice.* Chicago: University of Chicago Press.

Battin, M. P. 1983. The least worst death. *Hastings Center Report* 13(2):13–16.

Bayer, R., D. Callahan, J. Fletcher, T. Hodgson, B. Jennings, D. Mon-
sees, S. Sieverts, and R. Veatch. 1983. The care of the terminally
ill: Morality and economics. *New England Journal of Medicine*
309:1490–94.

Beauchamp, T. L., and L. B. McCullough. 1984. *Medical ethics: The
moral responsibilities of physicians.* Englewood Cliffs, N.J.: Prentice-
Hall.

Bemporad, J. 1978. From biology to spirit: The artistry of human life.
Journal of Medicine and Philosophy 3:74–87.

Benjamin, M. 1983. The newborn's interest in continued life: A sen-
timental fiction. *Bioethics Reporter* (December):5–7.

Benjamin, M., and J. Curtis. 1981. *Ethics in nursing.* New York: Oxford
University Press.

Beppu, K., and M. T. Tavormina. 1981. The healer's art: An interview
with Richard Selzer. *Centennial Review* 25:20–40.

Berger, J., and J. Mohr. 1967. *A fortunate man.* New York: Holt,
Rinehart & Winston.

Bergsma, J., and D. C. Thomasma. 1982. *Health care: Its psychosocial
dimensions.* Pittsburgh: Duquesne University Press.

Bernstein, R. J. 1980. Philosophy in the conversation of mankind. *Review of Metaphysics* 33:745–75.

Blum, H. 1976. *Expanding health care horizons.* Oakland, Calif.: Third
Party Associates.

Blustein, J. 1978. On children and proxy consent. *Journal of Medical
Ethics* 4:138–40.

Boorse, C. 1975. On the distinction between disease and illness. *Philosophy and Public Affairs* 5:49–68. (Reprinted in Caplan, Engelhardt,
and McCartney 1981)

Borgenicht, L. 1983. For this they go to medical school: Student reaction
to "Heartsounds." *Pharos of Alpha Omega Alpha* 46(3):32–36.

Brody, E. B., and J. F. Tormey. 1980. Clinical psychoanalytic knowledge—an epistemological inquiry. *Perspectives in Biology and Medicine* 24:143–59.

Brody, H. 1973. The systems view of man: Implications for medicine,
science and ethics. *Perspectives in Biology and Medicine* 17:71–92.

———. 1980. *Placebos and the philosophy of medicine.* Chicago: University of Chicago Press.

———. 1981. *Ethical decisions in medicine.* 2nd ed. Boston: Little,
Brown.

———. 1983. Brain death and personal existence: A reply to Green
and Wikler. *Journal of Medicine and Philosophy* 8:187–96.

————. 1985. Autonomy revisited: Progress in medical ethics. *Journal of the Royal Society of Medicine* 78:380–86.

Brody, H., and D. S. Sobel. 1979. A systems view of health and disease. In *Ways of health: Holistic approaches to ancient and contemporary medicine,* ed. D. S. Sobel. New York: Harcourt Brace Jovanovich.

Brody, H., and D. B. Waters. 1980. Diagnosis is treatment. *Journal of Family Practice* 10:445–49.

Bruner, J. 1986. *Actual minds, possible worlds.* Cambridge: Harvard University Press.

Bunzl, M. 1980. Comment on "Health as a theoretical concept." *Philosophy of Science* 47:116–18.

Burns, C. R. 1976. The nonnaturals: A paradox in the Western concept of health. *Journal of Medicine and Philosophy* 1:202–11.

Burnum, J. F. 1984. Dialect is diagnostic. *Annals of Internal Medicine* 100:899–901.

Callahan, D. 1977. On defining a "natural death." *Hastings Center Report* 7(3):32–37.

Cameron, I., and G. L. Dickie. 1985. The patient in poetry: An exercise in clinical problem solving. *Canadian Family Physician* 31:615–18.

Camus, A. 1972. *The plague,* trans. S. Gilbert. New York: Vintage. (Originally published 1947)

Cannon, W. B. 1963. *The wisdom of the body.* New York: W. W. Norton. (Pp. 305–24 reprinted in Caplan, Engelhardt, and McCartney 1981)

Caplan, A. L. 1981. The "unnaturalness" of aging—a sickness unto death? In *Concepts of health and disease: Interdisciplinary perspectives,* ed. A. L. Caplan, H. T. Engelhardt, and J. J. McCartney. Reading, Mass.: Addison-Wesley.

————. 1983. Can applied ethics be effective in health care and should it strive to be? *Ethics* 93:311–19.

Caplan, A. L., H. T. Engelhardt, and J. J. McCartney, eds. 1981. *Concepts of health and disease: Interdisciplinary perspectives.* Reading, Mass.: Addison-Wesley.

Cassell, E. J. 1976. *The healer's art.* Philadelphia: Lippincott.

————. 1982. The nature of suffering and the goals of medicine. *New England Journal of Medicine* 306:639–45.

Cassell, E. J., and M. D. Lebowitz. 1976. Causality in the environment and health: The utility of the multiplex variable. *Perspectives in Biology and Medicine* 19:338–43.

Ceccio, J., ed. 1978. *Medicine in literature.* New York: Longmans.

Chekhov, A. 1967. Uncle Vanya. In *Masterpieces of the modern Russian theatre*, trans. R. W. Corrigan. New York: Collier, pp. 175–223. (Originally published 1897)

Chrisman, N. J. 1977. The health seeking process: An approach to the natural history of illness. *Culture, Medicine and Psychiatry* 1:351–77.

Chrisman, N., and A. Kleinman. 1983. Popular health care and lay referral networks. In *Handbook of health, health care and health professions*, ed. D. Mechanic. New York: Free Press.

Churchill, L. R. 1979. The human experience of dying: The moral primacy of stories over stages. *Soundings* 62:24–36.

————. 1983. The place of the ideal observer in medical ethics. *Social Science and Medicine* 17:897–901.

Churchill, L. R., and S. W. Churchill. 1982. Storytelling in medical arenas: The art of self-determination. *Literature and Medicine* 1:73–79.

Churchman, C. W. 1968. *The systems approach*. New York: Delta.

Clark, B. 1978. *Whose life is it anyway?* New York: Avon.

Clouser, K. D., C. M. Culver, and B. Gert. 1981. Malady: A new treatment of disease. *Hastings Center Report* 11(3):29–37.

Cohen, A. K. 1968. Deviant behavior. In *International encyclopedia of the social sciences*, ed. D. L. Sills. New York: Macmillan Co. and the Free Press.

Cohen, H. 1961. The evolution of the concept of disease. In *Concepts of medicine*, ed. B. Lush. New York: Pergamon Press. (Reprinted in Caplan, Engelhardt, and McCartney 1981)

Coulehan, J. L. 1984. Who is the poor historian? *Journal of the American Medical Association* 252:221.

Cousins, N., ed. 1982. *The physician in literature*. Philadelphia: Saunders Press.

Cranford, R. E., and A. E. Doudera, eds. 1984. *Institutional ethics committees and health care decision making*. Ann Arbor, Mich.: Health Administration Press.

Culver, C. M., K. D. Clouser, B. Gert, H. Brody, J. Fletcher, A. Jonsen, L. Kopelman, J. Lynn, M. Siegler, and D. Wikler. 1985. Basic curricular goals in medical ethics. *New England Journal of Medicine* 312:253–56.

Culver, C. M., and B. Gert. 1982. *Philosophy in medicine*. New York: Oxford University Press.

Daniel, S. L. 1986. The patient as text: A model of clinical hermeneutics. *Theoretical Medicine* 7:195–210.

Daniels, N. 1979. Wide reflective equilibrium and theory acceptance in ethics. *Journal of Philosophy* 76:256–82.

————. 1980. Reflective equilibrium and Archimedean points. *Canadian Journal of Philosophy* 10:83–103.

————. 1981. Health care needs and distributive justice. *Philosophy and Public Affairs* 10:146–79.

————. 1982. Am I my parents' keeper? In *Midwest studies in philosophy*, ed. P. A. French, T. E. Uehling, and H. K. Wettstein. Minneapolis: University of Minnesota Press, 7:517–39.

Dennett, D. 1976. Conditions of personhood. In *The identities of persons*, ed. A. O. Rorty. Berkeley: University of California Press, pp. 175–96.

Deykin, E. Y., L. Campbell, and P. Patti. 1984. The postadoption experience of surrendering parents. *American Journal of Orthopsychiatry* 54:271–80.

Dickey, J. 1970. *The eye-beaters, blood, victory, madness, buckhead and mercy.* New York: Doubleday.

Dickman, R. L. 1980. Family medicine and medical ethics: A natural and necessary union. *Journal of Family Practice* 10:633–37.

Donne, J. 1941. Devotions. In *Complete poetry and selected prose.* New York: Modern Library. (Originally published 1624)

Dubos, R. 1965. *Man adapting.* New Haven: Yale University Press.

Duff, R. S., and A. G. M. Campbell. 1976. On deciding the care of severely handicapped or dying persons: With particular reference to infants. *Pediatrics* 57:487–93.

Edwards, R. B. 1981. Mental health as rational autonomy. *Journal of Medicine and Philosophy* 6:309–22.

Eisenberg, L. 1977a. Disease and illness. *Culture, Medicine and Psychiatry* 1:9–23.

————. 1977b. Psychiatry and society: A sociobiologic synthesis. *New England Journal of Medicine* 296:903–10.

Engel, G. L. 1960. A unified concept of health and disease. *Perspectives in Biology and Medicine* 3:459–85.

————. 1977. The need for a new medical model: A challenge for biomedicine. *Science* 196:129–36. (Reprinted in Caplan, Engelhardt, and McCartney 1981)

————. 1980. A clinical application of the biopsychosocial model. *American Journal of Psychiatry* 137:535–44.

Engelhardt, H. T. 1975. The concepts of health and disease. In *Evaluation and explanation in the biomedical sciences*, ed. H. T. Engelhardt and S. F. Spicker. Dordrecht, Holland: D. Reidel. (Reprinted in Caplan, Engelhardt, and McCartney 1981)

————. 1976. Ideology and etiology. *Journal of Medicine and Philosophy* 1:256–68.

————. 1978. Health and disease: Philosophical perspectives. In *Encyclopedia of bioethics,* ed. W. T. Reich. New York: Free Press.

————. 1984. Clinical problems and the concept of disease. In *Health, disease, and causal explanations in medicine,* ed. L. Nordenfelt and B. I. B. Lindahl. Boston: D. Reidel, pp. 27–41.

————. 1986. *The foundations of bioethics.* New York: Oxford University Press.

Eraker, S. A., J. P. Kirscht, and M. H. Becker. 1984. Understanding and improving patient compliance. *Annals of Internal Medicine* 100:258–68.

Erde, E. L. 1979. Philosophical considerations regarding defining "health," "disease," etc. and their bearing on medical practice. *Ethics in Science and Medicine* 6:31–48.

Fabrega, H. 1972. Concepts of disease: Logical features and social implications. *Perspectives in Biology and Medicine* 15:538–617. (Reprinted in Caplan, Engelhardt, and McCartney 1981)

————. 1979. The scientific usefulness of the idea of illness. *Perspectives in Biology and Medicine* 22:545–58. (Reprinted in Caplan, Engelhardt, and McCartney 1981)

Fabrega, H., and L. VanEgeren. 1976. A behavioral framework for the study of human disease. *Annals of Internal Medicine* 84:200–8.

Feinberg, J. 1974. The rights of animals and future generations. In *Philosophy and environmental crisis,* ed. W. Blackstone. Athens: University of Georgia Press.

————. 1976. Is there a right to be born? In *Understanding moral philosophy,* ed. J. Rachels. Encino, Calif.: Dickenson.

Feinstein, A. R. 1967. *Clinical judgment.* Huntington, N.Y.: Krieger.

Fingarette, H. 1985. Alcoholism—neither sin nor disease. *Center Magazine* 18(2):56–63.

Fisher, W. R. 1984. Narration as a human communication paradigm: The case of public moral argument. *Communication Monographs* 51:1–22.

Flew, A. 1973. *Crime or disease?* New York: Oxford University Press. ("Disease and Mental Illness," pp. 38–48, reprinted in Caplan, Engelhardt, and McCartney 1981)

Fost, N. 1981. Counseling families who have a child with a severe congenital anomaly. *Pediatrics* 67:321–24.

Frankfurt, H. G. 1971. Freedom of the will and the concept of a person. *Journal of Philosophy* 68:5–20.

Freidson, E. 1970. *Profession of medicine: A study of the sociology of applied knowledge.* New York: Harper & Row.

Gadow, S. 1980. Body and self: A dialectic. *Journal of Medicine and Philosophy* 5:172–85.

Geyman, J. P. 1980. Expanding concerns and applications of medical ethics. *Journal of Family Practice* 10:595–96.

Goosens, W. K. 1980. Values, health and medicine. *Philosophy of Science* 47:100–15.

Gorovitz, S. 1982. *Doctors' dilemmas: Moral conflict and medical care.* New York: Macmillan.

Gorovitz, S., and A. MacIntyre. 1976. Toward a theory of medical fallibility. *Journal of Medicine and Philosophy* 1:51–71.

Green, M., and D. Wikler. 1980. Brain death and personal identity. *Philosophy and Public Affairs* 9:105–33.

Grene, M. 1976. To have a mind . . . *Journal of Medicine and Philosophy* 1:177–99.

Grünbaum, A., 1980. Epistemological liabilities of the clinical appraisal of psychoanalytic theory. *Nous* 14:307–85.

Guttentag, O. E. 1949. On the clinical entity. *Annals of Internal Medicine* 31:484–96.

Hahn, R. A. 1983. Rethinking "illness" and "disease." *Contributions to Asian Studies* 18:1–23.

Hahn, R. A., and A. Kleinman. 1983. Belief as pathogen, belief as medicine: "Voodoo death" and the "placebo phenomenon" in anthropological perspective. *Medical Anthropology Quarterly* 14(4):3, 16–22.

Hampshire, S. 1983. *Morality and conflict.* Cambridge: Harvard University Press.

Hawkins, A. 1984. Two pathographies: A study in illness and literature. *Journal of Medicine and Philosophy* 9:231 52.

Haynes, R. B., D. W. Taylor, and D. L. Sackett, eds. 1979. *Compliance in health care.* Baltimore: Johns Hopkins University Press.

Hemingway, E. 1930. *In our time.* New York: Charles Scribner's Sons.

Hepburn, R. W. 1956. Vision and choice in morality. *Proceedings of the Aristotelian Society,* supp. vol. 30, pp. 14–31.

Hill, T. E. 1973. Servility and self-respect. *Monist* 57:87–104.

———. 1982. Self-respect reconsidered. In *Respect for persons,* Tulane Studies in Philosophy, vol. 31, ed. O. H. Green. New Orleans: Tulane University Press.

Hillman, J. 1975. The fiction of case history: A round. In *Religion as story,* ed. J. B. Wiggins. New York: Harper & Row, pp. 123–73.

Howe, K. R., and M. S. Jones. 1984. Techniques for evaluating student performance in a preclinical medical ethics course. *Journal of Medical Education* 59:350–52.

Hunter, K. M. 1985. Limiting treatment in a social vacuum: A Greek chorus for William T. *Archives of Internal Medicine* 145:716–19.

———. 1986. "There was this one guy . . .": The uses of anecdotes in medicine. *Perspectives in Biology and Medicine* 29:619–30.

Illich, I. 1976. *Medical nemesis: The expropriation of health.* New York: Pantheon.

Jacobs, G. 1964. Cybernetics, homeostasis and a model of disease. *Aerospace Medicine* 35:726–31.

Jonsen, A. R. 1982. On being a casuist. Presented at the conference on Clinical Medical Ethics: Exploration and Assessment, Knoxville, Tenn., August 17, 1982.

———. 1986. Casuistry and clinical ethics. *Theoretical Medicine* 7:65–74.

Jung, C. 1933. *Modern man in search of a soul.* New York: Harcourt, Brace, Jovanovich.

Kafka, F. 1979. The metamorphosis. In *The basic Kafka.* New York: Pocket Books. (Originally published 1915)

Kane, F. I. 1985. Keeping Elizabeth Bouvia alive for the public good. *Hastings Center Report* 15(6):5–8.

Kass, L. 1975. Regarding the end of medicine and the pursuit of health. *Public Interest,* no. 40, pp. 11–42. (Reprinted in Caplan, Engelhardt, and McCartney 1981)

Katz, J. 1984. *The silent world of doctor and patient.* New York: Free Press.

Kellert, S. R. 1976. A sociocultural concept of health and illness. *Journal of Medicine and Philosophy* 1:222–28.

Kelman, S. 1980. Social organization and the meaning of health. *Journal of Medicine and Philosophy* 5:133–44.

Kermode, F. 1967. *The sense of an ending: Studies in the theory of fiction.* New York: Oxford University Press.

King, L. 1954. What is disease? *Philosophy of Science* 21:193–203. (Reprinted in Caplan, Engelhardt, and McCartney 1981)

———. 1982. *Medical thinking: A historical preface.* Princeton: Princeton University Press.

Kleinman, A. F., L. Eisenberg, and B. Good. 1978. Culture, illness and care: Clinical lessons from anthropologic and cross-cultural research. *Annals of Internal Medicine* 88:251–58.

Koestler, A., and J. R. Smythies, eds. 1969. *Beyond reductionism: New perspectives in the life sciences.* Boston: Beacon Press.

Komrad, M. S. 1983. A defense of medical paternalism: Maximizing patients' autonomy. *Journal of Medical Ethics* 9:38–44.

Kopelman, L., and J. Moskop. 1981. The holistic health movement:

A survey and critique. *Journal of Medicine and Philosophy* 6:209–35.

Kraupl-Taylor, F. 1971. Part 1. A logical analysis of the medico-psychological concept of disease. *Psychological Medicine* 1:356–64.

———. 1972. Part 2. A logical analysis of the medico-psychological concept of disease. *Psychological Medicine* 2:7–16.

———. 1976. The medical model of the disease concept. *British Journal of Psychiatry* 128:588–94. (Reprinted in Caplan, Engelhardt, and McCartney 1981)

Kubler-Ross, E. 1969. *On death and dying*. New York: Macmillan.

Lamb, C. 1962. The convalescent. In *Essays of Elia and last essays of Elia*. New York: Dutton.

Lasch, C. 1979. *The culture of narcissism*. New York: W. W. Norton.

Laszlo, E. 1972. *The systems view of the world*. New York: Braziller.

Lawrence, D. H. 1955. A sick collier. In *The complete short stories*. Vol. 1. London: William Heinemann.

Lear, M. W. 1980. *Heartsounds*. New York: Simon & Schuster.

Levine, S., and M. A. Kozloff. 1978. The sick role: Assessment and overview. *Annual Review of Sociology* 4:317–43.

Lidz, C. W., A. Meisel, M. Osterweis, J. L. Holden, J. H. Marx, and M. R. Munetz. 1983. Barriers to informed consent. *Annals of Internal Medicine* 99:539–43.

Lipowski, Z. J. 1968. Review of consultation psychiatry and psychosomatic medicine. III. Theoretical issues. *Psychosomatic Medicine* 30:395–422.

Long, T. A. 1986. Narrative unity and clinical judgment. *Theoretical Medicine* 7:75–92.

MacIntyre, A. 1977. Patients as agents. In *Philosophical medical ethics: Its nature and significance*, ed. S. F. Spicker and H. T. Engelhardt. Boston: D. Reidel, pp. 197–212.

———. 1981. *After virtue*. South Bend, Ind.: Notre Dame University Press.

Macklin, R. 1983. Personhood in the bioethics literature. *Milbank Memorial Fund Quarterly* 61:35–57.

Maguire, D. C. 1974. *Death by choice*. New York: Doubleday.

Malcolm, A. M. 1984. To suffer a prolonged illness or elect to die: A case study. *New York Times*, December 16, p. 1.

Mann, T. 1944. *The magic mountain*. Trans. H. T. Lowe-Porter. New York: Alfred A. Knopf. (First published 1924)

Margolis, J. 1976. The concept of disease. *Journal of Medicine and Philosophy* 1:238–55. (Reprinted in Caplan, Engelhardt, and McCartney 1981)

Martin, M. 1985. Malady and menopause. *Journal of Medicine and Philosophy* 10:329–37.

Maugham, W. S. 1963. *Of human bondage*. New York: Penguin Books. (First published 1915)

McCormick, R. A. 1974a. To live or let die: The dilemma of modern medicine. *Journal of the American Medical Association* 229:172–76.

———. 1974b. Proxy consent in the experimental situation. *Perspectives in Biology and Medicine* 18:2–20.

Menzel, P. T. 1979. Are killing and letting die morally different in medical contexts? *Journal of Medicine and Philosophy* 4:269–93.

Meyers, J. 1985. *Disease and the novel, 1880–1960*. New York: St. Martin's Press.

Miller, B. L. 1981. Autonomy and the refusal of life-saving treatment. *Hastings Center Report* 11(4):22–28.

———. 1984. The Baby Doe rules: Can they be met? *Bioethics Reporter* 1:45–48.

Miller, J. 1977. *Living systems*. New York: McGraw-Hill.

Morreim, E. H. 1986. Philosophy lessons from the clinical setting: Seven sayings that used to annoy me. *Theoretical Medicine* 7:47–63.

Munson, R. 1981. Why medicine cannot be a science. *Journal of Medicine and Philosophy* 6:183–208.

Nordenfelt, L. 1984. Introduction to *Health, disease, and causal explanations in medicine*, ed. L. Nordenfelt and B. I. B. Lindahl. Boston: D. Reidel.

Novack, D. H., R. Plumer, R. L. Smith, H. Ochitill, G. R. Morrow, and J. M. Bennett. 1979. Changes in physicians' attitudes toward telling the cancer patient. *Journal of the American Medical Association* 241:897–900.

Olsen, T. 1961. Tell me a riddle. In *The best American short stories*, ed. M. Foley and D. Burnett. New York: Ballantine.

Parsons, T. 1951. *The social system*. Glencoe, Ill.: Free Press.

———. 1958. Definitions of health and illness in the light of American values and social structures. In *Patients, physicians, and illness*, ed. E. G. Jaco. New York: Free Press. (Reprinted in Caplan, Engelhardt, and McCartney 1981)

———. 1978. Health and disease: A sociological and action perspective. In *Encyclopedia of bioethics*, ed. W. T. Reich. New York: Free Press.

Pellegrino, E. D. 1979. Toward a reconstruction of medical morality: The primacy of the act of profession and the fact of illness. *Journal of Medicine and Philosophy* 4:32–56.

Pellegrino, E. D., and D. C. Thomasma. 1981. *A philosophical basis of medical practice*. New York: Oxford University Press.

Penelhum, T. 1967. Personal identity. In *Encyclopedia of philosophy,* ed. P. Edwards. New York: Macmillan, 5:95–107.

Perry, J. 1976. The importance of being identical. In *The identities of persons,* ed. A. O. Rorty. Berkeley: University of California Press, pp. 67–90.

President's Commission for the Study of Ethical Problems in Medicine and Biomedical and Behavioral Research. 1983. *Deciding to forego life-sustaining treatment.* Washington, D.C.: U.S. Government Printing Office.

Preston, R. P. 1979. *The dilemmas of care: Social and nursing adaptations to the deformed, the disabled and the aged.* New York: Elsevier.

Pritchard, M. S. 1982. Self-regard and the supererogatory. In *Respect for persons,* Tulane Studies in Philosophy, vol. 31, ed. O. H. Green. New Orleans: Tulane University Press, pp. 139–51.

Rachels, J. 1975. Active and passive euthanasia. *New England Journal of Medicine* 292:78–80.

———. 1986. *The end of life: Euthanasia and morality.* New York: Oxford University Press.

Ramsey, P. 1976. The enforcement of morals: Nontherapeutic research on children. *Hastings Center Report* 6(4):21–30.

Rawls, J. 1971. *A theory of justice.* Cambridge: Harvard University Press.

———. 1980. Kantian constructivism in moral theory. *Journal of Philosophy* 77:515–72.

Redlich, F. C. 1976. Editorial reflections on the concepts of health and disease. *Journal of Medicine and Philosophy* 1:269–80.

Reiser, S. J. 1980. Words as scalpels: Transmitting evidence in the clinical dialogue. *Annals of Internal Medicine* 92:837–42.

Rhoden, N. K., and J. D. Arras. 1985. Withholding treatment from Baby Doe: From discrimination to child abuse. *Milbank Memorial Fund Quarterly* 63:18–51.

Rollin, B. E. 1979. On the nature of illness. *Man and Medicine* 4:157–72.

Rorty, A. O. 1976. *The identities of persons.* Berkeley: University of California Press.

Rorty, R. 1979. *Philosophy and the mirror of nature.* Princeton: Princeton University Press.

———. 1982. *Consequences of pragmatism.* Minneapolis: University of Minnesota Press.

Ruse, M. 1981. Are homosexuals sick? In *Concepts of health and disease: Interdisciplinary perspectives,* ed. A. L. Caplan, H. T.

Engelhardt, and J. J. McCartney. Reading, Mass.: Addison-Wesley.

Sachs, D. 1981. How to distinguish self-respect from self-esteem. *Philosophy and Public Affairs* 10:346–60.

Sacks, O. 1983. *Awakenings*. New York: Dutton.

———. 1984. *A leg to stand on*. New York: Summit Books.

———. 1985. *The man who mistook his wife for a hat*. London: Gerald Duckworth.

Sapontzis, S. F. 1981. A critique of personhood. *Ethics* 91:607–18.

Sedgwick, P. 1973. Illness—mental and otherwise. *Hastings Center Studies* 1(3):19–40. (Reprinted in Caplan, Engelhardt, and McCartney 1981)

Sellars, W. 1963. *Science, perception and reality*. London: Routledge & Kegan Paul.

Selzer, R. 1975. *Mortal lessons: Notes on the art of surgery*. New York: Simon & Schuster.

Shaffer, P. 1973. *Equus*. New York: Charles Scribner's Sons.

Sheldon, A. 1970. Toward a general theory of disease and medical care. In *Systems and medical care*, ed. A. Sheldon, F. Baker, and C. P. McLaughlin. Cambridge: MIT Press.

Siegler, Mark. 1981. The doctor-patient encounter and its relationship to theories of health and disease. In *Concepts of health and disease: Interdisciplinary perspectives*, ed. A. L. Caplan, H. T. Engelhardt, and J. J. McCartney. Reading, Mass.: Addison-Wesley.

———. 1982. Confidentiality in medicine—a decrepit concept. *New England Journal of Medicine* 307:1518–21.

Siegler, Miriam, and H. Osmond. 1974a. The sick role revisited. *Hastings Center Studies* 1(3):41–58.

———. 1974b. *Models of madness, models of medicine*. New York: Macmillan.

Singer, P. 1983. Sanctity of life or quality of life? *Pediatrics* 72:128–29.

Solzhenitsyn, A. I. 1968. *The cancer ward*. Trans. R. Frank. New York: Dell.

Sontag, S. 1978. *Illness as metaphor*. New York: Farrar, Straus & Giroux.

Sophocles. 1979. *Electra, Antigone, Philoctetes*. Trans. K. MacLeish. Cambridge: Cambridge University Press.

Spiro, H. M. 1975. The tools of our trade—some comments on disease-disorder. *New England Journal of Medicine* 292:575–78.

———. 1986. *Doctors, patients, and placebos*. New Haven: Yale University Press.

Steinbrook, R., and B. Lo. 1986. The case of Elizabeth Bouvia: Starvation, suicide, or problem patient? *Archives of Internal Medicine* 146:161–64.

Stephens, G. G. 1981. Doctors at bay. *Continuing Education for the Family Physician* 16(2):15–16.

———. 1985. Clinical biographies: Issues in longitudinal care. *Continuing Education for the Family Physician* 20(4):260–75.

Stimson, G. V. 1974. Obeying doctor's orders: A view from the other side. *Social Science and Medicine* 8:97–104.

Strawson, P. F. 1958. Persons. In *Minnesota studies in the philosophy of science,* vol. 2, ed. H. Feigl, M. Scriven, and G. Maxwell. Minneapolis: University of Minnesota Press.

Strong, C. 1983. Defective infants and their impact on families: Ethical and legal considerations. *Law, Medicine and Health Care* 11:168–81.

Strull, W. M., B. Lo, and G. Charles. 1984. Do patients want to participate in medical decision making? *Journal of the American Medical Association* 252:2990–94.

Tavormina, M. T. 1982. Richard Selzer: The rounds of revelation. *Literature and Medicine* 1:61–72.

Temkin, O. 1963. The scientific approach to disease: Specific entity and individual sickness. In *Scientific change,* ed. A. C. Crombie. New York: Basic Books/Heinemann Educational Books. (Reprinted in Caplan, Engelhardt, and McCartney 1981)

Tolstoy, L. N. 1969. The death of Ivan Ilich. In *Great Russian short novels,* trans. A. R. McAndrew. New York: Bantam.

Tomlinson, T. 1986. The physician's influence on patients' choices. *Theoretical Medicine* 7:105–21.

Tooley, M. 1973. A defense of abortion and infanticide. In *The problem of abortion,* ed. J. Feinberg. Belmont, Calif.: Wadsworth.

Toulmin, S., ed. 1977. Mental health. *Journal of Medicine and Philosophy* 2:191–304.

Trammell, R. L. 1979. The nonequivalency of saving life and not taking life. *Journal of Medicine and Philosophy* 4:251–62.

Trautmann, J., ed. 1982. *The healing arts: Literature and medicine.* Carbondale: Southern Illinois University Press.

Trautmann, J., and C. Pollard. 1975. *Literature and medicine.* Philadelphia: Society for Health and Human Values.

———. 1983. *Literature and medicine* Rev. and enl. ed. Pittsburgh: University of Pittsburgh Press.

Veatch, R. M. 1973. The medical model: Its nature and problems. *Hastings Center Studies* 1(3):59–76. (Reprinted in Caplan, Engelhardt, and McCartney 1981)

———. 1981. *A theory of medical ethics.* New York: Basic Books.

Von Bertallanfy, L. 1968. *General systems theory*. New York: Braziller.

Weiner, N. 1954. *The human use of human beings: Cybernetics and society*. Garden City, N.Y.: Doubleday-Anchor.

Weir, R. F. 1984. *Selective nontreatment of handicapped newborns*. New York: Oxford University Press.

Weiss, B. D. 1982. Confidentiality expectations of patients, physicians, and medical students. *Journal of the American Medical Association* 247:2695–97.

Whitbeck, C. 1978. Four basic concepts of medical science. In *PSA 1978: Proceedings of the 1978 biennial meeting of the Philosophy of Science Association*, ed. P. D. Asquith and I. Hacking. East Lansing, Mich.: Philosophy of Science Association, 1:210–22.

————. 1981. A theory of health. In *Concepts of health and disease: Interdisciplinary perspectives*, ed. A. L. Caplan, H. T. Engelhardt, and J. J. McCartney. Reading, Mass.: Addison-Wesley.

White, R. B., and H. T. Engelhardt. 1975. A demand to die. *Hastings Center Report* 5(3):9–10.

Williams, M. E., and N. M. Hadler. 1983. The illness as the focus of geriatric medicine. *New England Journal of Medicine* 308:1357–60.

Wilson, E. 1947. Philoctetes: The wound and the bow. In *The wound and the bow: Seven studies in literature*. New York: Oxford University Press, pp. 272–95.

Wittgenstein, L. 1958. *Philosophical investigations*, trans. G. E. M. Anscombe. 3rd ed. New York: Macmillan.

Wolf, S. 1961. Disease as a way of life: Neural integration in systemic pathology. *Perspectives in Biology and Medicine* 4:288–305.

————. 1962. A new view of disease. *Transactions of the American Clinical and Climatological Association* 74:168–75.

Wolff, H. G. 1962. A concept of disease in man. *Psychosomatic Medicine* 24:25–30.

Woolf, V. 1948. On being ill. In *The moment and other essays*. New York: Harcourt, Brace & World.

Index

207